IN THE BEGINNING
MY LIFE WITH THE
MANIC STREET PREACHERS

IN THE BEGINNING MY LIFE WITH THE MANIC STREET PREACHERS

Jenny Watkins-Isnardi

BLAKE

Published by Blake Publishing Ltd,
3 Bramber Court, 2 Bramber Road,
London W14 9PB, England

First published in 2000

ISBN 1 85782 378 8

British Library Cataloguing-in-Publication Data:

A catalogue record for this book is
available from the British Library.

Typeset by t2

Printed in Great Britain by
Creative Print and Design (Wales),
Ebbw Vale, Gwent.

1 3 5 7 9 10 8 6 4 2

Introduction

This story is about a summer in 1987 when, for a brief few months, I was Nick Wire's girlfriend and became a singer with the Manic Street Preachers. What I'm offering is a slice of life of that time. It's not a sentimental account even though I had a close and warm friendship with Nick. The formation of the Manics cannot be separated from their social context. It was a hard time in a hard place, and false nostalgia would sound hollow, and we were young and took ourselves desperately serious.

Anyone who understands music and recognises sincerity knows the Manics are amongst the best in the world and without rivals in the UK. They have no need for gimmicks or presentation; they stand by their intrinsic talent and worth.

Someone said to me, when I was writing this book, that what I had to say would have little relevance compared to the mainstream accounts after the band achieved fame. Well, Nick had already written one of rock's all-time classics just before we met. In fact I was probably the first to hear 'Motorcycle Emptiness'. Genius seemed to erupt from those tempestuous teenage years.

I was lucky, privileged, to spend those few short months with the Manics. They are times I will never forget.

A big thanks to Steve Gatehouse

'I happen to think MSP are a good band ... And if you ever hear these songs you'll love them as well.'

Richard Edwards

CHAPTER ONE

We started with the Manics about the same time, my best friend and me. I sang with them through a brief summer in '87; Samantha went out with James for a few years. They got engaged then he said he had to marry someone else.

Last time I saw her she and I were at sixth-form college. Then, after studying, I left Wales for a farm in Uruguay. The Manic Street Preachers didn't figure in conversation among the South American cowboys. When I returned to my home four years later, I had no idea of their stature.

'Big, then, are they?'

Bringing me up to date on gossip, Sam tells me James

had phoned from the States. The wedding is in a day or so, and she isn't invited. It's nothing serious or personal, he said, just some publicity. At the moment it's top secret and she makes me swear not to tell anyone. It would ruin the effect.

James will marry a model or film starlet, they haven't decided. The only requirement is that she's very glamorous. 'They' are publicists organising the Manics' US tour and 'they' need to get a few headlines. Sam says it's not hard to imagine: Welsh women are dogs and James needed to go to the States to find a wife.

I try not to sound suspicious. 'He's never met this woman?'

'How could he? They don't know who she is yet.'

The only guests will be photographers. In a week there's a divorce and she reveals things in a tabloid.

This is just one of the scams 'they' have thought up. James is not as keen as Nick, who can be relied on for putrid quotes such as the one that he was glad Freddie Mercury had died. We had a laugh when Sam told me that one; Nick was brainy but not in the least vicious, in fact he's something of a pussycat.

Why had they chosen James for this marriage scam? Because, said Sam, scandal was one thing, bigamy another: Nick already had a wife; James was only engaged. It would make a good story about dumping the hometown sweetheart. How vile and nasty is this bunch of provincial punks!

'It gets better,' says Sam.

Until the marriage, she doesn't exist. Her engagement to James is bit theatre in the drama that will be the sudden, shock marriage. While he tours the world's stages, Sam is at a factory bench, anonymous. It's part of the PR bargain. Then he gets married, and it's discovered he was engaged to someone else all along. For now, James has to be ruthlessly single.

'How d'you put up with it?'

'If you think that's bad... '

Sam works on the same production line as Nick's wife; they assemble Walkmans. Nick calls her every night, cries down the phone. That's more like it, a sensitive Nick, much easier to picture than the Thatcherite thug slagging off the dead.

Nick's real ambition is to own a pet shop. James is at the end of his tether trying to keep his friend's mind off rabbits and goldfish. If Nick leaves, the band will fall apart. Sean is, of course, a vital figure but he's usually in the background. And Richey... ? Richey is something else; a late starter in the group without a proper slot or job description.

Is Sam a tinge jealous because she's stuck in that factory? The boys must be having a wild time. Not on tour, according to James. After a show they separate, split, go their own ways. James ends up in a hotel bar, gets drunk and watches night-time telly in his room. They all get homesick. Like most Welsh people they don't travel well. This doesn't sound plausible. Why do they do it? Must be the huge bucks.

Sean is on a big spending spree, in one pocket and out the other. Spend, spend, spend, generously. The other week he bought his girlfriend a new TV and video. But they call James The Rain Man or Rainy Day Man. When the Manics started earning James banked it, every penny. With what he's got, he could buy a modest semi-detached, in Blackwood. So the money isn't brilliant.

The only one I'd heard about was Richey. News of

some weird 'English' kid who cut himself even reached
South America. It couldn't be the same boy from years
ago? When I was with the Manics, he didn't even figure as
hanger-on. I remembered a shy, intense introvert;
someone clever and always absorbed in little drawings,
sketches, fliers for the band.

'Very different now,' says Sam. 'Darling of the
journalists, their Generation X; doesn't sleep, doesn't eat,
drinks... '

I have trouble imagining this changed, middle-class
Richey. But even James is worried. He's tried persuading
him to slow down, not to get caught in the publicist's
cliché.

James is a good one for advice — he could drink a fish
under the water table. Sam recalls his last home visit when
they got the 11 a.m. to Swansea. He went to the buffet car
to get breakfast and returned with double neat vodkas, for
himself.

About a week later I get a call from Sam.

'He's back!'

She's been in hiding for the build-up to his wedding.
Locked in her bedroom, said her mother, and physically
sick. On the phone she sounds pretty gleeful. James
couldn't go through with the stunt. His bride-to-be was a
big-jawed Texan and two hats taller than him. But that's
not why he's still unmarried. Sam had given an ultimatum:
her or fame in the USA.

'Do you fancy coming out with me and James?'

'The Red Lion, Blackwood?' That was where we
always went.

'No, he can't.'

I discover it's not because James has been banned. He

just doesn't go to Blackwood anymore. She won't say why. Maybe he's too famous for the place? We decide on a dim little pub called The Toby Jug in the village of Flower. It has a low ceiling and dark corners where middle-class people don't mind their p's and q's, and no one bothers you. Just the place to catch up on the things that happened since I left the Manics. And James is probably the most articulate and aware, the best one to tell the story.

My sister was about nine when I had my short career with the band. Sally recalls Nick coming to the house: a giant who stooped at the door, but was very kind and talked a lot. She doesn't remember sticking out her tongue or calling him names. No, she says, I've got that wrong.

She thinks I'm blasé about meeting James, and now she's nearly fourteen she says she should be allowed in the Toby. No one will notice, it's so dark.

'He's famous, been on telly. You'll be like a gooseberry with him and Sam.'

My mother urges her to drink underage, 'On the telly? Wow! You gotta go, may not get another chance.'

Sally wonders what he'll be like. Not to look at, she's seen pictures. Will he arrive in a white, stretch limo? Maybe he'll have a minder? That'll be boring. Perhaps he won't be allowed to speak, or he'll have a mask like Michael Jackson. Imagine all the famous people you pass on the motorway and we don't even notice.

'He's normal, ordinary. Likes fish an' chips.'

Well, he was ordinary. Now I'm wondering what to expect. It's so strange: to me, he can never be anything but the James I knew. Yet, he's obviously been through an investiture; it's what people now demand from him, to be something extra-ordinary. And the adulation, celebrity, aura makes a life of its own. In a way, he is a new creation; something made from the coupling of the fans' emotions and the image machine. But his essential self, the person I know, must be the same. That can't change, surely?

The pub is dim. When our eyes get accustomed to the gloom we see comfortable people on stools by the bar. If they are here, James and Sam will be tucked away in a darker corner.

'Pssst!... Here.' A white arm beckons.

I thought James would size me up, see if I was the same person. But he just sits back as if he'd seen me yesterday or we'd never met before. Though it's only been four or five years, he's got a hundred older. Not in looks — apart from a new hairstyle and crisp-cut clothes he is the same. But straight away you can tell he's skipped some generations, had a few life-times; moved way, way up the social scale. Confidence, is it? Or unwitting contempt for those still floundering down below?

They are both on whisky and Sam is tiddly. She lifts out a big yellow clock from her handbag and fiddles with the dials on the back.

'It talks in the morning. Says, "Vay-Cup!" He bought it for me in Japan.'

'Didn't he go to the States?'

'And Japan!' she says protectively.

'Tokyo is in Japan,' my sister stares, challenging, at James.

He nods agreement, then slips from his seat and goes to the bar. We watch the measures being tipped in his glass.

'Phew,' says my sister, 'he can drink a lot.'

'He's nervous with new people.'

6

In the Beginning

My sister looks at me as though I'm a fraud.

Back at the table his glass is way down, and he sips the rest quick, under Sally's intense search for cracks in immortality. I kick her under the table but she stares, unnerving. He is up and away again.

At the bar he downs a glass, and returns with a full one. After a sip he speaks, 'What's your favourite song of all time?'

Sally doesn't blink her eyes. ' "Islands In The Stream".'

'Dolly and Kenny. A mature choice.' Is he being ironic? 'And what's your favourite band?'

No hesitation. 'Guns n' Roses.'

'Yeah,' agrees James, 'brilliant. Axl Rose has a great voice, but the star is Slash. One of the best guitarists around. A great group but... '

My sister is devotional toward Guns n' Roses; usually there are no provisos or concessions, no dissent about their genius.

'... but as people... ' She should be clamping hands over her ears.

'... they are the dregs. Complete pricks. No morals whatsoever. Absolutely no scruples... '

Sally listens.

'They exploit women and have the word nigger in one of their songs. It's immoral. Worse is, they're completely manipulated by record companies. That would never happen to my group.'

'Did you meet them?'

James waves the question away. 'D'you know any other bands from South Wales?'

'Gene Loves Jezebel? Are they Welsh?'

'Men in drag, a pantomime. Can you name me a

7

serious band to come out of the South Wales Valleys?'

'Shakin' Stevens? Tom Jones! He's Welsh.'

'Not really a band, though, and he's via London to Las Vegas. There's not one, not one. The Manics are the first. We've got an obligation never to sell out.'

He gets up and Sam holds out her glass which he takes without speaking.

'Not like I thought,' says Sally, 'Quite nice, when you get to know him.'

Me and Sam are the gooseberries. Back at the table, he changes seats so he doesn't have to lean across.

Sally asks if he gets recognised. All the time, he says, in London. Loads of people coming up, autographs, or just to chat in crowded streets. She wouldn't like that, being pestered. James says he doesn't mind it in the least; they are the fans who buy the songs, the ones for whom the band have such respect.

If he doesn't want to be seen he goes to Cardiff. There, they never get recognised. Or if they do, people think it's naff to speak.

'I love Cardiff, except at Christmas. When it's packed with shoppers, I hate the fury of their spending; the aggression, the desperation to throw money away. I detest Cardiff at Christmas.'

'He's tight-fisted,' giggles Sam, 'an old Scrooge.'

'No. It's a con, a sham. And the working classes are conned the most.'

'I can't imagine not liking Christmas.' Sally is wondering if this is an effect of fame that makes you strange.

'Do you remember me from when I was little?' Perhaps she wants to run the clock back to when he was normal?

8

In the Beginning

He shakes his head, 'No.'

'I don't remember you either.'

They both stare at the table, as though suddenly noticing it's a disappointing style. Sally has a sly peep at Sam.

'D'you have groupies? Sort of, girls?'

James frowns, a little unfocussed. 'Know what I like best on telly?'

'*Baywatch*? Topper The Pops? My father watched Benny Hill, till he was banned.'

'*Cagney And Lacey*.' James slides from his chair. 'D'you wanna drink?'

'Glass of pop, please.'

At the bar, you sense he's been recognised because most of the men stare deliberately away. Only one of them talks, non-stop to the back of James' head.

'Cagney an' Lacey?' Sally sticks a finger in her mouth as if to vomit. 'Quick! Someone swap.'

'You're honoured,' says Sam, 'he was only going to say hello.'

James lowers himself next to where I was sitting and points Sally toward the bar. 'Drunk, asked if I liked the Shadows and Cliff Richard... You old enough for *Charlie's Angels*?'

'Course! It was on at nine, saw every one.'

'Well, that was the dregs, pile of plastic fake. *Cagney And Lacey* showed women, real women, carrying the weight of the world.'

'Yeah, and big padded shoulders.'

'That's cheap. The single one was so lonely and wanted children; the one who was married had money problems. She slogged long hours and because she was a cop she saw the worse. She worried about her kids growing up in the mess.'

'Too depressing for telly.'

'Not depressing, not at all. They were decent, good. Gave hope to the world because they were good... That's what women are like, essentially decent, and men are bastards, complete bastards. Excuse me, have to go to the Gents.'

He makes a detour wide of the bar, where the drunk man is demonstrating a slow quick-step of intricate footwork.

'Does he always say that?' asks Sally. 'Never heard "Gents" before, usually they say shithouse or bog.'

'Hey! Watch your language!'

'What's wrong, Jenny? Jealous?'

'Whatever for?'

'It's obvious. He didn't recognise you. Look at how you dress, you're past it.'

Samantha gives Sally a cool look. 'Remember what he said about being controlled, it would never happen to them? Bullshit. On tour, these feminists were told to tease the little girlie fans. Shove socks in their pants. Ask him when he gets back. Nick had football ones, looked like he was ruptured.'

When James comes out, no one says a word. We try to avoid it, but it's like there's an eye-magnet in his crotch.

'Sorry. Have I dribbled? Something up?' He gives Sam a ferocious glare. 'What've you been saying?'

Suppressed hysteria bursts on the table with tears and spittle. Sam tries to explain but the word sock sounds like cock.

James seems old with disillusion. He finishes his drink slow and in one swallow, then reaches for his jacket off the back of a chair. Sam gets up and follows, her

In the Beginning

shoulders still quaking.

I never saw him again, ever, except on telly.

CHAPTER TWO

The Cuckoo looks alluring from the outside, especially in that icy cold April of 1987. Warm, stained-glass windows with an orangey glow. It's a bit chapel like, and religion's just below the skin with us Welsh.

Sam, my best friend, pushes open the thick wood door. A rush of warm beery air puts life back in her face.

'Ooh, lovely.'

We make our way to the shiny bar.

Mel is at our heels, 'Half a snakebite, please.' The barmaid points to a small notice above her head. "No Underage Drinkers". Mel looks at me, I'm a year younger and a foot shorter, and no questions asked.

'I.D.?'

'Yeah,' she flashes a fake bus pass.

The barmaid squints at the picture, pouring Mel's drink.

The pub is divided by a glass partition. This first room is dimly lit and intimate, with respectable-looking couples.

Someone drops ten pence into the juke-box, selects the almost worn out track 67: 'Spirit of '76', The Alarm.

Beyond the glass partition, the atmosphere changes. A small, dingy room; cold, but buzzing with chatter. Students, most of them underage, cram the tables with pints of lager and cider with black.

Sam makes a beeline for a table close to the bar. We pull up chairs. A low smoke cloud makes the room close, cosy. It feels good to be surrounded by the Friday night crowd.

A boy that Sam shares classes with comes in and gets on a bar stool. James Bradfield hates the smokers, wants to avoid the scruffy students and their vile habit. Sam fancies him. She's not put out when a neat girl in a miniskirt and sweater takes the next stool along. It isn't James' girlfriend. Touching her tightly curled hair, the girl glances around. Her boyfriend must have missed his bus; she checks her watch.

The pub door opens and she cranes her neck. A local tramp shields his eyes against the light. The landlord allows him in to tease us because we're underage and can't complain. The door closes, and the girl cringes as the tramp goes straight towards her. Silent prayers of thanks are given by everyone who's not a sacrifice. The girl is rigid as he stands close; thoughtful, scratching his stubble. The tramp is studying the girl; James studies the tramp, absorbed in the spit that flecks the corners of his mouth.

In the Beginning

Suddenly, without warning, the tramp smacks a wet kiss on the girl's lips, and her cheeks flush. Then he turns abruptly and walks through clapping and cheers back to the door. Slipping from the stool, the girl rubs her face in a sweater sleeve.

'If Nick does come, I'm at home.'

James is thinking about the tramp. He would like to be one himself; homeless, careless, sitting on a park bench with a secret bottle in a brown paper bag. And sleep under a bridge curled up in a big, bold overcoat. Attached to no one, responsible for nothing, free.

Near us, a bunch of rowdy drama students slosh back snakebites, getting drunk fast.

'We ready then?' A boy stands up; big stain spreading below the zip of his Levi's.

'One more,' giggles a girl with ghost-white complexion spoiled by ruddy cheeks, 'one more for the road.'

'Plenty to drink at home.'

Another pale Goth gets up. 'No. Another here first!'

A tall blond walks in, rubbing his hands from the cold. He's got a sharp-boned hatchet face, and shivers under a thin lemon blouse. He heads straight for James and puts an arm around his shoulder

James looks up and smiles. 'Nick! Rachel was in. She's gone home.'

One of the drama students shouts across to the bar: 'James! My house. Mam's away.'

'Bet Rachel's mad,' says Nick, 'I'm half-hour late. Better get going.'

On the way out he stops at the fruit machine, unzips his jacket and feels for change.

'Come on, Sam!' calls a drama student, 'the more the merrier.'

'Have to give it a miss,' I say, 'promised Mam and Dad I wouldn't be late.'

'Me too,' says Mel.

James has a full pint. He tips it up, 'Ready to go!'

Sam knocks back her drink, 'Still okay to kip at your house, Jen?'

'Meet you in the bus stop. Don't be late.'

After the party-goers have left the place is nearly empty. Mel and myself decide to go on somewhere else, and when we leave the kid in the lemon blouse is still putting change in the machine.

We huddle in the bus shelter, April frost thick on the plastic panes, our breaths like dragon smoke.

'You'll have to get the next one,' says Mel.

The next is the last. If it turns up. I've already missed my connection and will have to walk home from Blackwood.

We've checked every chippy and take away in Risca, been up and down the main drag half a dozen times and Sam is nowhere. Mel lives near but it'll take me three hours to walk. And the last bus is notoriously unreliable.

'You could stay in my house but, well, you know, the animals.'

Mel's house is a zoo.

I'm just about to take the first heavy steps on the journey when the bus comes around the corner, lit up and beautiful like Santa's sleigh.

'Thank Christ,' Mel gives me a quick, shivery hug.

It's empty but for a woman with a shopping bag sitting near the driver. As the bus doors hiss, a tall figure emerges from the shadows of a shop entrance.

'Sit in the back,' says Mel, 'there's always sick in the

front of the last one.'

It's warm. The driver smiles. After I get my ticket, I settle snug in a rear seat. The tall figure is the gangly blond in a lemon shirt. He ducks on and slides into a side seat at the front. He has pale, graceful hands and they fold upon a green canvas bag that he sits on his lap. Opposite him, the woman stares hard out the window.

Inside it's beacon bright and the windows throw back reflections. I cup my hands to look at the street. The night is still going on. People spill from the pubs, tipsy and laughing.

It seems that as soon as we've started we stop. A scruffy kid stumbles up the steps and crashes into the counter. In one fist he holds a can, coins drop from the other.

'Steady now,' says the driver.

The drunk staggers along the aisle, pulling himself along the backs of seats. What seemed to be a map of Italy on his sweatshirt is big beer stain. Halfway down he stops and grins to himself. With a massive effort he tries to swig from the can. It reminds me of the game we used to play in Brownies: pin a tail on the donkey. Beer pours off his chin. The bus hits a pothole and Italy is drowned.

'Sor-ry,' he burps, 'sor-ry bow tha'.' He falls onto a seat.

The roads are empty of traffic and, apart from an occasional belch the journey is quiet. I lean my head against the cold window, close my eyes and drift off.

'Morticia!... Morticia!'

My eyes open with the drunk swaying in front of me.

'Hey. You, Morticia!'

I look around then glance at my reflection: straightened hair, black panda-eyes, flour face. And he thinks he's a genius to see a likeness.

'No! You Morticia. You are, you.' Bubbles pop from his red rubbery lips.

Down the front the woman grips her shopping with white knuckles.

'Morticia and... ' he pokes a finger in his chest, 'Gomez! Addams Family.'

The blond boy turns round to look, and he has an uncontrollable grin.

The drunk senses an audience. He points at me, 'She is... the Addams Family.'

The boy nods, still grinning.

'See, he knows!'

'Dave, sit down please,' says the driver.

'Morticia,' says the drunk. And he's snoring before he falls in the aisle.

Down the front, the punk shrugs and smiles.

A few minutes later Dave the drunk is up and stumbling fast to the front. The woman cringes into her seat, holding tight to her bags. The bus stops, Dave whooshes out with the opened doors.

We arrive in Blackwood bus station just after half-eleven. There's a man waiting, and the woman hurries off. They link arms and leg it fast as his limp allows them. Soon as I step down the bus reverses and the station is just silence and shadows. The blond boy had got off first and is just ahead, walking so slow it's like a loiter. Nah, he wouldn't try anything.

It's a mile and a half to home. I've a fair idea he doesn't live in my direction, but I think about asking him to walk me even though it would be miles from his way. Just when I'm catching up he glances around and takes off like a whippet. More Morticia than I'd thought, perhaps?

In the Beginning

Panting, out of breath, I put my key in the door and creep upstairs. The inflatable has already been blown up but there's no Sam to sleep in it. Before drifting off I wonder if she had any luck with that kid.

It's 2.30. I know because I've got the clock in my hand, the luminous dial next to my eyes.

Banging on my door woke me.

'What's wrong?'

'Downstairs! Get dressed. Quick!'

This time of night? Something terrible has happened.

There's a man and a woman in uniform. The woman has her hat off. They look huge in the bright living room; wrapped against the outside cold they seem hard, invulnerable. My mother and father are on the settee in their dressing gowns, looking guilty. What terrible secrets have these coppers extracted?

The man takes a black notebook from his pocket.

'Jenny?'

I nod.

'Your friend Samantha... '

'My God. What's happened!'

'Don't be silly,' says the woman cop.

'Can you say precisely when you last saw her?' A thin pencil hangs above the paper.

'She hasn't been home,' says my mam, biting her knuckle.

'Now we don't want a drama,' says the woman cop, 'she's probably tucked up in some friend's bed.'

Hm!

'Why did you came home on your own?' asks Dad.

'Because... did you want me to bring someone special?'

'Don't you show off, my girl!'

'Please, please. Can you answer the question?' says the policewoman.

I tell them about The Cuckoo and the group of friends.

'Are you or these friends taking any sort of drugs?'

'Hey?' My father jumps up. 'She wouldn't take drugs!'

'Routine, Mr eh... Have to ask. Well, Jenny?'

Should I confess? Will I confess?

'Tell the truth now,' says Mam.

There's a silence when I can hear my mother's heart pounding.

'No, nothing. Samantha, definitely not.'

Mam's shoulders slump.

'Is she pregnant?' asks the cop.

'Not to my knowledge. At least she hasn't told me.'

'And you're her best friend, so she'd say?'

'I think so.'

'You don't think she's pregnant?'

'She's not showing.'

'Is she with a boy?' The female cop gives a reassuring smile, like she understands these things.

Tricky. 'No.'

The policeman snaps shut the black book. No more questions.

'If you do know something you better tell us now.' It's not a plea but a threat. The woman has a French plait like a curled turd. It pulls her head tight, makes her voice shrill.

'Jenny, answer.' My mother makes me mad.

'Right then... ' The woman fusses, tucking the turd in her hat.

'I'll show you out,' says Dad.

They talk on the doorstep. My father's voice can't be

heard but the cops could wake the street.

'... do stupid things, don't they?... Don't they, do they?... We checked the attic in her house... What? You'd be surprised.'

Samantha didn't surface for a few days. There was a rumour that the police even dug up the garden. I didn't see her until the Wednesday after, sitting on a bench, at lunch time in college. The wind had changed warm, like spring, but she looked grey as though she'd been in jail. I suspected she was kept in, grounded, but she acted cool as if the big time had arrived. Kids walking passed snook admiring glances, and made sure we heard what they said.

'Was she really missing all night?'

'Someone said they dragged the river.'

'The police asked for a photo to put on the news.'

That was the big one. No one knew if it was true but even the rumour of a chance of getting on telly made Sam a celebrity.

She didn't volunteer what happened and I wasn't going to ask. We sat there in the sunshine; her like she was recovering in a sanatorium and me an unwanted visitor.

A stocky kid with a crew cut stepped out of a door whistling that Del Shannon song, 'Runaway'. Sam blushed, and I recognised him as the one she fancied, James. She was dying for me to ask.

He beckoned, a bit shy, and she bounced over. She was slightly taller and sort of leaned not to be looking down. They talk, then he handed her something and she looks across at me. When she comes back she has a grin on her face that's super-glued, no matter how much I scowl.

'Remember the punk, the blond one? Well, this is for

you.' She gives me an envelope that is radioactive green.

'He's split from his girlfriend, and fancies you.'

We start giggling.

'Aren't you going to open it?'

'Maybe.'

'Open it for goodness sake!'

'Who is he, anyway? I mean, I've seen him around but who is he?'

'There's three of them,' Samantha lowers her voice as though it's a conspiracy. 'James, you know him; Nick, the one who likes you; and another kid, called Sean. They formed a band. Call themselves something really naff, like Manic Preachers or something.'

'Jesus! You got yourself involved with religious nuts?'

'It's the name of the band. Are you going to open that letter?'

'A band? What sort of band?'

'Punk. But they think three members is crap. James says they won't make it without a lead singer.'

The envelope was securely gummed down and I nearly snap a nail opening it. There was luminous green note paper inside, not well folded. His writing is all shapes and sizes; capitals in the middle of words and very odd punctuation:

Dear Jenny,

I'm not sure, if you know who I am (I go around with Sean and James) but I know You I'm writing to ask you 2 questions

Firstly I'm a band called Manic StreeT Preachers and we're looKing for a new sinGer. Would you be interested in singing for us?

We are a bit, like Pop Will Eat Itself and Primal

In the Beginning

Scream. The second question is will you go out with me? If you say Yes to either of these questions please phone me.

Nick Jones.

I show Sam and her smile widens.

'Nick says it's better to have a girl in the band. Male musicians, female singer. A winning combination. Look at Blondie.'

'Why didn't they ask you?'

She gave me a resigned sort of look. 'You're first choice. Had to be someone local. They made a list. Someone who looks good... but not too rough.'

'What's that supposed to mean?'

'They're already thinking of the band's image. They want someone who knows how to behave.'

'Take orders, you mean? Be a good girl?'

'That's what Sean said. "Think we can get the Pope?" '

'There must be better than me; better looking? They don't even know I can sing.'

'Not to James. They've decided you've got something. Sean had suggested his girlfriend who sings in Oakdale choir, but her voice is too good. Exactly what they don't want, said Nick. Wrong image. Anyway, he already had you in mind.'

'Fantastic. He must have checked, found out I can't sing.'

'You have to phone him.'

'What for?'

'What do you think? Phone him!'

'To go out with him or to be in the band?'

Samantha is getting agitated. 'Both, you plonker! Go on, say you'll sing!'

'I don't know. What's he like?'

'You've seen him; tall... unusual.'

'Unusual?'

'Everyone else has their stuff in a plastic carrier; you've seen, everyone. But Nick's got a green canvas bag. You'd think he had the crown jewels. Like a woman, never without it. And it's, like, stuck to his shoulder, never comes off. Bet he wears it in bed?'

'I don't think that's odd.'

'He wears women's blouses. Mostly his mother's.'

'So what? I wear my dad's shirts.'

'Well, you're another weirdo!'

'Nah, don't think I'll phone.'

'Don't blame you, in a way.'

'Why's that?'

'He's not bad but... you can do better.'

'He looks alright, from what I remember.'

Sam pulls a face. 'Spiky hair with the roots coming up?'

'Been out with worse. That kid with the cabbage on his head.'

'He wears tight jeans, no arse.'

'But what's he like as a person? Might be a right prat.'

Samantha pulls me up. 'Come on, let's find a phone.'

We get out of the college and head along the main street. This business is too important to risk eavesdroppers.

'I'll wait outside,' says Sam.

The phone box nearest the college has a nauseous smell; a perfect level of dog shit fills the mouth piece. Luckily, I see someone else's nose print before it's too late. I take it as an omen: I'm not meant to call Nick. Sam drags me along to the next phone. She checks the next box, 'All clear, except for fags and pee.'

24

In the Beginning

I dial and the phone rings. A boy with a friendly voice answers. 'Yes, Nicholas speaking.'

It's hard to fit the image of spiky-haired scruff-bag to this refined telephone manner.

I introduce myself. And he sounds less stuffy.

'Oh, I'm glad you phoned.'

'Got your letter. I'm interested, singing in the group, that is.'

'Great...'

Was there a note of disappointment?

'Of course, you'll have to audition.'

'What? Didn't mention that in the letter.'

'Suppose you can't sing? I mean, you sound okay speaking but what if you sing like Sioux and the Banshees? We're not *Top Of The Pops*, can't just mime.'

'Well, I don't know. I mean...'

'Look, just sing, now.'

'What? In the phone box?'

'Go on. Sing, anything. Pretend you're in the bath.'

I drop another coin in the slot.

Silence.

'Jenny, still there?'

'I'm trying to think.'

'Don't. What's your favourite song?'

I put my hand over the mouth piece, open the phone box door.

'Sam!'

She is a few steps away, yawning and looking absent-mindedly at the passing traffic.

I wave my hand, frantic. 'Quick, come here!'

Sam pokes her head in.

'What can I sing?'

She looks bewildered, 'Hey? I don't know. Now?'

25

The money goes again, I fumble my purse for more coins.

'Think of something,' I hiss, 'you made me do this.'

She taps a knuckle against her forehead. 'I know!' Her eyes light up, 'Preacher Man, the Dusty Springfield song. It's to do with their name. Makes sense.'

I look at her blank.

Her grip on the door slips and it snaps shut.

'He's nuts!' she shouts above the noise of a passing lorry.

When the rumbling has died away I drop in another coin.

'Nick?'

'What's happening?'

'Okay, I'm ready.'

'Go ahead Jenny. Take your time.'

I clear my throat...

Drop in another coin and hesitate for a moment. This is costing a fortune, my lunch and bus money for the week. I'm more concerned about my emptying purse than getting in the band.

The phone box rumbles as a bus goes passed. Even with a finger in my ear there's just the noise of throbbing engine. I can't hear a word being sung.

I scream the last line...

'Okay! Okay!' interrupts Nick.

There's silence, then he clears his throat.

'Can you find another phone box?'

'What d'you mean?'

'Well, the sound's not very good in that one.'

'Maybe you could...'

'It's a joke. Listen, it'll be better with the band.'

'After all that? I've sung myself hoarse!'

In the Beginning

'I'll take you out for a drink, if you like.'

'Choosy where I go. Have to be somewhere nice.'

'Blackwood's a nice place. Meet you at the bottom of Chastens Hill.'

'When?' The pips start to go and my purse is empty. 'Where? What time?'

There's a click, the line goes dead. I hang up the phone.

CHAPTER THREE

We lived in a world about eight miles long and one street wide. It was part of a valley called the Sirhowy, and stretched from Blackwood in the north to Risca in the south, a snaky strip of land that we rarely went outside. Although there are dozens of valleys in South Wales, even those next to the Sirhowy were uncharted territory for us. If we hadn't seen them on telly, the people in the adjoining valleys might, for all we knew, have had rings through their noses and two heads.

Most of the time our world was considerably smaller than this. We occupied only the extreme ends of the stretch, Blackwood and Risca. In between was five or six miles that we only saw from the windows of a bus or, if unlucky, we walked through late at night.

Nick lived in Blackwood, Sean and James were from Pontllanfraith, we went to tertiary college in Crosskeys, and Risca was a popular place for a night out. In truth, the town of Blackwood merges with Pontllanfraith, and Crosskeys merges with Risca. So our lives were spent in just two places, each about the size of a generous prison yard. That was the extent of our known universe; in fact we probably knew more about Mars than the towns outside our area.

God knows where it is now but the Sirhowy valley used to be in Gwent. Over the years this county has had its name changed from Gwent to Monmouthshire then back to Gwent. At the moment it doesn't have a name, doesn't exist beyond a string of letters in a postcode. When it was a county, Gwent was in the far east of Wales, bordering England. But Sirhowy was the westernmost valley of Gwent, closest to 'real' Wales. It was a county of extreme extremes, schizophrenic in its differences. Near England was rolling countrified farmland; in the west were the steep urban corridors that formed part of the South Wales valleys.

Maybe this mix and mess, this confusion of geography, was the cause of a subconscious tugging of identities. Subconscious because, if confronted, people would vehemently deny the charge, but the way they act contradicts their denials. The charge is that the people of this county, this valley, secretly want to be identified as English. The evidence is that they put on twangs, iron out the sing-song melody of a Welsh accent and substitute the spivy tongue of a Mike Reid. In one of the region's towns can be heard cockney glottal stops as they say, 'Fu' th'

In the Beginning

En'lish!'

Something else unique about the Sirhowy valley is that it has the fastest river in Britain. They haven't actually timed it, but made their reckoning from the steep drop in altitude along the river's length. You'd have thought the tourist people would be boasting about this record, and get visitors in for the local economy. But to be fair there's nothing special to see, no scary rapids or raging torrents. When it's dry and the river shrinks to a squirt of washing-up liquid, there's a stink like it's flowing chemicals probably dumped by the council. It has been cleaned up though, and the river bottom looks well scrubbed except for some patches of rust. In fact, it's so well scoured nothing grows in it. Perhaps they used too much cleaner?

In the 1600s, when it was flooded with salmon and trout, the Sirhowy river had a mill built on it at a place called Gelli Groes, and it's still there today. Gelli Groes means, 'woods by the crossroads', and the crossroads is also still there. One of the roads leads to a church called Mynyddislwyn. This means 'Islwyn's mountain'. At the top is a church, still there, that was built in the 1200s. The site of this church is said to be pagan and near the church is a pre-Christian, Druid burial mound. So, in just one little area of the Sirhowy valley, very near James' house, there is a lot of pre-industrial history.

That sort of history is the one the Welsh Nationalists float around in, playing harps and reciting poems. And it has almost nothing to do with the cultural inheritance and experience of the Welsh valleys. Industrialism wiped away, smudged out, displaced and buried whatever quaint rustic ways may exist in the Wales of Welsh-speaking market town historians.

Jenny Watkins-Isnardi

In the late 1800s, the Reverend Monkhouse and Mr Fothergill built a furnace to make iron at the top of the Sirhowy valley. They were obviously a pair of brown nosers because they called the place where they built their operation Tredegar. This was in honour of Lord Tredegar. Over the next hundred years the Tredegar family very kindly allowed their name to be used throughout the valley, so now there's Tredegar House, lots of Tredegar Parks and even a Tredegar Clock.

The furnace business caught on and within a few decades, so they say, there were two dawns and two dusks; one lot made by the sun and the other by the glow from the fires. Except the one from the fires kept going all night and all day.

On top of the earth were ironworks and underground were the mines, for luckily there was a huge black stain of coal under the South Wales valleys. And even luckier for the bosses, women and kids were allowed to work in their mines. One owner bragged that women and girls, stripped to the waist, worked harder than slaves in the West Indies.

Not surprisingly in a place where you were better off dead, there were countless chapels and churches — still are. The preachers told stories about the afterlife, and said how wonderful the afterlife was for people who worked hard and didn't complain or answer back. But this afterlife wasn't a certainty, even if you slogged your guts out. Tredegar had a cholera epidemic in the 1830s. Whole families died and were buried on a bleak mountainside away from the town's consecrated graveyard. The cholera cemetery of Cefn Golau is still there, in parts. Most of the headstones have been vandalised but some inscriptions are still clear enough to make you weep.

The owners didn't have it all their own way. A bunch

of troublemakers known as the Chartists used to meet at a pub in Blackwood called The Coach and Horses (it's still there). In 1839 they went on a march to Newport, to put the frighteners on the bosses. But the bosses laid on an ambush and shot up the Chartists in a hotel called the Westgate; the bullet holes are still there. Those Chartists who didn't get shot were shipped off to Australia so they couldn't cause any more trouble.

Until the early 1980s things went smoothly. Every surface was black frosted with coal dust and big strong men were made glamorous with permanent eyeliner from muck they couldn't wash off. The idea of progress, that things could only get better, was handed down from generation to generation. People suffered in their own lives in the hope their offspring would be happier. Nothing unusual about that; most parents think their kids will improve on what they were born into, except the Royals.

But our parents hit pay dirt. Being teenagers in the 1960s, they cashed in all the investments their ancestors had made for the future; annuities of self-confidence, allowances for entertainment. My mother saw every group, from the Beatles to Dave, Dee, Dozy, Beaky, Mick and Tich.

The gods of time waited for our generation to come along then... SMACK! The Thatcherites. They reversed progress by going back to Victorian values, and introducing the ghost of Charles Darwin to the South Wales valleys. The mining communities, they said, were inefficient life forms that should be allowed to die out; we were a species that couldn't adapt to a new world order. It was all about survival of the fittest; we were used to beer and chips.

The coal had gone, everything inside had been ripped

out and it was like living on a crust. But not all Tories were mean-spirited bastards. Some sympathised and offered sound advice: 'On yer bike!' said Norman Tebbit, which was a poetic way of telling people to desert their towns and villages and leave the old and sick to look after themselves.

With all the miners and steelworkers on the dole, the Secretary of State for Wales said a 'culture of dependence' now operated in the Valleys. That is, we depended on State handouts: sickness and unemployment benefit. It was like telling a man who's made to kick down forests with his bare feet that, when he can't walk, there's not enough wood for crutches. Well, there was no work and no other source of money. What the Secretary really meant was, we should all starve to death, join the dodos.

Some people justified the closing of the mines by saying the place was cleaner and no one had ever wanted to work in the damn things anyway. But there was no choice about it, no alternative work to do. The best they could offer was, with no irony intended, 'there's light at the end of the tunnel'; meaning, things will get better. This was a very sensitive metaphor to use about dead and buried ex-mining communities, and to miners who'd spent their lives underground in the pitch-black. We were eight years into this tunnel when I started going out with Nick, and because he was not a rugby zealot the tunnel was darker for him than for others.

It may sound far-fetched but rugby played an important part in conditioning Valleys people to tolerate their terrible condition. Players and spectators accepted the brutality of the game and, no doubt, believed that the premises of that cruel sport applied to their own lives. Rugby made them stoic and proud to bear their suffering without whinging or marching on demos. This was

34

In the Beginning

because the Valleys had for well over a hundred years been religion mad. When people stopped formal worship and going to chapel, they were still possessed by religious obsession. Encouraged by teachers and civil servants, rugby became the new opiate.

Rugby was an Old Testament, hard-as-nails religion. It was well suited to people bristling with aggression and sensitive to insults, real or imagined. People whose every sense was tuned to the slightest offence, who would kick the shit out of you for a glance, because they had nothing except a small space by the bar, or a doorway or just the corner of a street. And the real things that attacked them were too big and too distant. There was an abundance of fear and self-loathing in the South Wales valleys.

Nick, James and Sean could have tried to become invisible, to avoid the attention of all the discontents. But it would have been pointless. The valley floor, from Blackwood to Risca, had a river and a road, some rugby fields, a few shops and rows of terraced houses. Life was squeezed in tight and there was no room to hide. Besides, there wasn't anywhere to go except pubs and you only went, for financial reasons, on a certain day. Everything was compressed in time and place. Nick's solution to the violence was to be brightly conspicuous, wearing clothes that provoked sneers and jibes but not a thick lip.

Probably there was as much chance of dying from monotony as being done in by a religiously rugby fanatic. We went to pubs because there simply was nothing else. The big events, such as bands, were in Cardiff. It was only twenty-odd miles but we'd be running out like Cinderellas before the end to get the last bus or train.

By day Blackwood had three pubs and two cafes. By night it had a few pubs. The two cafes were owned by

Italians, and they had huge cappuccino machines that steamed like angry locomotives. Everyone in Blackwood adored the Italians because they were good people; friendly, sociable and very, very clean. 'Just like us Welsh,' we kidded ourselves. During the war some Italians were interned in camps. The Italians had supported the communities more than most indigenous Welsh, yet they were rounded up like cattle. It was one more terrible, unforgivable injustice. To our credit, thousands signed petitions and brought pressure to get them released.

The two cafes in Blackwood are called The Square and The Dorothy. They reflect a microcosm of the town's class system. The Square is appropriately named because of the types it attracts rather than its shape, for it is very definitely oblong. In the morning business types take tea and toast. For an excellent, well-cooked lunch you can have office workers, the odd solicitor and local shop owners. And through the day there's well-to-do retired types catching up on gossip. The owners must be brilliant to work for; the same women have been dashing about the tables in the same black-and-white outfits that were high fashion in the '50s. Capanini is a revered name.

The Dorothy was a small self-service run by two dark and hairy brothers, about in their thirties. The younger of the two was part of a folk duo, good on the acoustic. The Dorothy didn't sell cigarettes because the brothers were against smoking. But there was no patronising sign saying not to smoke. In reality they'd have had no clientele if smoking was banned. The Dorothy's customers were a nervous lot, and ate pasties and drank coffees in a dense fag smog.

The atmosphere attracted the worn and the weary. You could have written the bible of bad luck stories from the defeated faces that pulled on fags like it was the only thing that kept them alive. There were push-chairs and prams and kids about thirteen with their babies. And there were old men in scarves on summer days, bent over coughing their lungs up.

We loved The Dorothy; it was our place, our unofficial club. On Saturdays, after a trawl of the town's second-hand shops, it was where everyone ended up. And there was talk on everything under the sun that was important to us: what was Number One? Who was shafting whom? What should be Number One? Who should be shafting whom? The Dorothy was fantastic, unique. If it had stayed open all night, whole families would have been orphaned. When God writes the book of things he got right, there'll be a whole chapter on the two brothers.

There might have been a few closet Tories but only the really stupid ones put their hands up. Being Conservative around Blackwood was like a criminal offence, your only excuse was to plead insanity. The odd friends who showed Tory tendencies we thought of as eccentric or just born daft. In Welsh they say, 'Twp'. A lovely word to describe Tories.

That was it, really. Hardly anyone took drugs, except for a daring drag of weakened weed. There was a disco in an adjoining valley but it was so rough you'd need life insurance. Along the valley there were as many pubs as chapels and we stuck to just a few; mainly The Red Lion in Blackwood and The Cuckoo in Risca.

We all knew each other. It was like the circles when you throw a stone in a pond: at the middle are your closest friends, and the connections and affections get weaker the further from the centre. On the edges are just faces you know. But you're aware of everyone, absolutely everyone, because the pond is so small and the edges are the sides of the valley.

CHAPTER FOUR

Nick is meeting me in Blackwood. It is a warm evening, still and sunny. The stroll from my house to the bus stop has hot urban smells: fumes, tarmac. As I wait, cars crowded with Valley wits blare past, heads out of windows: 'Yr fuckin' weirdo!' 'My granny got better clothes 'n that!'

Getting my ticket from the driver I notice a girl waving near the back. Amanda-Punk, ardent feminist. She shifts over for me to share the ten-minute ride. Dressed in black, T-shirt, jeans, leather jacket, she wears her hair in a foot-high blonde mohican. Her eyes are coated thick in shimmering blue mascara. She is scary. The previous weekend she'd floored some lippy guy with one punch.

'Where you off then, Je'?'

I tell her I was seeing Nick.

She looks puzzled. 'Who's that? The skinny one, legs like bent skewers? Good lookin' girl like you? Do better 'n that.'

The bus goes up a steep incline, along a short, level stretch, and drops down into the next valley. Chastens Hill, gateway to Blackwood. I make my way down the aisle. Glancing ahead out the window, I see Nick, hands in pockets, waiting by the kerb.

As I step off the bus, a wristful of bangles slips over my hand and rolls down the slope. Nick is off like a flash, chasing after them, getting down on hands and knees to collect them up.

We walk the short distance to Blackwood High Street, Nick in a second-hand dark blazer and black drainpipes. Under the blazer is a woman's T-shirt, brightly coloured with daisies. He takes long strides, and it seems his torn and battered daps must fall apart.

Blackwood is quite rich, in Valleys terms. No shops boarded up, no beggars, hardly any daylight muggings. The great Neil Kinnock was our MP.

There are four or five pubs a few minutes' walk apart. 'Four or five' because one or another is always being closed down or re-opened; a drugs bust, beer gone to the dogs. Most of the pubs are fall-down-drunk by ten at night. Rugby and football sorts go to get unconscious as fast as they can, either with drink or fighting.

Nick likes the more sedate Red Lion, a bit of the way up market. It has a juke-box but not so loud you can't talk. And funnily enough the middle-aged couples are more tolerant than kids at other pubs. It was odd for us to drink there; raging rebels in the heart of Valleys petite bourgeoisie. Still, not as odd as those hulking thick rugby types who once ridiculed Nick and now listen rapt to the Manics!

Inside The Red Lion it is dark and silent, almost empty. Two blondes sit by the bar, Barbie-doll hair and off-the-shoulder tops. They stare at their reflections in the bar mirror, sipping their snakebites. Nick stands near them, waiting to be served. Three peroxides, one with inch long, jet-black roots. Everyone was blond back then.

He comes back with two half-pints of lager and lime.

'What have you been up to?' I ask.

'Got up late. This afternoon, James' house. But he kicked me out. Got hysterical because his mam was in the bath.'

'Hey? Does he think you've got X-ray eyes or something?'

'Had visions of me seeing her in a bath towel.' He laughs.

'Seems a bit strange.'

'Always been paranoid about things like that. I don't take any notice. Really it's because we've been with each other every day this summer, getting on each other's nerves. Even the best of mates get fed up. Imagine being married?'

The place starts to fill up. Nice, decent people. Husbands talk to wives about kitchen units and vacuum cleaners; girlfriends talk to boyfriends about souped-up Escorts and nippy little Fiestas. Someone puts 'God Save the Queen' on the juke-box.

'He was on telly the other day,' says Nick.

'Duke of Edinburgh?'

'He's lost it. You could see it in his eyes. Used to have that incredible stare, really impressive. He's just crap now.

41

They were brilliant though. The Sex Pistols were the best. Poor Johnny, poor old Johnny Rotten. Who do you like now? Any of the new stuff?'

'Quite like the Waterboys.' Even as I said it, I sensed it was the wrong thing.

'Oh God, you as well! Another hippy. James loves them. Yuck! All that trumpet music, just hippies.'

'I like them, that's all. I don't analyse why, or who they are or what they sound like. Can't you just like a sound without thinking about it?'

'No, that's rubbish. Music's too important. It's got a history, a social setting, complexity. You have to think.'

I would have to remember as well. For Nick sometimes contradicted himself, especially if he wanted to sound profound or controversial. Maybe I did think but I wasn't going to speak my thoughts. There was silence. But he couldn't be quiet for long.

'You going to stay around here, live in the area?'

'Probably not.'

'Nothing, is there? Nothing round here.'

He becomes thoughtful, almost brooding. 'I hate the closed-minded mentality. It's stifling, dead. God, if I stayed I don't know how I'd end up.'

'What's the alternative?'

'For sure it's not putting up with what they've taken,' he looks about the pub, at the quiet-spoken, decent people discussing holidays and Christmas presents. 'They must love it, the stinking politics, empty future. There's nothing but decay. And the Welsh are the most conservative people on earth, always living in the past.'

'You feel strongly then?'

'You must have the guts to break away. There's nothing here if you're ambitious.'

42

In the Beginning

Suzanne Vega comes on singing 'Luka'. I get up to buy the next round.

'Sit down.' He proudly fishes a fiver from his pocket and irons it flat on the table. We are rich.

'Is it fake?' I whisper. He looks offended.

'I'm probably going to hell for this fiver.'

'God knows where Thatcher and her crowd are going, then.'

'They'll redefine hell.'

'So, why are you damned?'

He drains his glass. 'Originally I got two quid from my neighbour for mowing her lawn. But I couldn't hold on to it, spent straight away. So I asked my dad. Said he was skint. That was it. No money, no chance of meeting you tonight. Then I remembered the catalogue money. Mam keeps it in a biscuit tin. Doesn't send it till Tuesday, I'll try and put it back.'

'All kids nick from their parents.'

'Do they?' He looks surprised, relieved.

His fiver was well spent but it went quickly. When we leave, it's still light and sunny. Walking up the High Street we pass a tattered copy of *Smash Hits*. Nick picks it up and flicks through the pages. He stops at an article on Madonna. Photographs show her in a flaming red flamenco dress.

'She's going down hill,' Nick says, 'Her last record was terrible. "Get Into The Groove" was excellent.' He throws the magazine into a bin; environmentally conscious even then.

We pass a young bloke in a Dennis the Menace red-and-black knitted sweater, and stop for a brief chat. He keeps flicking greasy black hair out of his eyes.

'How d'you know him?' I ask when we've walked on,

'seems like a slime-bag.'

'Got the biggest record collection round here, like a record library. Music's a serious business.'

Near the bus station are public toilets that stink from some distance.

'What a ronk!'

'They'd smell sweeter, only I had a good solicitor,' says Nick.

'Sorry?'

'He got me off from cleaning them.'

'I didn't know it was legal to make people clean toilets.'

'Community Service... Remember Rachel?' She was the girlfriend who had dumped him.

'After we split I went to a club in Newport, I was so depressed... The place was hot and smoky, and I got totally pissed. Wham! sang, "Wham Bam, I am a Man", girls in pale silhouettes danced around their white handbags. The record ended. Next the Clash screamed from the speakers. The dance floor emptied. I began a furious pogo. The floor was wet with spilt beer. A giant leap and crash, I fell flat. One of my friends dragged me up. They tried to get me to leave. One more drink. They left without me. No money, and the place was swirling. I tripped down the velvety carpeted stairs, passed the beefy bouncers in tux and bow ties. They sniggered and taunted, "Poofter". I stumbled out the entrance.

'Newport was teaming with drunks. A dangerous place. A boy and girl were having a stand up fist fight. They broke off. The girl tells the boy to piss off. He storms away down the street. She screams after him, ordering him to come back. He walks on. She cries. I walk past her; sad, more depressed.

In the Beginning

'I'm skint, alone, pissed off at the fag end of a night in this ash-tray of a town. I just want to be out of there, be home. Down a poor lit alley there's a blue Escort. I lean against it, look inside, inspect the lock, look in the window again. It's not new enough to have an alarm. There's not a soul in the street. Check the lock again. What the hell.

'Were they watching me the whole time? Was I too drunk to notice? One minute I'm trying to get in an old blue Escort, the next I'm in the back seat of a cop car.

' "Remove your boots and take out your laces," they said at the station. In case I intended to hang myself. I wasn't that fed up.

'The worst thing was telling my parents. You feel such a shit for letting them down. They both came to court with me. That's where the toilets come in. The magistrate sentenced me to three months... cleaning the bus station toilets.

' "But your honour, your honour... "

' "Be quiet," said my solicitor, and then got me a remission.'

'What did the others say,' I ask, 'James and Sean?'

'James went into a sulk. Said he was the rebel, the one in the band with a reputation. Should have been him before the court... you know, James Dean, rebel with a cause.'

I'd missed my bus listening to his confession. Nick offers to walk me home. On the way we pass the beer garden of The Red Lion. Earlier it had been full; now only a couple remains. Nick waves. The boy looks embarrassed, waves shyly back.

'Who's that?'

'Louise and Richey.'

'Friends of yours?'

Jenny Watkins-Isnardi

'No, hardly know the boy.'

CHAPTER FIVE

Nick's house is at the top of a big hill. It's hell to climb, a sheer rise. I'm going up to meet his mother for the first time, and to audition for the band.

My heart is pounding and I'm panting. Funny. A few months earlier, a friend of mine was ready to kill to get him. Kill Nick, that is. And I remember saying he wasn't worth a breath.

It was an end-of-term party in Newport. Those from around Blackwood met up at the bus station. The coach is already twenty minutes late. The wind and rain slash through, running the mascara of Punks and Goths, males and females indiscriminately. No one takes an umbrella or overcoat to a disco, the lurex tops and velvet dresses are already soaked. Me, Mandy and Cheryl shelter down wind of Mel. She's big, nearly six foot. If she'd been built into the bus station, it would be a lot less draughty.

Nick and his friend James are standing apart from everyone else. They are sort of defying the storm, or pretending it's a hot sunny day. Nick is wearing black drainpipes and a shimmering gold blouse, obviously his mother's, with bat-wing sleeves. He is a study in 'cool', facing the wind like he's sailing down to Rio on the front of a yacht. Most of us think he looks a right prick. But Mel stares at him adoring, as though he's the Führer, the superman.

The bus pulls in. On the side it says 'Merlin Coach Company' and it is about the same age as the sorcerer. It'll be magic if we don't break down before Newport.

The driver is a fat and fuming, red-faced git in detest-kids mode.

'Good to see you, Drive!' someone shouts.

'Get on, quick!'

Mimi can't make the first step because she's bound like a mummy in a tight latex skirt. Drive revs up and pretends he's going to slip the engine into gear, terrifying Mimi. Paul, a big hunk of a kid already starting a beer pot, chucks Mimi over his shoulder and dumps her in the aisle.

Before we pull off, Drive discovers he's not in such a hurry. He tells us how much he hates pixies and oddballs; he's not having drug dealers and junkies on his bus! And we're not going anywhere unless the person smoking — God knows what! (Embassy Regal) — gets rid of it. And what's more he doesn't want a peep, not a sound, not a squeal or a titter, or else he'll take us to the nearest police station.

In the Beginning

After making this fine speech, he squeezes his beer gut into the driver's cubby-hole, which is below aisle level. Because we're looking down on him he fumes even more and the back of his neck is red as a four-bar electric fire.

Martin and Paul have just shared a Stella twelve pack. Not to make a noise, Martin puts his hand up, hoping the driver will see in the mirror. If he did it's ignored.

'Please, Drive, can we make a stop?'

You can almost feel the driver gloating, relishing the thought of a bladder busting.

'Please, Drive?'

His friend Paul starts to moan. 'Pissing myself.'

The girls are really sympathetic.

'Half an hour yet, lads.'

'Have to hold it in, boys.'

'Just think of water, lovely cool swishing water.'

Martin unzips his fly and points his willy at an empty can.

'You wouldn't dare?'

There's a noise like a low-flying jet.

'You dirty sod!'

The can overflows and frothy liquid creeps down the bus. Breathing stops and all eyes follow as the stream edges toward the driver's well. If only there was an incline but it's downhill all the way to Newport, and just the one place that pee can go. Then a long leg stretches out and a big Doc Marten directs the flow under a seat and toward the door.

'Well done, Mel.'

Cheryl takes a bottle of vodka from her handbag.

'Just smell it, quicker and cheap.'

Behind them, Dave and Debbie open cans of Miller and drop in aspirins. The cans are passed around with

49

green plastic straws.

By the time the bus reaches Newport most of its passengers are pissed. Drive refuses to park outside the club, drops us round the block. We stumble off and stagger against the freezing wind. When we get to the nightclub door we're nearly all sober.

The main hall is enormous with different tiers of dance floors and flashing lights around the edges. From the high ceiling hangs a big silver ball and tiny glass squares wink to the beat of the disco.

Nick and James head for the ornate brass bar. The bar-boys are pulling pints in skimpy red shorts and T-shirts. Nick orders two halves of lager and lime. Close by is a man in stay-pressed and Fred Perry, with a tidy blonde on his arm.

'Circus must be in town,' says the man.

'How original. Never heard that one before.'

As Nick turns away he bumps into a very tall girl who stands there just smiling. He mumbles something, plonks the lager into her hand and hurries for the nearest door. Mel bursts into tears.

Nick finds himself in a smaller, scruffier room. In a poorly lit corner a group of Goths are congregated around a shiny table. Head to toe they are in funeral black and the girls sip dark rum and coke. A muscular boy in T-shirt, jeans and trainers staggers by slopping beer from the five pints in his two fists.

He belches in their direction, "alloween come early!'

There's not the flicker of smile on the Goths' crimson lips.

'Fucking oddballs!'

One vamp rolls her eyes and pouts her mouth on a cigarette, another lifts a pale hand as she yawns theatrically.

'Bunch of Lesbo-witches!'

Nick gets himself a drink and stands near a table where a boy in PVC jeans and silver-skull belt lounges back into his biker jacket. In his mirrored sunglasses is the limp image of his girlfriend. He puts a Marlboro to his black mouth and studies his languid poise in her sunglasses. They are silent, fixated with their reflections.

A DJ slob in a slack, stained shirt plays depressing Indie music. Nick gets another drink. On the small dance floor shufflers with rhythmless feet step to the dreary beat.

Nick feels a huge contempt for everyone and everything. He is getting another drink when the music stops and The DJ announces The Cure, 'Boys Don't Cry'. Even though he hates the fat bastard who sings it, Nick loves the song. Suddenly the dance floor is a swarm of Robert Smith clones in white shirts and clumping black boots with the tongues out. Thick eyeliner and red lipstick beneath dyed-black back-combed hair.

'Wankers,' mutters Nick, feeling even more pissed off. He gulps the lager and strolls back to the big room.

Soon as he's through the door, he's surrounded.

'Thank Christ you're safe!'

'She's outta control!'

'Pissed!'

'Out of her mind!'

'Mad!'

'And she's got a knife.'

No need for Nick to ask who they mean.

'You're having me on?'

'She carries a flick knife in her bag. Said if she can't have you, no one can.'

As Nick is looking for somewhere to hide, Mel

appears, mascara, washed by crying, all over her cheeks.

'NIIICK!'

Someone pushes Nick through a door. A few brave people try to block her path, and soon give way when they see the knife. She follows him out, chases down a purple corridor. Nick dodges into a Gents. Sweating, panting, he leans his head against the cool white tiles. She wouldn't dare come in.

The door opens, 'There's a nutter outside waving a knife!'

Nick rushes into a cubicle and disappears headfirst through a high and tiny window.

The air on the bus is 70 per cent proof, even the driver seems to be in a stupor. He is about to pull off when two girls in tight minis and stilettos come running into the headlights. They wave their arms like there's been a murder. He rolls down the window.

'Please.' It's Cheryl, out of breath. 'Just wait, two minutes, our friend, can't get her out.'

'You on this bus?'

'Jen!' shouts Mandy, 'You better come. Locked herself in the bog, she has.'

A slime-bag bouncer says we are not allowed back but if we're stuck for somewhere to go, we can wait for him in his flat. Cheryl pleads; Mandy's all for beating the bastard up. He's not all that big, she says. One of the double doors opens and down the corridor come waves of tortuous screaming. Mr Boss-of-the-Club wedges the door with a shiny shoe. He's dripping in gold and sickening perfumes.

'Kev. We gotta trouble in no. 2. Some slapper, she locked in.'

'Mel!' shouts Cheryl, 'It's okay Mel, we'll get you out.'

'With-a you, is she, girls? Better you come.'

In the Beginning

We make our way down the purple passage. Kev stares after us like a meal that's walked off his plate.

Cheryl gets on hands and knees, twists her head under the cubicle door.

'C'mon Mel, the bus is waiting. They're all on except us.'

Mandy has asked for a bunk up and leans over the top of the door.

'Get out you stupid cow! You wanna walk home in the cold?'

I join Cheryl on the floor, 'Mel, please, just slip the catch.'

'He hates me.' Mel is sitting on the bog, mascara dripping in a pool on the floor.

'No, Mel, Nick's just shy. On the bus he said, he said... ' Cheryl struggles with her imagination.

'He said you're a stupid fucking wanker and if you don't get out he'll come down and piss on your 'ead.'

Mel cries, quietly, shoulders shaking.

'Please, Mel... ' Cheryl, who was a swimmer, has a swimmer's big heart. She would squeeze under to comfort her friend but she also has a swimmer's big shoulders.

Suddenly Mel jumps up. She shoves her head down the toilet; retches and farts, blasting us from the door.

'You dirty sod!'

The retches change to sobs.

'Poor thing,' Cheryl lays back on the floor, 'He wasn't worth it Mel. Not worth jail.'

'Leave her, stupid cow. The bus'll be gone.'

'Please, Mel, come out, please?'

Mel lifts her head from the toilet bowl and looks around unsteadily. She sees her friend staring up with moist, pitiful eyes, and bursts out laughing.

Cheryl shoots out.

'Laughing? The fucking bimbo's laughing!'

She shoulder charges the door.

'Hey, hey. He cost-a good money!... You don't come out I'm call the cops. They got-a dogs.'

The catch slides. Out steps Rocky Horror Mel, six foot, and stooping to look small and fragile.

'You fucking tramp!'

Her metallic dress is ripped, silver tights gaping, holed. She sees a reflection in the mirror and slumps to the floor. We grab her arms and drag her to the door.

The bus is still waiting. The doors open with a whoosh of the driver's foul language. The wait has woken him up.

'Five fuckin' minutes you said! Been here twenty, bastards. Got a fuckin' home and a fuckin' family, kids your bastard age, not like you fuckin' bastard lot... '

We get on to loud clapping and cheers. Mel is pleased with herself and tries to make a bow but she's knocked into a seat. Most of the journey she's being sick into her handbag or calling out like a sheep, 'Niick... Niiick ... Niiiiick-key.' Then she drifts into sleep.

By the time we reach Blackwood the bus is nearly empty. Most people have been dropped at places coming up the valley: Risca, Wattsville, Crosskeys. The last drop was the street where Neil Kinnock and James Dean Bradfield had houses. A couple of Goths get off with James, but he hurries from them when he's down the steps.

A quarter of a mile beyond the sign, almost hidden by bushes, that announces Blackwood, we enter the dead town. The remnants go bleary-eyed down the aisle. Half-asleep, cursing the cold and regretting not taking a coat.

The bus is deserted except for us three girls.

In the Beginning

'Make her ger-roff.'

'I'm not. Had enough for one night.'

'She can go home with you, Mand.'

'No way. Mam'll be ape-shit with her like that.'

Perhaps Mel's in a coma. For all the shaking, prodding and pinching she might as well be a big bag of spuds. The bus had motored past her terraced house where all the lights were off; parents and pets sound asleep. (Mel's mother loved animals. When it was cold and wet she let the horse shelter in the passage. It wasn't unusual to be greeted by a neigh when you knocked the door. If it snowed you walked through a farmyard of dogs, a cat, a duck, the horse and a goat.)

The driver is backing out when he notices there's people still on. His scream notches to the final cog on his temper, 'Get Off! NOW!'

Authentic, no arguing with. We tiptoe with heads bowed then, shivering, watch the tail lights swing out of the station.

'That was a shitty thing to do.'

'She deserves it, stupid cow.'

At the deserted depot back in Newport, the driver has a quick look at the litter in the aisle. He glances at his watch, and decides on an early clean up in the morning. Outside, he tries the door to make sure it's secure.

An hour or so later Mel is having a bad dream. She's been kidnapped by a madman, held captive with her head in a vice. Opening her eyes, it's still dark and she can't move. It's no nightmare; she's stuck, gripped by something firm and velvety. Panic-stricken, she gropes to try and free herself and discovers her head is wedged under the arm of a seat. She wrenches free and leaps up as memory comes trickling back. Racing down the aisle, she trips over an empty vodka bottle, scrambles up cursing everything from alcohol to deserting friends and criminally neglectful drivers.

She is still pressed against the door like a Tom and Jerry cartoon when the driver appears yawning at first light. Whatever impression Mel made, kids on his bus after this said he was kindness and politeness itself.

At the top of the hill is Nick's house, a neat and solid semi. I get my breath before opening the little wooden gate. Between two compact and trimmed lawns is a tidy path to the front door. The bell has musical chimes.

A woman with shoulder-length, wispy blonde hair answers. I had not expected Nick's mother to look like this — vivacious and attractive.

She is welcoming and warm. 'Jenny? Come in, come in.' I'm led along a sunlit hallway. 'Nick's waiting for you in the kitchen.'

She is very tall for a Welsh woman, big-boned with heavy yet graceful movements.

'How was the walk? It's a killer, that hill. Gives me palpitations.'

There is no trace of a Welsh accent, her voice is refined and gentle.

Nick is leaning against the sink sipping a mug of tea. 'Alright, Jen?'

In stark contrast to his mother, he speaks with the melodic local lilt. He is a picture of drabness: red jeans, purple-and-orange striped shirt, green socks.

'Cuppa tea?'

The electric kettle is on a pine Welsh dresser. Nick's mother switches it on then nudges her son out the way to rinse a mug under the hot tap.

In the Beginning

Propped on a pine shelf is a big pin board. Stuck on it are 'Save the Whale' clippings, postcards of Greenpeace's Rainbow Warrior and various badges to do with environment and social issues. In the top left corner are two strips of passport photos. Nick's mam sees me looking, goes across and touches the photographs fondly.

'Look at his hair. Orange!' A very stern-faced Nick, taken in the harsh and shadowless light of a photo-booth.

'And this is my other boy, Patrick. He's older. Been living in the States a few years. Works with children.'

'Is he a teacher?'

'Oh, no. Helps look after kids whose parents are in the Forces. Can't teach there, needs O level maths for that.'

'Bloody ridiculous,' says Nick, 'What's he need that for? Doesn't want to teach maths. I haven't got one. Funny thing, maths. Odd the people who're good at it.'

His mother is still staring at the pin board. She looks thoughtful.

'Never any trouble, him or Nick... Though there was a time when Nick just shut himself off. Wouldn't come out for days, hours on end in his room We were worried sick.'

'Don't exaggerate, Mam.'

'And that was when... '

Nick groans, 'Oh, God.'

'... he stopped eating meat. Got so thin. Can you imagine? Thinner than now. Once he passed out, collapsed. Took him to the doctor's. Anaemic, the doctor said. Told him to start on meat straight away. Didn't have the right build for it. Remember Nick? That's what the doctor said.'

'Jenny's a veggie, aren't you Jen?'

'How d'you mean, braindead?'

'Got a sense of humour! She's alright, though, isn't

she? Small but not too thin. You ready for that tea?' She pours boiling water into the mug, dunks a tea bag a few times before throwing it into a yellow peddle-bin.

'C'mon then, bring it up with you,' says Nick.

Back in the passageway, he opens a door and pokes his head around the frame.

'Hello, this is Jen.'

His father lowers a newspaper for a moment and smiles.

At the top of the stairs Nick points to his room. 'Take my tea on in, be there now.'

The door handle is shiny white ceramic. I sense rather than see that the room is cramped, oblong. It is dark and dismal, nothing bright or light in here. The only window is small and almost hidden by heavy curtains. I part them slightly. The walls are covered with dark velveteen wallpaper, like might be in hotel lobbies. There is nowhere to sit except the narrow bed which fits snug between a wall and a pine wardrobe. The bed is neatly made with a quilt and blanket carefully tucked beneath the mattress. I lift the pillow to use as a back rest against the wall. Underneath is a pair of blue pyjamas, carefully folded. I arrange the pillow back where it was and sit prim on the edge of the bed. Everything in the room is in its place. Along one wall are some shelves with odds and ends placed exact, so you know not to touch. On a small worktop is a desk lamp. Under the window is a sweet jar with a few coppers on the bottom. The blue lid has a slit and is fixed permanent with bandaging of brown tape.

Before I've looked at the walls, Nick comes in rubbing his hands together. He stoops to switch on the light which gives a dull yellow glow. A smell has come into the room with him: sharp, clean, almost disinfectanty.

In the Beginning

'It's the best,' he says, 'Astra. Well, it's my mam's actually.'

'Hand cream?'

'The guitar. Plays hell with the skin, practising every day. I hate rough hands.' This comes out almost like an apology and I get the impression he immediately regrets saying it.

'Anyway, like I said, my mam's really. Just borrowed a bit.'

Something crashes through the half-closed door, leaps and sends Nick sprawling to the bed.

'Where've you been?'

A huge yellow Labrador slathers spittle on Nick's chin. Nick reaches up and hugs the dog to him.

'Isn't she gorgeous?'

I'd jumped up as soon as the door banged open. 'She's big.'

'Big and beautiful, aren't you Bonnie? That's why I love her.'

They wrestle to the floor, then the dog breaks free and bounds about the small space, her tail flapping wildly.

'Sleeps here, with me. Doesn't like the kitchen floor, do you Bon?'

Nick's mug of tea goes flying off the desk top.

'Okay Bonnie, that's it... That's enough!'

The dog stands stock still and stares at Nick.

'No room for you in here. Go on, out you go.'

Like an obedient child, she goes straight to the door and runs down the stairs.

'She's well trained.'

'Not trained, no. We understand each other, or rather she understands me. Animals are so much smarter than humans, got all the qualities we lack.'

'Like what?'

'Honesty, they don't lie. True feelings; trust, reliable. You got any pets, Jen?'

'Yeah, we've got a cat.'

'Ugh! Cats? Hate the damn things. So sneaky and sly.'

'Thought you said animals were honest and trusty?'

'Well, cats are horrible. Only friendly when they want food. Just take, never give in return. Evil, vile creatures. Make my skin crawl... Not like Bonnie, she's a real friend.'

'You think friendship is just convenience, mutual benefit?'

'How d'you mean?'

'I scratch your back, you scratch mine. You think friends are supposed to do things for each other; balanced out, like on a scales?'

'Hey? Talking stupid.'

'No I'm not. Friendship's not like a business. You don't do favours for each other like an exchange.'

'Don't get so wound up. I was talking about cats not people... I'll play you something. Music soothes the savage breast.'

On the floor, by the side of a black mini hi-fi is a stack of LPs and singles. He holds up a yellow-and-pink LP cover with greasy grunge faces peering out.

'Pop Will Eat Itself?'

The Poppies chant from the tiny speakers. Then Nick knocks it off and there's silence. I look at the wall, trying to think of something to say. I'd never seen blue velvet paper before, at least not in a boy's bedroom.

Nick reads my thoughts. 'Yeah, I know. it's dire. But it would take too long to get all the pictures down.'

There are hundreds; pictures, posters, photographs. Even the wardrobe is plastered. Loads are of pretty pop starlets.

'Debbie Harry's cool. Looks terrible without her make-up. Not bad for her age, though.'

'I bet she's the same age as your mother. Does she need make-up with that face, those cheek bones?'

'Yeah, not bad. But she is crap without the war-paint.'

Next to Debbie is Patsy Kensit in big colour. A slender figure in filmy miniskirt and a head tilted, coy. I hadn't taken Nick for a fan of Eighth Wonder.

'Yeah, I know, the music's shite and Patsy's not the best singer in the world. But she seems lovely and looks gorgeous, that's more important.'

Peeking out from between Patsy's ankles is a chalk white face with blackened eyes and blood red lips. The hair is spiked so fierce it could disembowel a horse.

'Put that for Patsy to shit on. Ugly cow. She's got a hard soul, don't you think?' He reaches across, grabs a corner and rips it away.

'Fucking Goth weirdo!'

'You don't like her, then?'

'Talentless git. She was nothing but gimmicks. I loathe Goths.'

'He had talent.' Nick nods to Morrissey holding a bunch of white gladioli, in National Health specs and a hearing aid.

'Had talent?'

'Liked the way he messed with gender in his lyrics. Gone downhill since that brilliant *Top Of The Pops* performance when they sang "The Boy With The Thorn In His Side". Danced with red carnations in the arse of his Levi's. Brilliant!'

'You think he's lost it?'

'Either a very big liar or a very big wanker.'

'How come?'

'Says he'll stay celibate for the sake of his art, songwriting for the Smiths.'

'What's wrong with that?' In the photo, Steven Morrissey's left arm is raised above the gladioli. The armpit is hairless, clean shaven. That must be messing about with gender, I guess. Nick doesn't explain why he's either a big liar or a big wanker. Instead he lifts the turntable arm very carefully from the record and sets it gently down on the rest. He takes the record off and blows across the surface before inserting it in the cover. On his knees, he flicks through the pile of records then holds up the Sex Pistols, *Flogging A Dead Horse*; the cover photograph is a big brown turd. I shake my head.

'Okay, easy listening... Here, one of my all-time favourites.'

He puts a disc on the turntable.

'Brilliant,' says Nick, 'absolute classic.'

Joe Strummer belts out 'Should I Stay Or Should I Go'.

'Don't get this bit, though. What're they saying in the background?'

Nick listens close to the speakers then shakes his head, 'Can't make fucking head or tail of it. Still the best Punk band ever, apart from the Punk Gods themselves, that is.'

'Let me guess?'

He nods to the wall above his bed and row after row of '70s Punk idols: the Clash, Buzzcocks, Ramones and, of course, the Sex Pistols. It is a gallery of the damned, some of the prints are frail and fading: the people in them, a decade out of date, are aged and worn.

'No need to guess, there's only Sex Pistols.'

In the Beginning

One picture has a plastic cover, the bodies beneath are oddly preserved; young, scrawny, scary. Johnny Rotten raises a finger, ice-blue eyes freezing the lens. Nancy, in fishnets and shiny patent heels, supports (out of it) Sid with scarred, razor-thin arms bared for his admirers.

Nick goes up and plants a kiss on Sid's leering lips, 'My idol. My absolute idol... Such a Punk Rocker! Lived his life exactly how he wanted. Didn't give a shite about no one. Except Nancy, loved Nancy.'

'Yeah, loved her to death, didn't he?'

'You're dead right. What passion! He had to kill her. God, what romance! Makes me faint to think about it. Better than Romeo and Juliet, better than Tristan and Isolde, better than... '

Nick tells a story of epic love and tragedy. A story that has nothing to do with the degradation and the sordid deaths of Sid Vicious and Nancy Spungen. I tell Nick he's a thick romantic, no better than a Goth.

'You just don't understand! The rock 'n' roll thing, that's how it should be. Anarchy, complete anarchy.'

'Seems strange,' I say, 'a Welsh Valleys boy identifying with these cockney spivs.'

'Spivs! You're winding me up. True working-class heroes, they are.'

'Still seems odd. Such a big cultural divide.'

'How d'you mean?'

'Well, what have you got in common? Different backgrounds, different upbringing, different cultures.'

'There's a bigger difference between you and me. I hate this fucking shit culture! What culture is Welshness? It's a fraud, all cosy, full of beer and rugby. You are too close to your parents. Break away, shock 'em.'

From outside the window come little squeaking

sounds. Nick wrenches the curtains apart.

'Skateboarders!'

He follows their progress down the hill.

'I was skateboard champ of Woodfield-Side. Stopped just before I went to college. It embarrassed my dad... They put everything in order, don't they? Do this at one age, something else when you're older, something else when you're older still. Everything's in compartments, regimented; it's part of the training, like a robot. Rich bastards never have to grow up. And little kids are the true anarchists.'

'My parents are not like that.'

'No, mine neither. Still got the skateboard. Sprayed it myself, fluorescent paint. Work of art it is. Should have seen me, could do anything; jumps, flips. Then people started shouting things like, "get a job, you lazy twat". Reach seventeen and you're supposed to stop enjoying yourself. My dad worried what the neighbours would think... He didn't actually say it but, I got the message: "Act like a man". Hate all that macho-pressure crap. What does it mean, hey? Be a man! Jesus.'

'Didn't take you for the active type, sporty.'

'Too right! Football, cricket. In the team, brilliant I was. Then I discovered girls... '

Outside, a brittle voice is raised, shouting. Nick opens the window to hear what's being said.

'... bloody lunatic! Doing my bit when I was your age! They respected the streets then! What's it coming to, hey? Hey?'

When we look out, there's an old man, bent over a walking stick. A couple of kids listen, mouths open and docile, one with a skateboard under his arm. They don't seem to have much idea how to answer his question.

64

In the Beginning

'Poor old sod. Terrible to get old, ennit? You got grandparents, Jen?'

'Don't seem to exist in Wales, do they? All die off. What about you?'

'No, none of my dad's parents, and my mam's English.'

'Hey?'

'An evacuee from the war. They died when she was young.'

'That explains the accent then?'

'Yeah, real cockney my mam, no Welsh blood there. We've got a foreigner in the family.'

'What about this audition, you trying to put me off?'

'Not at all.' Nick kneels before his record pile, 'Know the words to "Since Yesterday"?'

'Yeah, I think so.'

He flips through the singles, 'Yuck! What's that doing there?'

A record frisbees off the wall and onto the bed. It's a Damned single with atmospheric writing coming out of Gothic smoke.

'Fucking Dave Vanian, so ugly! Should be melted in hell.'

He puts something else on the turntable. 'First, listen to the Primitives, get an idea of the sort of voice we want.'

Tracy-Tracy sings 'Thru The Flowers', her voice smooth and eloquent. But the record is short, it finishes before I've taken it in.

'Can you manage something like that?'

I nod, knowing that I'd never ever even sung in the bath.

'Right, Strawberry Switchblade. I'll say "Now" when you have to start. Okay, then?'

Johnny Rotten glares down. I think of him auditioning

for the Pistols, lounging by Malcolm McLaren's juke-box singing Alice Cooper's 'School's Out'. Here I am standing rigid by Nick Jones' mini hi-fi about to try Switchblade's 'Since Yesterday'.

The record plays through while I stare dumbly at it revolving.

Nick puts it on again. He shouts louder this time: 'Now!'

He is patient, replaces the needle for the third time. 'I know it's not easy. I know, believe me... '

He goes to the window, looks out. 'I won't watch, won't turn around. Just listen, promise.'

I shut my eyes and press one ear closed. Then I'm singing with Jill and Rose, the three of us in our polka-dot frocks.

When I open my eyes Nick is staring at me. He doesn't speak straight away. Then he looks at the record lying flat and still, and he's going to ask me to do it again.

'Yeah, okay. I'm happy with that.'

'So that's it, I'm in?'

'Well, we'll see what James and Sean think.'

CHAPTER SIX

Nick is on the pavement looking bored, Saturday shoppers step around and over his gangly legs. He acknowledges me by lazily lifting his hand. I apologise for being late. He is indifferent, stands up with a reluctant unfolding of his long body. Before we begin the walk to James' house, he wipes the backside of his red jeans, buttons the collar of a lemon shirt.

'You could be drunk on these fumes.' I try to break the ice. Blackwood has a Friday night hangover. His reply is lost as a shell-suited woman hauling carrier bags forces us apart.

The valley is an endless street of towns and villages.

Jenny Watkins-Isnardi

Between Blackwood and James' place in Pontllanfraith, is two miles of main road and crowded housing. Above the town's gritty air, the hillsides are oddly green in the July sun. Each valley is quite unique. Nick's seems warmer and less hostile than mine, perhaps because it's nearer England?

Leaving the town, Nick is more relaxed.

'Had your results yet?' he asks.

'Not yet.'

'Piece of piss. Did you swot?'

Stupid question, nobody admits to swotting for exams. I shrug.

'I didn't get maths, nerd's subject. My brother's the same, that's why he can't teach in the States.'

'But he's living there now?'

'Yeah, he had a different test, an AIDs one... Everything's a test, isn't it? Always have to prove your worth. They try to wreck your self-esteem. That's James' pet hate. All bollocks, he says.'

Nick has forgotten. At the end of our walk is another sodding test. An audition to sing with his band. He'd asked me, I guessed, because I looked the part: pale and punkish. My self-esteem is shrinking with every step.

At the red brick library, our path is blocked by a man with white hair and transparent skin. He mumbles something. Asking directions?

'Sorry?'

'I said, "What's the most interesting book in the world?" '

Nick stares, disbelieving.

'The Bible?' I guess.

'No. *Gulliver's Travels*, and I'll tell you why... '

'We're a bit pushed.' Nick grabs my arm.

In the Beginning

'Where else could that happen? That's the bloody pits closing down.'

The law court is also red brick. For some reason people lower their heads and hurry past. We stroll, defiant.

'What're you reading now you've finished college?' I ask.

'Reading? I stay in bed 'til it's time for *Lace*.'

Lace: afternoon TV from the Jackie Collins book; pick of the plastic surgeon's art, empty minds and made bodies.

'Can't believe you watch that crap!'

'Hey? All those women in leather suspenders. Fantastic.'

'God, Nick. That's pathetic.'

'I'll watch what I like. Done my exams, time to relax. If I was a girl, I'd be in front of the mirror all day with my suspenders.' He's winding me up, I think.

Ahead is something decked out in camouflage; iron-stud boots, black tam. A tight little figure who won't take any shit from the world. He is weighed down and only making little steps. We soon catch him up.

Nick pats his head, 'Good disguise mate, nearly didn't see you there.'

An angry face whips round, big moustache and burly brows, eyes flashing hatred.

We run. Behind us is a frenzied drum roll of clip-clopping. I imagine sparks shooting up from the pavement. When the sound is safely distant, Nick turns and blows a kiss.

'You're not short, for a girl.' He says, reassuring. 'Welshmen are, though. It's why they get a complex.'

'Welshmen are short girls?'

'It's terrible being tall sometimes. I have to duck so they don't feel threatened.'

Jenny Watkins-Isnardi

Not far from James' house are the Council Offices —
spacious grounds, huge parking, grand steps leading to
local democracy. It's well planned.

'My mam knows someone working there.'

I'm impressed. 'In with the bigwigs, is she?'

'The big mops, more like. She's a cleaner, keeps the
whisky bottles nice and shiny.' He makes a gesture like
detonating dynamite. 'I'd soon polish it off. Lucky sods.'

Close now to James', my stomach is churning. I'd
seen him and Sean about but we'd never spoken.

'Hope my voice is alright.'

'Why? It's all shit.'

'Your music?'

'Our music? No. The business.'

I hadn't heard him joke about music before. 'I thought
you wanted to make it big, sell millions?'

We are in James' street, a terrace of grey stone
turning black with traffic grime. Through a gap in the
houses is a distant cricket pitch with white figures frozen
still in the sun. We stop, watch, wait for movement.

'Know what I really want? To be the biggest, most
famous. We'll make an album, a sublime, brilliant album.
Then the band will split and I'll kill myself.' There is no
irony in his voice.

'Yeah?'

'Sid Vicious, the way he died, young, famous,
gorgeous. I'll die young and beautiful.'

'Wow, dramatic.'

'I can imagine my funeral. Massive. Family and
friends, crying because I was so young, so talented. Loads
of flowers. Beautiful and sad.'

Something happens on the field. The bits of white all
move in unison, like someone had pulled a string.

70

In the Beginning

'I bet you'll change your mind if you ever get big. Never want to end, you won't. I can see it now: middle of the road, cabaret, comeback concerts.'

'All that fame shit! I'll die young. A work of art. The papers will be full of it.'

I remind him of a song he'd written about dreaming of drowning water and thinking of enticing knives, which ends optimistically, declaring that he never would as he's not that stupid.

'Yeah, well, the music industry's still a crock of shit. Marx predicted what would happen. Heard of Karl Marx?'

'Prat!'

'What did he say, then?'

'He said, "Fuck off!" '

'Not quite. Successful businesses get bigger until just a few dominate. In music it's MTV and Virgin, they'll own everything... world stars are corporate puppets. God bless the Beatles who've fought to keep their songs being adverts.'

We're outside a door with peeling paint. James has nicknamed his row Coronation Street, in homage to the dismal soap. He answers the knock, looking down at the floral carpet, and leaves us to fix the catch. I wait in the dark passage until Nick nudges me on.

Two rooms have been knocked together, divided by an archway. One window faces the street, the other looks onto a lane and a sprawl of allotments. The room is full of light, and noisy with chirps and chirruping. On a sideboard is a line of bird cages, each cage crammed with bright yellow canaries. The floor beneath is a mess of seed and droppings.

James noticed me looking, 'My dad's... Mam hates them, threatens to let them go in the street.' He sits on the

far windowsill, skinhead, tight black jeans and Doc
Martens.

When James was little, Nick told me, he rode a
windowsill in a cowboy hat. His dad had bought him a
mouth organ. He spent hours in the Wild West. Jesse
James?

Sean is behind some drums. A disappointing, puny
kit, nothing like the fancy stuff you see in videos. He looks
neat and compact, with a scrubbed shiny face. Nick had
told me Sean had a spot and was fanatical to get rid of it.
He grunts a greeting.

Nick plugs his bass into an amplifier and sprawls in a
worn Chesterfield armchair. He takes a plectrum from his
pocket. The chair is next to the drum kit. Sean rolls out a
beat on the snare and flourishes a cymbal, he pauses,
twirls the sticks round his fingers. James is adjusting the
mic stand. I stand by the door, an onlooker, outsider.

Nick says, REM's new single, 'It's The End Of The
World As We Know It', is brilliant. The best they'd done.

Sean pulls a face. 'It's crap! The worst REM ever.
Shit!'

James looks over, grinning. 'It's... not all that good.'

'Total shit. After "Radio Free Europe" they lost it. But
what do you expect from a Simple Minds fan?'

The strength of feeling unnerves me. Christ, are they
going to fight before we start?

'Bloody good band, Simple Minds.' Nick tunes the
bass, nonchalant.

James put his mouth close to the mic, 'Testing, one-
two-three. That okay?'

Sean and James are much more spruce than Nick,
who looks lazily thrown together. Even their movements
are more precise, more crisp. Nick says something I don't

In the Beginning

understand and James adjusts an amplifier.

'Testing, one-two-three.'

It sounds exactly like the first, but the others nod approval.

I am still by the door, my stomach in a tug-of-war.

Nick looks up. 'We all ready?'

It includes me. No, I'm not. I don't know these other two. Am I paranoid, or did they dislike me on sight? I edge unsure toward the mic.

'Jenny, you stand there.' Nick points to a spot on the patterned carpet away from the others. 'Put the mic there, James.'

'No. She might as well sing in the garden.'

'Sound better if she's further away.'

'Singing solo?' The mic stays where it is, close to the other three.

'Alright Jenny?' James smiles, genuine, warm, 'Don't worry.'

I want to hug him.

'Come on then.' Nick is impatient.

Without looking, he shoves a grubby piece of paper in my hand. The lyrics are scribbled rough, a jumble of small and capital letters. As I'm staring, trying to read, the bass and drums start. There's a golf ball in my throat and the words on the sheet are fused into one long sentence. James nods my cue...

It's a ballad/duet by Nick. The title, 'Can't Be Happy Without You', is a scramble of letters.

I must have sung something. Next moment James is beside me, taking over. Then James moves away, his eyes closed. This time I hear my own voice. The music ends. James nods, smiles. Nick's face is expressionless.

Before I catch my breath, the opening chords of

Strawberry Switchblade's 'Since Yesterday' burr out. I gulp, and sing. James moves in, we share the mic for the alto chorus. His voice is brilliant, the harmony blends like cream.

Soon as we finish, Nick wants it again... He's still not satisfied.

'C'mon, once more!'

The room is hot, airless.

'Wait, I'll get her some water.' James runs downstairs to the basement.

Sean shouts after him: 'I'll have pop!'

There is silence, then an apologetic reply: 'Have to be water.'

'Pop-man came yesterday!' Sean stares fuming at the floor. 'There was a bloody crate!'

He goes on quieter, talking to himself. 'Typical. No fucking pop. In summer for dick's sake!'

The sun is streaming in through a window but the atmosphere is dark, sour. Nick glances at me, eyebrows raised.

'We'll eat!' says James, 'Who's hungry?'

Nick forces a hand into a tight hip pocket. 'The chippy?'

James is back in a few minutes, belts down the stairs with steaming bundles. Then he's rushing up, handing out. Mine are on a plate. He's gone again, soon as the food's dispensed, rushing to the basement. Nick and Sean stand, shoving in handfuls of chips. I sit, prim as a vicar's wife. In less than a minute the stairs creak again.

'Not hungry?' I ask.

'Yeah, had the same as you.'

James' back is to Nick, who deaf mimes 'He's shy.'

My plate is still heaped as Nick screws up his paper

and lobs it at the settee. 'Right then, we ready?'

'Give her a minute.'

Sean is still angry, 'C'mon James, we're always fucking hanging round for you.'

I stuff an un-vicar-like gob full and go to the mic. James has his guitar slung over his shoulder.

'Our Zodiac Mindwarp song,' says Nick, 'belt it out. Scream!' He gives me another scrawled scrap of note book.

This time it's fast, frantic. The start is like Echo and the Bunnymen's 'The Cutter'. The room is too small, the pulses, threatens the walls. I want to just listen, be crushed in the noise. But I have to sing, solo. The words jumble and tumble, come out spitting and twisted. They stop playing. Nick glares.

'It's so quick,' I say.

'Eh, yeah.'

We try it a dozen times. I can't get it, can't get in. Punk is impossible, like chasing leaves in a raging storm.

A peeved Sean says to call it a day.

Nick shakes his head. 'We get it right once, all through.'

There's a groan behind the cymbal, 'Okay for you.' Sean holds up a hand that clutches in spasms, 'You're not holding the fucking sticks!'

They try again. The guitars race, the beat lags, my voice croaks. It tapers to a desultory fade.

'Bollocks,' says Nick.

When I come back from the toilet they are packing away. No help wanted. I stand around on the edge of their disappointment.

'Well, if you don't need me... '

Nick walks me down the passage, opens the front door. Traffic is streaming past. On the opposite pavement kids play hopscotch, their shadows short, crouched.

'So... enjoy?'

I shake my head. 'Too bloody tense.'

'You made an impression.'

'The way I eat chips?'

'Less friction with four.'

'Could have fooled me.'

A few doors down, a car pulls up. Strapping kids pile out and a tidy-looking father and mother.

'Making that bastard racket again!' They gang around their shopping as though challenging us to steal it.

'I'll have the little bugger!'

Nick pulled me into the doorway. 'He's got pigeons.'

'Right.'

'On his allotment, half a mile away. Says they won't home because of the music.'

'Right... Less friction with four? What's that mean?'

'Means you're in. Lead singer, decided when you went to the toilet. James thinks you're a bit weird but likes your voice.'

'I'm weird? Can you have women preachers?'

'We'll change the name, might bring us luck.'

CHAPTER SEVEN

There's one lamp left unsmashed, its light reflects the splinters of glass under the swings. The roundabout spins slowly, carrying Nick from dark to light then back into shadow; round and round. He is gripping a red Spillers bag and his face is sick and set, white as a mask.

We are in Tredegar Park, Risca, Saturday. In one direction are a few acres of grass and flower beds. If you listen there are low sounds, whispering and moans, completely hidden by the night. In another direction, past the swings, is the massive shape of Moriah church, five years short of a hundred birthdays. Across the road from the Moriah is The Cuckoo. We left it crowded and throbbing with music. Left suddenly because Nick had been chucked out for fighting.

'It was bloody wrong, wasn't it?'

Before I can answer he is carried away. When his face returns it is lined, angry.

'Why?' he says, 'Why bloody me?'

'Because you're different, you stand out.' I think of the crisps just opened and the lager and lime left after only a few sips. 'Anyway, you bloody deserved it.'

It wasn't even a fight. You couldn't have one in that place, so packed on Saturdays you'd crick your neck on a head-butt. He'd put our drinks on the table then changed his mind about crisps for himself. At the bar there's a space between a skinhead and a Goth. They're both big and facing each other. Nick must be the only one in the pub who hasn't noticed the electric charge across that gap. He walks straight in, and it's a wonder he's not blown straight back out.

I go up to get him away. 'Nick, come on.'

The Goth has a bloodshot eye, and picks mascara from the corner with a blackened fingernail. He's trying not to blink but can't stop his cheek twitching. The skinhead is drinking from a bottle of Nuke, his arm massive and a tattoo stretched tight along the muscle.

I grab Nick and pull. As he falls off balance there's a crack of glass. The floor around us is suddenly empty and Nick, his back to the bar, just stares at me. The bottle has flown to bits leaving the skinhead holding a short stub of the neck. In the Goth's hand is a thin-bladed knife. The twitch gone, he's got a snake stare of concentration.

Nick is turning slowly to see what's going on when someone steps from the crowd and pushes him. The blade clatters and skids across the floor sending people hopping

78

like it's molten metal.

There's a big dispute after, whether Nick would have landed on the knife. Some claim he reached out and twisted it from the Goth; others said that was instinct, if he hadn't knocked the knife away he'd have been stuck on it.

'It was him! And him!' shouts the barmaid as the landlord comes bustling up. Then, for good measure she points at Nick. 'An' he was something, as well.'

'You're all banned. Out!' The landlord waves his arms about but keeps his eyes on the floor in case someone disagrees with the punishment. Nick turns around for justice but everyone seems to be arguing their version of what happened. On the way he collects his red bag and I glance at my lager and lime and packet of crisps, still life on the table.

The roundabout comes to a stop with Nick facing into the dark. He raises his head, looks toward the shapeless black of hills that enclose this valley, his shoulders sag.

'Doesn't make sense, not right.'

'If you're tall you get noticed, simple as that.'

'No, that's not it.'

I tug the bar to pull him round. He looks defeated, pathetic, clutching the bag like it's keeping a grip on his feelings.

'I'm the one should feel bad. What did I do?'

He sniffs, wipes his nose with the sleeve of his shirt. 'Someone could've been dead.'

'You did well, then.'

'I hate this sodding place.'

The park gate squeaks. Something white glides along the path toward the swings. We hold still and watch unseen. A girl pulls up her skirt and climbs onto a seat. She strains out her legs and the chains creak, at first slow then fast and faster. She goes high, higher, facing the ground, then the sky, higher than the hills.

'Christ!' Nick is mesmerised.

The gate slams. We hear the clip of hard heels but see nothing until the reach of light. A figure in tight denim, big busted. She stands, hands on hips, following the arch of the swing. Then she bends and slips off a shoe.

'You're a cowing liar.'

'No, I never did.'

'You're a liar!'

She throws, misses, hobbles to pick it up and throws again.

'Will you fuckin' slow!'

Something else appears. A boy, scrawny in a tight T-shirt.

'Beck, you coming down? I don't love her, honest.'

The shoe floats up, curves between the chains.

This time she collects it and clouts the boy on the back of the head. He swivels and punches her face, knocking her down. She gets straight back up and walks lopsided out of the light.

'No, wait. Christine!' The girl scrambles off the swing and chases, 'Christine! Am I still your friend?'

The boy picks up the shoe and follows.

There's quiet except for the occasional distant passing of a car. Nick hugs his knees. From somewhere in the dark there's a quick torrent of swearing, drowned by a scream. The scream dries to a cough then a trickle of sobs. Pressing his hands tight against his head Nick pinches up the skin into a fantastic face lift. His eyes bulge like he's mad.

80

In the Beginning

'It's the hate. We must hate ourselves to do this. It comes from the past, the ugly past. All we know is aggression and hate.' His stare is fixed on his shoes.

'Don't be stupid. You just got thrown out of a pub, that's all. You're always dramatising.'

'Minds suffocated by these fucking hills. Don't you feel imprisoned?'

'Why should I? Not chained to anything, am I?'

'We're trapped, right at the bottom. Lower than pond life... We only exist when enough of us are killed. Even then only the freakish make news. Mine disasters are best but they don't happen these days, so we don't exist.'

'You talk enough crap for someone who doesn't exist. Were you drinking before you came out?'

He spits and hits his foot.

'Old people think we're all on drugs. I'm surprised you didn't say I was.'

'No, you're much too old Nick.'

'Old Nick, the Devil himself. Scares me, my name.' He puts on a strange voice: 'It's spoooky, eeevil.' Frightening himself as much as me, he stands and looks around. 'Is it gone darker?'

Nick had told me that he'd spent months on his own in his bedroom, isolated, alone, not interested in anyone. He'd been obsessed with writing songs and poetry. At the time he'd said, I remember wondering if it's what happened with boys or if Nick had had some sort of crack-up. Most of the time he was the most down-to-earth and normal type you could imagine. But, just very rarely, it was like an imbalance would set him off in one direction and he just kept going and going down that way; like his thinking went into a tunnel and he had to keep going along no matter where it led.

Jenny Watkins-Isnardi

At that very moment, I felt scared. 'C'mon, we'll get some chips.'

He holds up the carrier bag. 'I can't, someone's collecting this.'

The noise of the gate makes us both jump. Odd, it never sounded the same twice. This time there's a groan, like it's reluctant to open. Along the path comes the tap of a three-legged man or maybe someone on a crutch. It stops just on the rim of shadow where light catches the shiny surface of a walking stick.

'Dan,' says Nick.

Daniel dresses smartly in a suit with all the buttons done up tight. He's able-bodied, even powerful looking, but walks with a black ornate cane. And he must have big brass balls because everybody sneers and smirks as he parades through Risca.

'Danny!'

The walking stick raises in acknowledgment. Crossing the lamp light he looks Victorian. Closer, you can see he's plastered with make-up because of his terrible acne.

'Heard there was trouble in the pub tonight.' He takes out a battered ten packet of Regal.

'What was it, Neanderthal or Cro-Magnon?'

'Which came first?'

'Haven't the fucking faintest. I only know this place is stuck in the Heavy Metal age. Imagine if you took away their beer and rugby? They'd be on life support. Well, most are already.'

Maybe it's the second-hand suits from charity shops that make him seem worn and old. 'Pissed off are you?,' asks Nick.

'No more than usual in this bastarding hell hole.' He scrapes something from under the roundabout with his

82

cane; a frog, flat and baked hard. 'They should just let this place die, fucking extinct anyway. Ever get the feeling you're the only one alive?'

'Never mind. Uni in September, you'll be gone.'

'Hopefully.' Danny tries to stab the frog but the stick's too blunt. 'If I get the grades.'

'You're dead cert, guaranteed.'

He gives up trying to stick the frog and whacks it into darkness.

'Not for the grades I want... Not going unless they're straight 'A's.'

'Is that so?' Nick stands up and for some reason clutches the plastic bag like he thinks it'll be stolen. 'Well... you worked hard.'

'More or less... '

'What happens if you don't?'

'I don't go, do I?' Dan raises the stick to his eye like a telescope. He looks along it toward a distant hill and pulls an imaginary trigger. 'Boof! Fuckin' fate, ennit?'

There's silence, awkward, embarrassed. Then Danny says he has be off.

'You didn't give him the bag.'

'He's not the one.' Nick stares at the spit stain on his dap.

'D'you think that's an excuse, about getting the right grades?'

'Course. He's bloody trapped.'

'Maybe he's afraid?'

'What of, his shadow?'

'Have you noticed how people moan and moan about work, boyfriend, parents, but they won't change things? Then again... it's a little pond and he's a big fish.'

Nick balances his backside on a metal strut. 'Yeah,

maybe.'

'Which?'

'What?'

'Which d'you think? Moaner or big fish?'

'I think. I'm pissed off. Danny's a coward not a fish.'

'Let's see what happens when you have to go.'

'Give me the grades and a grant, I'd be off tomorrow.'

'Nothing here to keep you, then?'

A shadow appears by the lamp, coming from a different direction to the gate. It hesitates, unsure.

'Nicky?... Nick?'

'Jenny!'

Nick jumps up. 'Headless, that's you!'

We meet under the light. He shakes hands with Nick. His clothes are smart, not local; even his shadow has a sharper edge.

Headless is a couple of years older than Nick and has moved to London. Nick's mood is transformed, all smiles and a bit bashful. 'They said you were home.'

'My sister's birthday.'

'Oh yeah? Wild! Where is she?'

'Her birthday's tomorrow.' He is an art student, an escapee, a hero.

'How's London with the election? They like Kinnock?'

'Kinnock? Don't see much of him. What about the group, Nick? The Manics still manic?'

'Jenny's gonna sing with us.'

'Aw, wild!' Headless looks at me. 'You must be chuffed?'

And then at Nick. 'She up to it?'

'So, who's big in London?'

'Fuzzbox, d'you like them?'

'Fucking shit.'

In the Beginning

'Good punk band. Thought you were the punk-meister?'

'They're pox. Fakes, like Cyndi Lauper, Sioux, Kate Bush.... I fuckin' hate fakes.'

'God, Nick. They didn't tell me... Are you bitter or what?'

'No, I don't think so. No more than normal.' There's a rustling noise in the fencing of shrubs just beyond the swings. Nick stares into the shadows.

Headless pulls up his sleeve to show a woman's watch; delicate, dull yellow. Undoing the clasp, he holds it to the light and reads the symbols on the back. 'Real gold, solid. It was my gran's. Want to try?'

'God, she had big bones.' Nick jangles the watch on his wrist.

'Looks good on you, keep it.'

'Don't be daft, probably a heirloom or something.'

'Nah, not really my nan's. I bought it in a flea market. There's loads in London, you can get anything.'

'Yeah, well, we got bargain shops, heaps. Only things doing well here.'

The noise is there again; scary, goose pimply, a sort of brittle slithering that makes your imagination go nuts. Behind those bushes is the Moriah with God knows how many thousands of dead spirits sitting in its pews. I suggest we go for chips.

'Why don't you come back with me, Nick, to London? Plenty to do there.'

'Nah.'

'You could come as well,' Headless says to me as an afterthought.

Nick opens the red carrier bag and pokes about whatever is inside, 'I'm all set,' he says, matter of fact,

'University in a few months. Can't mess up, can I?'

'Jesus, Nick. That's what they planned for me. It's just to keep them happy. Is it for you or them? And what happens after Uni, teaching?'

'We'll all end up buried in Blackwood, so what's the odds?'

'Make some detours first, for God's sake. You're depressed, Nick. Stick around here and you'll go mad.'

The bushes explode. A shadow charges across the playground, a bull's head smashes through the swings. Me and Headless duck by the roundabout.

'Christ, Gozzgog.' Nick sounds relieved.

I look up and see a massive Duran Duran hairdo silhouetted against the sky.

'They said you wanted to see me.'

Me and Headless stay down around the roundabout.

'Yeah. I want you to give something to Rachel.' Rachel is Nick's ex.

'Scared the shit out of you, didn't I?'

'They're in this bag.' Nick holds out the red carrier.

'And I scared the daylight crap out of you two.' Gozzgog nudges Headless with a cuban-heeled boot. When Headless gets up, his eyes are taller than Gozzgog's but his head is a few inches shorter.

'They say you can see a person's soul in their hair,' says Headless.

'Well, fuck, take a good look.'

Nick smoothes the carrier bag, 'Will you give it to her?'

'Will I!' He takes the bag, sits down and tips out the contents. There's posters, neatly cut out articles: the Alarm, Zodiac Mindwarp, the Beastie Boys, the Damned, the Mission...

86

In the Beginning

'What's all that for?' I ask.

'I want to stay friends, no harm in that.'

'No harm at all,' says Gozzgog, 'we're mates, I'll give it to her.' He holds some posters up to the light. 'Oh yeah,' he purrs, 'she'll love them.' Amongst all the stuff is a luminous pink envelope.

'That's private.,' says Nick.

'Not between friends.' Gozzgog starts to open the envelope but Headless knocks it from his hand.

'Don't be nosy.'

Gozzgog blinks, surprised. 'Tell the London poof to fuck off where he came from.' He scoops the papers and some dirt into the carrier bag. The park gate bangs.

'He's vile. Why'd you give the stuff to him?' I ask.

'God help. He's Rachel's best friend.' Nick slaps Headless on the back, 'A London poof! You've made it, then?'

'I'm a foreigner already, only been gone a year.'

'Mustn't leave, see. They don't like it if you do.'

CHAPTER EIGHT

The summer they electrocuted the Rosenbergs was queer and sultry. How can a summer be queer? Sylvia wonders what it would feel like to be burned alive, all along her nerves.

The book is almost touching James' nose as he reads aloud: startling prose about startling things — exections, electrocutions. He is short-sighted, won't have glasses because he's self-conscious. He still recalls the embarrassment of wearing brown NHS specs when he was a kid. There is a small, discreet distance between us, so our thighs do not touch. When the bus lurches, swaying him over, he grips the seat in front to stop our shoulders nudging.

He pauses and stutters slightly, ' "I... thought it must be the worst thing in the world." ' Then he looks up, not quite making eye contact. 'They gave her electric shocks.'

I find this a bit heavy first thing in the morning. 'Yeah? Just a story though.'

'No it's true. Her life.' He shuts the book and points to the name, Sylvia Plath, on the cover.

'She cracked up and they gave her electric treatment. Listen to this.... ' He flicks through the pages, points a finger and reads a passage about the author having metal plates strapped to the side of her head. ' "There was a .... Whee-ee... ". '

He stops suddenly, aware of heads on the top deck of the bus, turned to a sound that's like a squealing pig. After closing the book, he stuffs it into a carrier bag.

'What day is it?'

'Wednesday.'

'Shit! English first thing. Bloody teacher calls the register out loud. Tells everyone my name.'

'How else she gonna do it, telepathy?'

'She's the only one shouts it all.'

'James Bradfield? Got a nice ring to it.'

'She says the middle bit as well.'

He whacks his head with the Spillers carrier. Whatever the 'middle bit' is turns him into a head banger.

'That bad? Don't tell me: Aneurin? Lloyd?'

He squirms. 'Worse, much worse. Dean... James Dean Bradfield.'

'Wow! James Dean, your real name?'

Leaning close, he puts his hand to his mouth, 'My dad. He loved cowboys, and rebel films. James Dean was his hero.'

90

In the Beginning

Then he relaxes a little, sinks down in the seat. 'Could have been worse. He liked John Wayne as well... John Wayne Bradfield. God, think how I'd have to walk and all the loonies queuing to beat me up.'

'But you don't like the name, James Dean?'

'Hate it, prattish. James Dean: rebel, cult hero. Not exactly me, is it? Feel such a fake.'

He looks in his carrier, ruffles through some papers. 'What else have I got? Can never remember today.' Unfolding a creased and cracked timetable, he traces a finger along Wednesday. 'Oh God, Pete piece-of-piss for drama. He's hopeless, his class is a dawdle. We found a big pile of page three girls in his drawer. Shocked us; don't deserve respect, do they?'

'Sad buggers, teachers. Who'd want their job, end up like that?'

'Yeah.' James looks out the window. He seems glum, perhaps thinking about not becoming a teacher and not finishing up like Pete piece-of-piss. Whatever he thought, when he looks back in he's more cheerful.

'See telly last night?'

'Nope, I was out with Nick.'

'Brilliant film. One of my favourites, had Matt Dillon, can't fail. If I was a girl I'd dream of snogging him all night. Got those cheekbones, like Nick's. Seen that film about fifty times.'

'What's it about?'

'A club, El Flamingo, summer in the '60s. Dillon has this job parking cars and he's eighteen... '

The words come spilling out.

'... Really, it's about making choices when you're young. You know, important choices.' James was quite a bit older than me, almost a year. I didn't have much idea what he was on about.

'Yeah, sounds horrible.'

'Knowing what you want to do with your life.'

'What to do, hey?' The weekend was miles away.

'Important to know what you want, isn't it?'

'Very.' Would I have chips for lunch or a yoghurt?

'Look at people around college. Easy to tell the ones who'll end up in shite. Fancy dying in this shit-hole? Years go, before you know it you're too old for anything. I heard kids talking about pension plans! Might as well make a coffin and jump in; living dead.'

He becomes quiet, turns his head, stares again out the window. He's talked himself into a bad mood. After a wait, when the conversation seems to be over, I take a *Melody Maker* from my bag. Before it's opened James snatches it. 'Excellent! Won't be a minute.' He flicks straight to the Indie charts, scans quickly and reels off bands I've never heard of.

'*George Best*! It's there, brilliant!'

'Heard of him. Footballer?'

James stares at me, unsure if I'm joking. 'Eh, yeah. But I'm talking about the album: Wedding Present, *George Best*. In at 47, fantastic band, such passion. They're going to be huge!'

He's about to hand the magazine back then changes his mind. 'Just want to check the Pop charts... oh good, Bananarama... And Kylie!'

'Kylie Minogue?'

'Love her to bits. I'm her number one fan.'

'Even with Jason, those duet things?'

'She's so tiny and gorgeous. I could eat her.'

'Oh well, my sister's a Kylie fan, she's ten.'

'Good taste, your sister.'

In the Beginning

He stabs a finger at a big picture spread; a very tall man with a pony-tail stands over the rest of the band like he owns them.

'God, I hate them. Seriously weird. One ended up in a nut-house; another disappeared, went walkabout. And that woman... ' he almost punches her face, 'always swishing her bloody skirt, cooling her fanny. Makes me spew.'

'Better turn over then.' I thumb through the pages. 'There, they're pretty good.'

'The Waterboys?'

'Thought you liked them?'

He grins, sheepish, as though being caught out. 'Well, yeah... "A Boy Called Johnny", that's a classic. You know the song's about Patti Smith?'

It seems odd he relishes raving about Kylie but is shy to admit liking the Waterboys. He closes the magazine carefully. 'They're just a bunch of hippies really.'

So that was it, he had a low opinion of hippies. No matter how good a band's music was, if there was a sniff of hippiness it cancelled out their merits.

He returns to looking out the window. The clouds are darker now and spatters of rain streak the dirty glass. His mood is changed again, he seems happier, more content.

I open the magazine to the Gig Guide.

'Gene Loves Jezebel are in Cardiff. Going to see them?'

James glances quickly. 'Fuck off!'

'Don't you like Welsh bands? Everyone in college is going.'

'All the girls, you mean. Disgusting. Please close the page.'

'What's the problem?'

'Can't bear to look, plastered in make-up, revolting.

Even wearing lipstick. That's not a band, it's sex-on-sticks. Rather throw a tenner down the bog. Wouldn't go if you paid me.'

'Don't worry, no chance of that.' What a jerk! Turning small talk into a bloody lecture.

'Please don't mention them again. Puts me out for the day.'

I wasn't going to mention anything again. If the gap between us had been the Grand Canyon, it wouldn't be wide enough. He stares out one window, I stare across the aisle and out the opposite.

At the next stop a boy dressed identical to James comes up the stairs: tight white T-shirt, tight red jeans, Doc Martens and a hand-knitted cardigan. He stops, leans across and pokes James' shoulder. 'Alright?'

James was still huffy. 'Miles, see you later.'

The boy carries on down the bus and gets a book from his Spillers bag.

'Sorry,' James nudges my arm, 'it was stupid. I get too wound up. Buy you a coffee, make up for it.'

Crosskeys College cafeteria is bleak. It's a fish tank looking onto a main road; inside there's tables like desks and a few vending machines. The space is all straight lines and angles, hard. When we get there, the floor already has a dandruff covering of bits of polystyrene. The place makes you edgy, nervy; if you don't smoke, you break up coffee cups.

James had asked the boy on the bus to come. He had something to do and said he'd be along later.

'Notice his ear?' says James.

'Bit discoloured, was it?'

We sit with our machine coffee, gritty and bitter.

In the Beginning

'Miles was an original,' says James, 'in the band at the beginning.'

'Really?' Nick might have mentioned him before. But whatever he'd said about this Miles didn't stick in my mind as important. 'So, what was it like, what happened, in the beginning?'

James leaned back in his chair, looked out at the traffic and the rain.

'Nick was always clever, confident about his A levels. Knew he was headed for university. A degree and a good job was certain. It was all too predictable. Like those plays I had to study, where the fate is already decided. Nick said there's no point if you know the end. And where's the excitement?'

I nodded my head, confused. Maybe because I hadn't read the plays.

'The stories he'd written, lyrics, poems, practising the guitar. They'd all be a waste... Nick made a list, mainly old school friends, that he'd like to form a band with, then narrowed it down. Miles, bass; Sean Moore, drums; Nick, rhythm; me, lead guitar.'

'And who came up with the name?'

'Manic Street Preachers? Me and Nick.'

'What does it mean?'

'I dunno. Perhaps we'd seen some loony with a bible around Blackwood... We did Sex Pistols, Clash, Blondie. We were raw energy. It took a while for Nick to show me his own lyrics. I knew straight off they were brilliant, good as any of the cover versions we were doing. Then we worked together, putting them to music.'

'So you were playing gigs?'

'No, that was just practices. One of our first appearances was with another band, Funeral in Berlin. We rented a place in Blackwood, The Little Theatre. It's a bricked-up old chapel with the pulpit ripped out and a stage put in. Stinks of damp.'

James broke off the story as his friend, Miles, plonked himself down at the table. 'I was just telling Jenny about one of the first gigs.'

'Oh yeah? Told her about this, then?' Miles touched his ear. Now I was aware of it, it looked deformed. The lobe was purplish and swollen, the skin flaky, like he'd caught it in a door.

'Better if you say, it's your ear.'

'It's dead, can't feel a thing. Rotting off, I expect.'

'What happened?'

'Well, wanted to be the part, didn't I? Shaved my head but didn't look hard enough so I locked myself in the bathroom with a sewing needle, a safety-pin and a bag of ice. Sterilised the needle and pin with steam off the electric iron.

'Took a couple of ice cubes and pressed 'em on my ear. Stung like mad. Then it went numb. Got the needle and pushed; won't go in, so I have to screw it, like. Wouldn't believe how tough the skin is, and just as I break it the feeling comes back. Christ! Nearly passed out. In the mirror there's this pasty face with blood underneath. The needle's halfway through, and it's hard to get out, all slippery. Anyway, must have been making a noise because there's a knock on the door and my mother asking if it's something I've eaten. Flushed the toilet and yanked the needle. Before the cistern's full I've jammed in the safety pin. Next thing I know, I'm puking down the bowl and my mother's asking was it what she cooked... '

'You haven't finished yet,' says James, 'what about the flyers?'

In the Beginning

'Oh God yeah. I'd said I'd give out the little photocopies we did. They were handmade, advertising us in The Little Theatre. Well, I left it to the last minute and went to Blackwood with this big, throbbing ear and a bloody T-shirt. Stood in the High Street trying to give these things out to Saturday shoppers. Before you knew it, they were crossing the road not to pass and I had the pavement to myself. Then some bloke came out and said if I didn't clear off he'd call the cops.'

'So how did it go, the performance?'

'I don't want to hear this,' says Miles. 'See you.' He gets up and slings his Spillers bag over his shoulder.

'Wasn't that bad. Funeral in Berlin was on first. All in black. The singer was fat, loud and dead common. And he was sweating and tone-deaf. The song was about nacrophiliacs, nymphomaniacs or insomniacs. That's how it rhymed, all the way through. Nearly all the audience was Goths; any colour as long as it's black. When "The Bin" finished their last number the place was half empty. There were some kids drinking Strongbow. Nick was so nervous; leaping like mad to "God Save the Queen". They started throwing cans, and Nick's jumping, ducking and weaving. Well, that wasn't so bad. But someone busted up a piano, threw a chair at it. Miles still feels terrible, that's why he won't talk about it. We got banned, anyway. Can't play there again. Pity, it's a nice little place even though it stinks.'

'What happened with Miles? Why did he leave?'

'He just turned up for a practice and said he was leaving, wanted a solo career. Nick begged but Miles was adamant. That was it, no point in three of us carrying on. Then someone, Nick I think, came up with busking in Cardiff. A sort of test to see if just the three of us would be okay.

'Nick's dad took us because his car had the biggest boot. But there was only room for Sean's drums. Me and Nick had our stuff on the back seat, and we somehow sat on the floor. He dropped us off in St Mary's Street, a few hundred yards from The Hays Plaza. Sean threw a wobbly, said he'd look a prat lugging his stuff through the city so he left all his stuff in the boot, took a tambourine. We had no amplifiers. Ever heard punk without amplifiers? We tried to make up for it by all singing together. Didn't impress anyone. We had 32p after three hours, and 30p was what Nick put in as a float.'

James was renowned for sitting in the canteen, drinking coffee and being bored. It was time for class.

'You staying here?' I ask.

'I shouldn't. They threatened to kick me out. Me and Sean had a scam going, borrowed bus passes from two kids who lived in Newport. We'd bugger off for the morning, go to record shops. Never bought anything but we got a music education. We'd go to a pub, a real dive. Make half a lager and lime last hours. Nick came sometimes. If he had money it went in the fruit machines. Brilliant. We'd talk about being on *Top Of The Pops*, even what we'd wear. Then Nick would spoil it by saying he'd kill himself when we'd made it. Bloody stupid. Absolutely serious he was.'

Was James having me on, about Nick? Winding me up? There was a famous story of James' audition for the drama class. Pete-piece-of-piss told the twenty or so hopefuls that they weren't allowed to speak but had to draw attention to themselves. Something original, unusual. Most kids started stripping off, which was probably what Pete had in mind when he thought up the test. James was so shy he just lay on the floor. Then he

In the Beginning

closed his eyes and started shivering and quivering, and seemed to be having a fit; tongue drooling, and his face in spasms. They didn't know if he was pretending; someone forced a ruler between his teeth. Even the nurse they called thought he was epileptic. Perhaps it was real, perhaps he convinced himself? Maybe he was too embarrassed to snap out of it? No one recalled him having another fit, though.

'Bugger it,' says James, 'more coffee?'

'Have you got money?'

The place was starting to empty, reluctant kids dragging their feet and bags toward the door. Before long just a few die-hard stay-aways are left.

'I can afford it. I'm rich!'

'What've you been fiddling, then?'

'Had to get a job.'

This time we have hot chocolate, powdery and very sweet; delicious. First two lessons are now history. By way of thanking James, I tell him everyone thinks he's dead lazy in college.

'Bloody cheek! Know the Memo in Newbridge?' Did he mean the Memorial Hall, near Crumlin, on the way to Six Bells? These were tough names, they made people tremble in the soft towns to the south.

'I do weekends in the Memo.'

'Gerron! Is it bad as they say?'

'Well, last Saturday was Rockers' Night... Go through the doors of the club at quarter to six. Those doors are famous, huge, like castle things, white but stinking dirty. Jane, the woman I work with, is already there wiping glasses. She's always smiling. But she's got nothing to smile about. Two kids, and her husband's out of work. Weekdays she's a dinner lady. Counting her job in the club, she

99

works every day and never complains.

'I take off my jacket and put it under the bar. First thing is check the bottles. That's easy. Only thing they drink is Diamond White and Nukey Brown. Next is the hard one, pluck up courage for the cellar. It's like Frankenstein's crypt. The steps down are rotting and it's damp, cold. Flick the switch and the bulb stays dead. Back up the stairs, get the torch by the till. The batteries are gone, taken out for the radio. Jane throws a box of matches. God, I hate this. The draught on the stairs blows the matches out. So you walk down in pitch-black, afraid a step might give. At the bottom, strike a light and prey the barrels were changed in the afternoon. There's so much rat shit and spider crap, all you want is get back up the stairs, quick.

'Me and Jane have half a lager before Mr Big arrives. The glasses are soft plastic so they won't cut. The night's show lug in equipment, dump it by the small stage and come straight to the bar.

' "You the Gun-Slingers?" says Jane.

'Three men and two girls. The men have hairdos like architecture, overhangs with dye and gel. One of them orders three Jack Dan doubles and two shandies. The girls take the shandies to the stage and start setting up the stuff. The men whack the drinks back and order more.

'Mr Big, the sec, comes in, looks around, ignores everyone and goes to his booth by the door. Inside, he takes off his green blazer and waits, tapping a pencil against the chipboard shelf, looking out. People start to stream past. His eyes are careful, scrutinising each one. Then suddenly his pencil beats a drum-roll on the front of the booth.

' "Members only! Members only! You strangers?" Two

girls freeze in their tracks.

‘ "Need a member to sign you in!"

‘ "Don't fuckin' know no one."

‘ "You'll have to wait."

'They stand to the side. The DJ plays Guns n' Roses, "Welcome to the Jungle". Mr Big sees a trusty member, aged a hundred and six.

‘ "Will, will you sign these young ladies in?"

‘ "Her with the hair but not the other."

‘ "Don't mind d'you Sha'?"

'Left at the bar is a lone Gun-Slinger, seeing off doubles. "Still get nervous see, on a big night."

‘ "Lays 'n' Hentlemen! All the way from Merthyr, a rock legend and sensation making their debut at the Memo... " A thrash of drums. The singer skips to the mic in tropical shorts and neon shirt, undone to his hairy beer gut. He air-guitars the opening to "The Final Countdown".

‘ "Good, this. Play it well we do," says the stray Gun.

‘ "Shouldn't you be up there too?" asks Jane.

‘ "Wouldn't mind another drink."

‘ "Yeah, that's what I want." A bloke with his head hunched in his coat, swaying with an empty glass in his hand. "Left me she did. Said I was potching." His eyes are red, watery swollen. "Gutted I am, gutted."

‘ "Can't believe it," Jane reaches over and folds down his collar, "Not the type. You, potching?" He has a ring of love bites almost circling his neck.

‘ "Well, just the once, like."

'A fading rocker with patched denims and grey ponytail comes to the bar. "Shite this lot. I seen the best ever. Know that don't you?"

'I shake my head. "Rolling Stones?"

'His beefy fist nearly melts the plastic pint. "Fucking

101

Stones, who're they? Quo! Like 'em?"

' "Oh yeah, very intricate."

' "Don't like the sound of that."

'A woman totters up behind and jabs him in the back. "Larry! You pissing me about? Asked for a brush, I did."

' "Sorry doll, this fuckin' kid... "

' "S'cuse me love." The woman leans across to Jane. "Haven't got a hair-brush have you? Only I got this problem... " She reaches up and shakes her beehive. "It's getting a bit thin in the middle. See? Gonna collapse on me."

'Jane opens a counter drawer. "Think I've got just the thing... " She hands the woman a can of Pronto, quick-acting spray.

' "You're a doll. Ta, love." The woman leans over at the hip, gives her head a good gassing.

' "So just watch it," says Larry, being pulled away by his woman. "Intricate? What sort of fuckin' word's that?"

'Handy, that spray. Our main weapon in case of attack. I never used it, but legend said it set like superglue, and you could freeze someone in mid-head-butt. We got other stuff as well, air freshner that stinks like ammonia. I use that on Compost Corner. That's where the dope heads spliff. Hazy as the Milky Way. Now and then something red-eyed comes from under the fog and goes to the bar or bog. When the smell gets too bad I spray it like crops. They cough and splutter but can't complain because the stink would carry to Blackwood cop shop... '

I interrupt his story. 'You don't smoke, James?'

'Nah. I need the adrenaline, strive on stress. Don't like dope, makes you too relaxed. Rather a drink. Mind, I gotta say, the smokers don't cause trouble. There's a Chinese takeaway outside the Memo. But you don't have to go that

102

far for a fight. You can have one before you cross the road: girls most often, they don't seem to need the preliminaries, or maybe they're just impatient. In the chip shop, though, it's guaranteed. Half the fun of going in is hearing the pre-fight build up. Really original it is:

' "What you starin' at?"

' "These tiles on the floor."

' "You lyin' cunt! Don't like my shoes, do you?" Biff! Bash! Smash! If there's no one they've got a grudge against, they pick on the poor sod behind the counter, and she's Italian.

' "Egg flied lice an' ch-rips preeze. An' make it sh-nappy." Makes you proud, it does. One bloke even told her to shove her ch-rips up her Chinese arse! Terrible, isn't it? They don't bother to clean the window. Not worth it when there's a new pane every week. I blame education. They don't teach 'em proper these days, in schools and colleges. Fancy bunking off to Newport?'

CHAPTER NINE

It's my second walk along James' street. I can't remember the number so I'm looking for plastic flowers. Again I pass the fading Labour poster in Neil Kinnock's window. The house seems deserted, a symbol for the time. Across the road is a small used car place, no more than a yard and a few vehicles. The salesman looks over, shielding his eyes from the sun. Finding nothing of interest he goes back to wiping the dust from a cronk.

I must be near James' place. The father of the funny family comes out on the pavement and stares after me. Turn around and he'll ask if I want a fight. The trouble is that three or four windows have flowers and without looking in it's difficult to tell if they are fake. I'll have to take a chance, were they purple or pink? I press the bell on pink.

Jackpot. I hear feet belting along the passage. It can only be James. He answers the door in olive-green T-shirt and black jeans.

'Sorry I'm late.'

He looks down at the doorstep. 'Don't worry, we're just sitting round.' Remembering why I've called, he stands aside to let me in.

The low sofa and baggy armchair have been pushed tight against a wall. The room looks bigger, less cluttered, even though the free space is taken up with amps and microphones. The drum kit is to the side of the cleared area, off centre stage. Sean smiles from behind a big cymbal. 'How's it going?' His face is scrubbed and shining, his hair almost radiant black. Nick is kneeling on the floor in a white shirt with huge turquoise spots. His guitar is slung on his back like a rifle. In his hand is a lead, and he is looking at the rows of sockets on an amplifier.

'Late,' he mutters, without turning round.

'Right, we're ready to go!' says James and immediately runs downstairs to the basement kitchen. Sean gets out of his seat and lifts a cushion off the settee. He crams it into the hollow of the big drum.

'What's that for?' I ask.

'Two things. Muffles the bass drum so it's not so echoey and ringing. That means, in a way, it's more exact and oddly enough sharper, more accurate.' I hadn't expected such an explanation, let alone a couple of sentences.

'What's the other thing?'

'Keeps the noise down. Neighbours.'

In the Beginning

James has returned and, without speaking, hands me a glass of water. I always feel like saying, how kind, how thoughtful are these little acts. But I accept the water with just a nod.

Nick gets up rubbing a knee. He bends then straightens it, and there's a loud click. The wide guitar strap cuts into his neck, which looks raw from the sun. Is that why he's irritable? He hooks a thumb and adjusts the strap over his collar. I sense Sean grinning at me behind his big cymbal.

'What was this adventure you had yesterday, Jen?'

Nick bangs down on a bass string. 'For God's sake, are we ever gonna start?'

'Tell you later.'

James is at the mic. 'Testing, two, three, four.' He beckons me over.

'Are we now darn well ready?' asks Nick.

'Will someone say what we're doing?' I plead.

'Should have been here earlier.' Nick thuds the bass. There's a clanking and crashing of rhythm guitar and drums. I recognise the opening to 'Since Yesterday', just. Before the chorus, James moves to the mic. His voice is tender. Perfectly pitched for the high la-la-las.

Halfway through Nick stops.

'What's wrong?' asks James, to the accompaniment of desultory drums.

'Jenny's too slow coming in. Okay, try again.'

When the song is finished, James says he had a burning in his chest.

'Hope it's not your heart,' says Sean, flat, without emotion.

'He's getting old,' says Nick, 'we'll try something slower: "Can't Be Happy".'

107

Jenny Watkins-Isnardi

James closes his eyes, concentrating, waiting for his entry. When he sings, his everyday protective armour falls away. Shyness, reserve, suspicions disappear. He forgets himself. His voice is honest and raw. Exposed. He sings with his soul.

The song finishes and there's a pool of silence that the rest of us are reluctant to disturb. James turns up the volume on his guitar. His left hand presses strings way up the neck, right hand flicks the plectrum. High-pitched, piercing notes cut quick and razor-sharp. He stops abruptly, plays the exact same notes again and wah-wahs the tremolo. He picks faster, careening the trem; the room fills with a revving wail that bounces around the walls.

'For fucksake!' Sean screams above the noise, 'The neighbours!'

The silence following this seems to throb. Nick smiles warmly, proud of James. Then there's a Clang! Clang! Clang! of the door knocker.

'Christ! Who's that?'

'Can't they see there's a bloody bell?'

'He was on the doorstep,' I say, 'that nutter. He's in a blind rage, I expect.'

'Hell.' Nick ducks down by the settee. 'You go, Jen. He wouldn't hit a girl.'

Sean is crouched low behind the drums. 'I wouldn't bet on it.'

James slips out of his guitar strap. Clang! Clang! Clang! He freezes.

'Well, he can't break the door down.'

'No? Smash that ruddy window though.'

I walk on tiptoe toward the curtains. 'What's wrong with these people? Why are they so aggressive?'

'It's the woman's genes,' whispers Sean, 'her whole

family are fuckin' nuts.'

'Nah, it's living round here,' says Nick, 'enough to crack anyone up.'

Peeping out, I see two frumpy women with handbags. One of them has a pile of magazines under her arm.

'Why haven't I gone mad, then?' asks Sean.

No one replies.

One of the women leans forward. Clang! Clang!

From further down the street comes a man's voice. 'They are in, the bastards. Keep knockin'.'

'It's alright, just a couple of Jovas,' I call.

James stands behind me, looking over my shoulder.

'Answer before they knock the fucking door down,' says Sean.

'It's your house as well.'

Clang! Clang! Clang!

Nick gets up from hiding and stands behind James. 'Got a bloody nerve, haven't they? I mean, you know, persistent like.'

'Is anyone fucking going?' Sean throws his drumsticks and marches toward the passage.

We crowd by the living room doorway.

'There's a bell here, see.'

The buzzer sounds in the passage, making us jump.

'It seemed not to be working,' says a woman's voice, sweet and well-spoken.

'Well, it seems to be okay now, don't it?'

'There was rather a loud noise, we wondered if it could be heard?... Mummy and Daddy not in?'

'Mammy and Daddy is not in, no.'

'Ah! When the mouse is away? Student, are you? My son's also in college.'

'Good, I'm glad. What d'you want?'

'We have a message... '

The man's voice from down the street interrupts, 'In fuckin' jail, they oughta be! Locked up!' A door slams.

Sean doesn't give the woman a chance to continue. 'Look, just gimme a *Watchtower* thing. I like them, they're funny.'

Sean sits on the settee with the rest of us pressed close. He turns the pages and stops at the drawings, taking longest over big ones with crowds. 'Either they've got crazy grins or they look at the sky dead worried. It's like they live in a mental asylum and they're scared of Martians.'

'They're so boring,' says Nick.

'Yeah,' says James, 'to be good you have to be boring. You have to be boring to get into heaven, so think how boring heaven is? And it goes on forever.'

'To get into heaven you gotta wear a three-piece suit and have a perm, and if you got a rucksack it's better.'

'But no make-up,' says Nick, 'that's me out... Christian Rock? Contradiction in terms.'

'Cliff Richard,' says Sean.

'Jesus!' James jumps up as though his bum's been stung. 'He's the package, Sir Cliff Tory Richard.'

Nick lifts his guitar from the floor. 'Dad reckons we're condemned never to get the government we want.'

James nods agreement, 'Yeah, it's torture being lumbered with what the English vote. That's why these Jovas do so well. It's either them or top yourself.'

'You depressing sods,' says Sean, 'I don't wanna talk politics.'

Nick plucks a deep bass note. 'Unavoidable, mate, with Death's Head re-elected.'

At the centre of the magazine is a picture to colour in.

In the Beginning

It shows people and animals sitting around a big lake with palm trees and snow-capped mountains in the background. A man with a bowler hat and umbrella has an arm around a lion.

'Surreal ennit?' says Sean. 'Feel sorry for the lion, though. Looks like they get tranquillised in heaven.' Over the page is a maze puzzle. At the entrance of the maze is a sort of neon casino sign, saying 'Enter', and in the middle is a big head and beard, and arms outstretched, welcoming. 'Not much of a prize, is it?'

I point to the sides of the puzzle where the wrong paths lead to fires and monsters with lots of heads and a great many teeth.

'Better than this.'

Sean traces a finger along one of the routes. His first try takes him off the end of a precipice into a waiting, gaping tooth-filled mouth.

'Pathetic,' says James, 'I can think of worse than that.'

'Like what?'

'Thatcher, for a start.'

'Yeah, they need to update hell a bit.'

Nick is sitting in the baggy chair, absorbed in running the fingers of his left hand silently up and down the frets. 'Anyone see the Style Council thing last night?'

'On telly?' says James, 'Yeah, it was alright.'

'Alright? When they did, "Walls Come Tumbling Down", it was just brilliant!' Nick sings the lyrics into his chest, barely audible.

'He was good in the Jam,' says James. 'When they did "Underground" on *Top Of The Pops*... talk about passion. It was unbeatable, amazing.'

'I'd give an arm and leg to do stuff like that. Fantastic words.'

Jenny Watkins-Isnardi

Sean is not interested in Paul Weller. 'Heard Echo and the Bunnymen's latest?'

Nick screws up his nose, 'McCulloch's voice is... I don't know, not right. Sounds awful on that "Lips Like Sugar"... Eh, I've got a version of "Train In Vain" for you to listen to.'

James and Sean both nod, silent. Nick grips the little yellow plectrum and clears his throat self-consciously, although he has no intention to sing. It's a heavier, clunkier version of the Clash song. James and Sean watch, still as statues, their eyes following the fingers of Nick's left hand pressing out the bass. It's slow at first but then gains momentum and gallops toward the end.

We all smile. James nods, strumming his guitar. 'Play the chorus again.'

As Nick picks through the bass line, James plays rhythm. He hums along with the tune, adjusting and correcting his pitch.

'Back again, from the beginning.'

This time James puts in the lyrics. As he sings, he is staring fixed and mesmeric at Sean. But Sean shakes his head. 'No James, too low.' James closes his eyes, picks the song up in a different place. There's laughing. James opens his eyes. 'Too high, you sound castrato.' Sean strains to mimic the high pitch. Nick joins in and they both howl like cats.

'Shurrup, You'll have the Jovas back!' shouts James.

He tries again and finds the pitch.

'Okay.' Sean picks up his sticks, mimes a silent rhythm beating the air. Then he closes his eyes and hits the skins. He repeats the same pattern half a dozen times then nods his head. 'After three... '

He clacks the sticks: one, two. James takes the mic, I

112

stand to the side, arms folded.

The music comes in slabs of heavy rhythm. A bit slower, it would be old Rolling Stones R&B. They are concentrating intensely with complete conviction, when Nick suddenly stops.

He slips the strap and leans the bass against a chair. Ducking low he creeps over to the window. James' guitar frizzles out and the drums slow to a one-stick beat. Nick peeps over the sill. 'Brewer!' he hisses. Sean gets up and walks toward the window. A pale, lank arm waves Sean to a crouch.

'What's he doing?'

'Lookin' at cars, the flash bastard.'

Brewer, lead singer with Funeral in Berlin, is nodding, hands in pockets, to the salesman. The salesman fiddles with his cuff-links, shirt sleeves sticking out like Christmas crackers.

'Make a nice couple, don't they?'

Brewer's donkey jacket, with NCB on the back, makes him stoop. His legs look so fragile he could do with another pair to support the coat.

'How can he afford that!'

They are in front of a car that reflects the sunlight metallic blue; the salesman dabs his cuff now and then onto the sparkles.

'Where'd he get the money for a car like that?'

'Where'd he get money for a car?'

'Where did he get money? They never have bookings, not real bookings.'

'Perhaps his father found a job?'

'Can't be paying on HP. They do a check.'

'I don't understand. Doesn't make sense.'

'Wouldn't you like a car?' I ask no one in particular.

'It's no big deal.'

They turn and stare at me.

'You're old enough to drive, why not have a car?' They ignore the question and look back to the window, as though I suggested they buy the Tardis or Starship Enterprise.

'Ah, look!' cries Nick.

The donkey jacket is getting into a sick-looking little car with no hubcaps and sad, lifeless red paint.

'Fucking cheapskate.'

'Wanker!'

'Wouldn't be seen dead in that heap. Just goes to show... '

James is first back. He makes adjustments to the amplifiers before picking up his guitar. Sean and Nick are still engrossed in the sunlit scene across the road. 'C'mon, you two. Having a mother's meeting?'

Sean returns to his kit, rubbing his hands together and smirking, 'Love a bit of gossip, I do.' He starts drumming the intro to "Dear God". Nick gets up stiffly, rubs his knee and there's that click as he stretches his leg. He takes long strides in a loping skulk as he ducks back to his chair.

The song is one of the few originals they do; suicidal lyrics penned by Nick. As James is playing the opening bars, Nick calls across to me:

'On your own, Jen, solo.'

The music gets faster. The words trip over my teeth, awkward, clumsy. Nick stops. We start again, from the beginning. I concentrate but it's like doing a tongue twister backwards in a foreign language. 'Entice' spits out as 'Invite'. We stop again. Nick is fuming mad, he won't look at me; I have offended his writing. He turns to James.

114

In the Beginning

'Show her.'

James looks embarrassed, shakes his head.

'Show her for Christ sake, we'll be here all night!'

It's no wonder I can't sing. The bass is random thumps and bangs, the drums thrash with no rhythm and the guitar detonates explosives. Yet within the chaos is James making sense of the scramble. He knows when to pitch words against the noise or let his voice be smashed by the guitar and drums. Sean suddenly lets go his sticks.

Nick turns on him, still pumping the bass. 'C'mon!' If he had a whip he'd crack it. Sean pulls an agonised face and rubs his left shoulder. 'What's wrong?'

'Arms, killing me. Let's have a whiff?'

'D'you mind?' James asks me.

I smile, the surprised and dumb smile of an outsider.

'Yeah, you don't realise,' says Sean, 'looks easy on *Top Of The Pops* but it's bloody murder.' Nick lolls back in the chair, legs draped over the sides. He is immediately relaxed, eyelids drooping, hands clasped loosely over the big turquoise spots.

'Is that your mother's?' Sean stays behind the drums. He twists the silver clasps on the side of the snare, and tests the tightness by tapping with the tips of his fingers.

'Might be, not sure.'

James can't stay still. He fidgets and buzzes about like a bee after pollen; in and out the fat beams of sun that shine through the window, dense with a myriad tiny specks. The room is warm and airless. I perch myself on the edge of the sunken settee, my legs itching in thick woollen tights.

Against the opposite wall is a dark Formica sideboard. Behind the smoked glass are posed lines of polished figures: a girl with the sun on her cheeks and a floppy pink hat, three cute puppies by her buckled shoes. A couple dancing; the boy in fitted jacket and knickerbockers, his partner light as a ballerina, skirts flounced and flowing in an imaginary breeze.

James comes to rest on the settee and follows my gaze. I sense his seething embarrassment, his frustrated anger. Samantha had told me how he hates what he thinks is cheap and vulgar. He feels like knocking the ornaments to the floor, smashing their heads. He looks about the room; from the rolling seascape framed on a wall to the vase of plastic at the window. He turns his head to the chirping, shitting canaries.

Sam said he'd like to torch the place, burn it to the ground, watch it disappear in billowing smoke. He would put a match in the mess of allotments at the back of the littered lane. The whole street, including Neil Kinnock's house with its flash Habitat fittings and leftover London furniture: the parish, district, council or whatever it's called, he'd like a hot angry, spitting bonfire. He feels the shame of poverty, of living in a forgotten province; a place scraped bare, that has no excuse to exist. He feels the guilt of knowing that his parents and their parents and theirs have been enslaved and all their toil has come to this. And he feels you are given just enough hope to be told there is no escape.

'Which d'you like best, James?'

'I think I like the shepherd carrying the lamb.'

'But his head is missing.'

'Yeah.'

Sean brings over the chrome kitchen stool he uses with the drums. James has offered to make tea and we listen to his footsteps hurrying down the stairs.

'So what happened, then?' asks Sean, 'I heard it was

In the Beginning

an expensive trip.'

'I wonder which story you heard?'

'The bus didn't turn up.'

I could have told Sean the same version I'd said to everyone who asked about the Star Burst Festival near London. The bands included Gaye Bykers, That Petrol Emotion, Voice Of The Beehive, Pop Will Eat Itself and Dr. And The Medics. All favourites of me and Sam. The £17.50 took a lot of begging and scrounging but it included a bus from Cardiff, and we couldn't wait.

My father took us at first light to meet the coach. He made us double-check the place and the time. No one else was waiting at this spot but we persuaded him it wasn't cool to be this early, so he left us shivering on the corner of Westgate Street.

When it was nearly time and still no one had turned up, we felt excited being the only ones from Cardiff. There was another queue, down the far end of the street but they must have been going to a different place because that wasn't the pick-up point for Star Burst. And, coincidentally, a bus did turn up about the time ours was due, and that queue piled on.

Sam sort of suggested we might run and check but I said if it was our bus, all the people would know we'd been standing in the wrong place. So, when it drove passed we pretended to be window shopping, at half-six in the morning.

Sean nods. 'Christ, that's really tough. I bet you feel terrible?' There's not a hint of sarcasm. 'Any chance of getting the money back?'

'Doubt it; our fault.'

'Yeah, but even so... you wouldn't deliberately do that.' Now I can't tell if he's taking the piss or is really sympathetic.

James comes in with a tray of teas. Below the glass doors of the cabinet is a shelf cluttered with trinkets and photographs. In a small silvered frame is a boy with a basin fringe of straight, dark hair. He stares from behind NHS glasses, gawking at the camera, wide cake-hole mouth. James hands me a flowery mug, glances at his ten-year-old self and gives an embarrassed, tight-lipped smile.

Sitting too far back, I sink into the settee. Tea slops onto my lap. 'I should've said, the springs are gone.' James grabs the mug from my burning hand. Sean throws the cloth that's used to pack the microphones. Nick looks on, slurping.

For a while this is the only noise, and Nick is as oblivious as a snorer. Suddenly James drains his mug and rushes into the passage. He speeds flights at a time up the stairs. Footsteps bound above us, and then he is jumping back down and into the room. He stands in front of Nick, holding a tattered paperback. 'The Lunch.' Nick looks at him, puzzled. 'William Burroughs, *The Naked Lunch.*'

'You found it? Excellent!'

'I read it ages ago.'

'Who's that?' says Sean.

Nick holds up the faded cover.

'Yeah, and I read it before him. That's the bloke with weird titles. What's the other one? *Dead Fingers Talk*, or something.'

Nick turns over the pages, 'The writing's even weirder!'

'He made sentences from bits of newspaper,' says James.

'Shot his wife. Made her put an apple on her head, like William Tell, and missed. Didn't go to jail, though. Said the trick went wrong. Who'd wanna go to the States?'

'Wonder if we'll tour?' says James. 'Why's your brother there, Nick?'

'Don't really know. Looking for a job? Well, there's nothing here.'

'Funny place to go.'

'How's that?'

'Most head for Newport. Cardiff, at a push.'

'Yeah, I suppose. P'raps he thought the States had more to offer?'

The basement door bangs shut.

'Wind,' says Sean.

James speeds down the stairs. We hear James and a woman's voice.

'His mother.'

The tap is turned on and water pours into the stainless steel sink.

'Making her tea.'

Something, a tin, falls and rolls across the floor.

'He's putting the shopping away.'

'Good to his mother,' says Nick.

'She'll be asking who's up here. If he says a girl, she'll tease him and ask your name and if you're pretty.'

'Thinks every girl's his girlfriend.'

I feel uneasy. 'Will she mind me being here?'

'Not at all,' says Sean. 'Knows her son's a good boy. Always did his homework, never messed around.'

'It's funny,' says Nick, 'she's so proud of him. He loves books and uses big words. Sticks at things, sees them through. She's glad he's in a band with his best friends. Already started a scrapbook, convinced he's gonna be famous. But James is sort of removed, can't share. Secretive, she says he is.'

119

'No, not so much secretive,' says Sean, touching a spot on his chin, 'more, like... puts up a barrier. Well, yeah, secretive.'

'Talking of which... we're making a change.'

'That's not a secret.'

'Well, no, not any more.'

'It never was a secret.' Sean sits back relaxed, hands behind his head, hair immaculate.

'No, I know. But Jenny didn't.'

'How could she? She haven't been told.'

'Well, then... until someone's told, it's secret, ennit?' Nick waves his big hands about expressively.

'No, there's lots of things we're not told but they're not secrets. Like, for example, there must be loads in different languages and we just can't understand. Don't mean they're secrets.'

'You're just being stupid, Sean! I'm not on about that kind of thing. What I'm saying is, if you don't tell somebody, deliberate. You're keeping a secret.'

'But, it's not deliberate. We're not keeping it from her.'

'Well it is a bastard secret till she knows!'

In the quiet that follows, there are footsteps on the stairs. Not hurrying, scurrying but heavy, measured.

'Oh, shit.' I push myself forward to the edge of the settee, ready to bugger off.

James grins round the door, 'Mam said stop fighting or she'll sort you all out.'

'It's Nick, making a big thing about changing the name.'

'What d'you think of it, Jen?'

'Haven't a clue what they're on about.'

Nick breaths a deep theatrical sigh. 'Now we've got a girl lead, they want to change the name to Betty Blue.'

he Manics hit London.

The band live in action during their early years.

Generation Terrorists photo shoot, 1992.

Top: The boys from Blackwood.

Below: The band in Tokyo, for the *Motorcycle Emptiness* video shoot.

Top: Backstage at Birmingham University, February 1992.

Below: With Traci Lords.

Nicky signing autographs outside the *TFI Friday* studio.

The band at the MTV Europe awards, 1998.

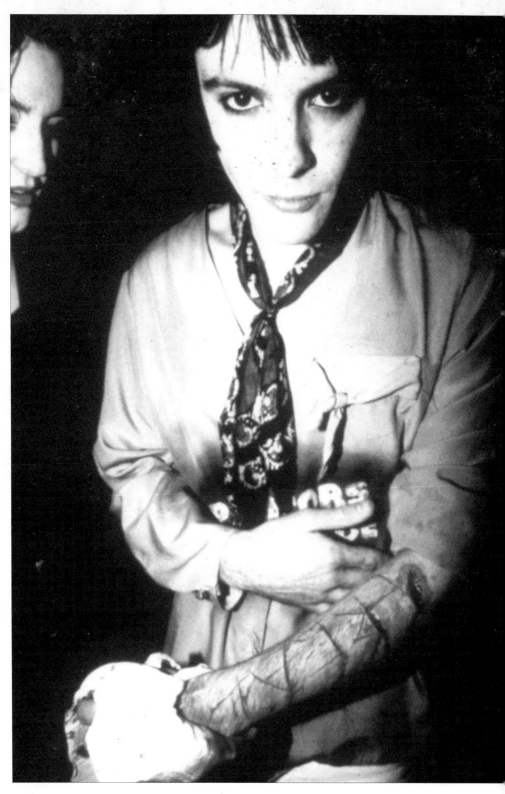

Richey: the one who was not part of the original line up. This shot was taken after he gouged the words 'for real' into his arm with a razor blade during an interview with a journalist.

In the Beginning

'They? We all agreed!' says Sean, 'But it's mine, my favourite character, Betty Blue, from the French film.'

'Are you sure?' I feel flustered. 'I mean, Manic Street Preachers is so... different.'

'Nah,' says Nick, off-hand, 'it's only a ruddy name.'

'I'm flattered.'

'Why?'

'Well, changing it for me. Like... I dunno, an honour.'

'Hey?... it's not being changed only for you. Betty Blue's a good name. I like it.'

In spite of Nick acting like a moron I feel included, part of the group.

'Tell you what,' says James, 'show her the video, how a good singer is.'

'Ah, yeah, spewy. Where's the remote?'

James pulls the curtains. By luck a slice of sun shines on the dancing couple in the cabinet. 'You had it last, Sean.'

'No, I didn't.'

'Yeah, last night.'

'He's such a plonker.' Sean smiles at me confidentially, a new ally.

'For goodness sake.' Nick kneels in front of the telly, presses Play on the video. Zigzag lines flicker across the screen.

James belly-flops beside Nick. 'Strange this, doesn't happen with the remote.' He pokes rewind. There's a loud clunk.

'We lost a remote once,' says Nick, 'Turned up a year later in... '

'What's this!' Sean's hand is pressed down the side of the cushion. With a guilty grin he eases out the remote control.

121

'See!' James looks across to me. 'Told you. That's his telly chair.'

Steve Wright is looking cool in a chunky sweater under hot studio lights. He welcomes us to *Top Of The Pops*. We are quiet and attentive, absorbed by an ageing moustache and dead eyes. Then Sean's thumb flicks something at the screen. 'Gerroff, you old bastard!'

The picture fast forwards to the Primitives. Their singer, Tracy, is figuresque in a cut-tight black suit. Like a miniature Monroe she pouts, flutters her lashes, shakes her suicide-blond hair.

'Manage that, Jen?' Nick is sitting up, hugging his knees into his chest.

'Anyone can fuckin' mime,' says Sean.

'No, she's not miming. Brilliant voice.'

'So, why's her lips not moving to the words?'

There's a push to get close. Two noses almost touching.

'No, I tell you, she's live.'

'Yeah, course. She is alive, but she's fuckin' miming.'

Nick shakes his head. 'No, never.'

'Jenny can't see!' James shoves the other two out the way. 'Tell you what, she's really small. Below five foot.'

'Nah, never. Taller than Jenny. What height are you, Jen?'

James saves me the bother. 'Everyone's shorter to you, Nick.'

'My mam's not.'

'Her purse is though,' says Sean, cryptically. He presses fast forward, and Steve Wright Jackie-Jumpers through the quick flicker of acts. 'How'd you lose a remote for a year, Nick? I can't hardly believe it.'

'Where did you say it was found?'

122

In the Beginning

'Stop!' Nick grabs the remote. 'I like this one.'

'Oh, no.' A universal groan as Marti Pellow tilts his head coy to the camera. 'Sweet Little Mystery' comes across sweet and sexless.

'Fuck! These make me puke! Puke, puke, puke.' Sean does a show of sticking a finger down his throat. 'It's nothing. It's like... fuck all. It's fuckin' air.'

'Supposed to be.' Nick is engrossed.

'When we're on, we'll fuckin' murder it! Won't know what hit 'em.'

'Not supposed to be anything.' Nick talks staring in a trance at the screen. 'It's new every minute, not burdened with history. If Pop had tradition it'd be dead.'

'Shit! What was all that?' Sean gets from his chair to sit on the floor in front of Nick. 'Sometimes you frighten me.'

Nick presses the Off. 'So what d'you think of that cover then?'

James tugs open the curtains. For a moment we sit squinting like newborn bats. 'Which one?'

'The one I done, "Train In Vain".'

'Yeah?... Not so bad.'

'What d'you think, James?'

'Sounds respectable. Needs beefin' up, though.'

'Beefin' up?'

'Yeah, for sure. Something missing.'

'Such as?'

'It's thin.'

'What's this, a fuckin' soup kitchen? What d'you mean it's thin?'

'I dunno, needs some spice.' James looks mischievously at Sean. 'Could do with a bit of trumpet.'

'Crumpet?' says Nick.

'TRUMPET!'

Sean stares back murderous. 'Fuck off.' He doesn't like to be reminded of his days playing cornet in the Welsh National Youth Orchestra.

'Up for one more run through?' asks Nick.

Sean glances at his watch, 'Suzanne Vega's playing Newport, I'm a bit pushed.'

'Hey? She's not there for two weeks. You walking via London?'

'Promised to get tickets for Rhian.'

'I suppose she's too busy? And you're paying?'

Sean shrugs. 'I suppose.'

'How've you got the money? Honest, you're daft as a brush with her.'

Downstairs in the kitchen a cupboard door slams.

James looks jittery. 'Yeah, maybe it's time to pack in.'

Like a subtle sheepdog, he guides us toward the passage. I just have time to pick my cardigan from the arm of the settee.

'What about all the stuff?' asks Nick.

'Don't worry, I'll take care of it.'

The catch clicks as soon as the last heel is over the doorstep. The street is deserted except for the car salesman. He glances up for a moment at the three kids who will never be customers of his; scruffs, freaks, with no ambition and no hope of affording his motors.

CHAPTER TEN

Amanda-Punk listens, elbows on the table, her chin in her palms. She's really pretty if it wasn't for that mohican — the sides of her head are smooth as egg cups. Opposite Amanda, Rhiannan, Sean's on-and-off girlfriend, slides her glasses up the bridge of her nose; her voice is clear and deliberate. She wants Sean to hear. She reads about some traveller putting a blanket on the hot sand to sleep.

At a nearby table, a man in a yellow sweatshirt listens closely as he pretends to concentrate on stirring his tea. There's a hole cut in his shoe, on the side by the big toe and a bit of red sock pokes through. He is shiny bald with black-framed glasses, and as he swirls the spoon round his cup he has a stupid grin like he understands something secret.

Rhian puts the book on the table and shouts the last words of the sentence, before slamming Jack Kerouac's *On The Road* on the table.

The Dorothy ceiling fan creaks in the heat. Sean wipes his index finger along the line of sweat on his top lip. He gets up unsteady and Rhian scowls at his back as he makes for the drink machine with the picture of a dog with its tongue hanging out.

Also here are James and Nick. This is part of the Saturday ritual, always the same: spend the morning deciding what to wear and getting ready to hit Blackwood High Street. The hair is hardest. You'd never think it took so long to get that 'hasn't been brushed in years' effect, that 'just left to rot'. But it must be exact, precise. Too much and it looks managed, a stage effect. It has to be so precise that your parents take offence, they think it's an insult to the way you were brought up and the soaps and shampoos in the bathroom.

We meet up, and usually there's no mixing of the clans: Goth and punks are as separate as oil and water.

In the High Street it's Woolworth's for records, the big newsagents for music mags and Barnados for clothes, though recently a string of places have been opened, like the Red Cross and the Cancer Shop. From Woolies to the last charity shop takes up until late morning. The afternoon is spent in The Dorothy.

The talk never dries up. We discuss telly, films, books, bands and local gossip. Never politics, really, because no one watches the news or really reads the paper, at least they won't admit it. In winter the cafe windows steam over, the hubbub of the outside street disappears. Inside

In the Beginning

it's cosy, with kids who're skint sharing cappuccinos, and shivering and complaining each time the door opens.

Today is a Saturday and slap-bang in the middle of summer. It's a scorcher and college has finished. The tables are busy with students. Regardless of how much the sun shines, everyone wears Doc Martens or monkey boots. Most kids are drinking cherry- or raspberry-flavoured slush-puppies. Two boys, obviously rich, sip pink milk shakes in tall glasses through candy-striped straws. They're next to the window, the best place to sit.

The windows look out on to the High Street. The bottom half of the panes have cane blinds, individual hanging sticks that you can push aside to look out. Sean always hogs the seat next to the window and is forever shifting the blinds. Inside, the walls were once white but years of fags have made them dirty beige. Apart from a line of wicker lamps suspended from the ceiling, the L-shaped room is simple and unadorned. It's not obvious why The Dorothy should become the place to be, apart from the two brothers who own it. Nick likes it because of the fruit machine at the back, near the unisex toilets: a sip of tea and a quick gamble. The allure for me is the seating. The booth-like tables and benches have been fixed to the floor since the '50s. The burgundy vinyl seats are padded and comfortable. With a bit of imagination and keeping the cane blinds closed, you could be sitting in Italy or France.

Nearly all of us who come here are dreamers. We vow to avoid the 9 till 5, never get married, to travel, become actors, writers, poets, rock stars. A rock star is the ultimate. The Dorothy is full of the future's big names. Everyone is in a band of sorts, or doing something for someone in a band. There must be more groups per square mile in Blackwood than anywhere else on the planet. The

127

talk about bands is serious, and what matters most is image and attitude. No matter if you can't actually play anything, that's irrelevant. What's vital is how you'll look and how you'll act. That has to be spot on, dead right. Just a little either side of the right image is naff, copycat, catch-up stuff.

The ones already in a band swan about the place as if they've already made it. God knows what they'd be like if they actually got a booking. When there's a rehearsal somewhere public it's the talk for weeks, and they're so cocky it's as though they've been signed up for mega bucks.

Everyone knows the two most important groups are Funeral In Berlin and the Manic Street Preachers. The Funeral In Berlin boys are super cool with serious attitude. They refer to girls as 'bits of stuff' and a long-time girlfriend is just 'seeing someone'. They can drink ten or twelve pints and not throw up and they've seen every Goth and Indie band ever to play in Cardiff. And, hey, there hasn't been a band yet good as Funeral In Berlin. When the big deal is struck, F. I. B. will strike it.

Nick, James and Sean don't have this, 'I'm in a band' air. They rarely spout off in The Dorothy, though they discuss it plenty when they're by themselves. Come to think of it, that's all they ever do talk about. Maybe it's too important to throw around just to impress or make small talk? But with other people they are unpretentious, almost humble. That's not to say they don't believe in themselves, because they do. It's as if they know something the rest of us don't. As if they're waiting, biding their time; like it's fated, they know what will happen.

Nick says, 'It's the mouthy ones with all the right gear are the idiots. They'll never make it.' He never minces his
128

words and prides himself on being outspoken.

Today, though, he's hardly spoken at all since arriving at The Dorothy. He could be in one of his sulks. Before coming here we called in the Wishing Tree chip shop. Nick asked me to get the fritters, as usual, but I refused because it's me every time. He hates going in, because the owner's son knows Nick's brother, Patrick. They always ask Nick for news. Nick went in and they asked tons of questions. They spoke about Patrick with a lot of affection, like he was something of a saint. No, it's not the chippy. Nick is looking out at a strip of street between the bamboo canes. He seems absent-minded, thoughtful.

The chain holding the 'Closed' sign on the door rattles. A skinny kid who used to be in Crosskeys college comes in, dressed tidy in radiant white jeans and a black T-shirt. At the counter he buys a Kit-Kat. On his way out he passes our table and nods shyly. 'Nick.'

On the pavement he peels the foil back precisely and takes a neat bite of the chocolate. Then he's gone amongst the women shoppers and their carrier bags. James looks at Nick. 'Was that hello?'

'He must've seen you,' says Sean. 'Nick's a celebrity.'

Rhian has slipped out of her seat and combs her finger through the ends of her brown hair. She stares at Nick. 'I saw you. What the hell were you thinking of?'

She doesn't give him time to reply. 'Why did you do it?'

Nick looks at her without any expression, 'I just felt like doing it.'

'Boys can be so silly, can't they?' Rhian hitches her holdall higher up her shoulder. 'Ready Mandy?'

Amanda waves to me at the door. 'See you Jen.'

'What was Rhian on about?' asks James.

Jenny Watkins-Isnardi

Nick replies with the same deadpan look. 'She must've seen me on telly.' A radio that was humming away in the background seems suddenly loud and sharp. John Paul Young sings, 'Love Is In The Air'.

James looks at Sean, and puts a hand over his mouth to cover a wide smirk. 'Fucking shit music!' Sean must have had a serious fall out with Rhiannan. When he's miserable he cheers himself by spending money. James watches, as he slides a tray along the shelf by the counter. The coffee machine spits and hisses. James follows every move as Sean points at the display case of pies, pasties, doughnuts and egg custards.

The centrepiece of Sean's feast is a steam-heated pie that gives off mouth-dripping vapours, the soft crust is soaked in rich gravy. Before cutting into the pastry, Sean glances at James. The knife releases a funnel of savoury smells

'Bad luck fat boy, you're on a diet.' James gets up quickly. I think he's going to smack Sean and steal the pie. Instead he goes to the counter.

'Cut it out, Sean.' Nick is so pious sometimes, as if we're all his children.

'Cut it out,' mimics Sean. 'He'll be sorry for laughing, I haven't half started yet.'

James places a Pyrex cup and saucer and stares down at it glum. Sean shakes the sugar bowl under his face.

'What's the matter, afraid of getting fat? Go on, have some.'

Lately James has taken up swimming and running. Every night he disguises himself as a fugitive, all in black. Then he runs a circuit of the valley in a test of physical stamina and mental discipline. There's temptation all around: pubs, chippies, takeaways. But he doesn't stop.
130

In the Beginning

He's conscious of his body shape and wants to be hard and muscular. His nightmare is ending up like a lard-arsed Mickey Rourke, the actor he once loved. So no more junk food, goodbye greasy chips, curry and Peter's pasties.

'These pies,' says Sean, 'they gotta be the best.' He takes the cap of crust off showing the juicy insides. Then he digs the fork in and lifts a chunk of meat. James sips his tea, the little finger delicately crocked. Sean seems to lose interest in the teasing and uses his knife to part the bamboo curtain.

'Christ, did you see that! Bev Thomas, used to be a right stonker. Now she's a right fat cow.' He grins a mouth full of food at James. 'Still got nice tits, though.'

'The Fine Young Cannibals are covering a Buzzcocks.' Nick often broke into conversations like he's been orbiting on one of Jupiter's moons. He speaks flat, deadpan.

'It's alright, too.' James is glad of the change of subject.

'No it's not.' Maybe that's why Nick has been moody all day? One of his favourite bands has been covered. Surely he couldn't take it that seriously?

Sean pulls his cappuccino in front of him, closes his eyes and sniffs at the chocolate-stained milk. Then he pushes it toward James motioning him to smell.

'You like Frankie, don't you Jim? Would you believe it? Frank Sin-fuckin'-atra.'

'He's got a pure voice,' says James.

'What the pissing hell does that mean? Pure voice? Like, there's nothing in it? Pure my arse.'

'Gonna try my luck.' With an effort Nick slides from the bench like he hasn't got the energy to get up. Soon as he's out of earshot I ask what's wrong.

'Pre-menstrual,' says Sean, 'makes him a moany cow.

131

Just ignore him.'

'He blew the allowance on a fruit machine,' says James, 'didn't last an hour.'

'And, that telly night is still playing on him... ' adds Sean.

A week or so before, James and Nick had gone to The Studios. Nick thought about the cameras panning the audience at the end of each show, and wanted to be on TV. S4C, the Welsh language channel, showed a live comedy hour every week. We found out about The Studio from a big notice in college that advertised a night's entertainment with free transport and drinks. The first few times, the courtesy coach was standing room only. But it soon dropped away because the actors were always cocking their lines up and there would be retake after retake. Besides which it was all in a foreign language and we were bored shitless.

As soon as you get off the bus, in fact, there is a sort of mental apartheid. The studio assistants gabble away in Welsh and the ones who understand were first to the drinks and refreshments while we stand around like the proverbials at a wedding. It's all very civilised and proper but the whole time it's like being in a foreign country. We are referred to as, 'non speakers', which must be their euphemism for leprosy. All we have to do is make the right sounds at cue cards. Oddly enough these are written in English, and some of the gags are obviously so bad that the Welsh speakers have to rely on the cards as well because sometimes the timing is right out.

Anyway, Nick and James had been the only ones on the coach. There's no guide for the seats in the studio and they settle under huge lights that burn into their necks. James spies a kid in uniform carrying a tray of drinks and

In the Beginning

says he'll get a couple of lagers. Nick is fumbling with something in his pocket.

'Gyda or heb calch?' asks the boy.

James looks blank. The boy repeats, 'Gyda or heb calch?'

When he realises James is a non speaker he asks roughly, 'With or without lime?'

Nick takes a sip and pulls a face. 'Gnat's piss.'

A man with a clipboard comes officiously towards them and jabbers away nineteen to the dozen. He gesticulates, speaking quickly, and his tone says it's urgent. James stares down at his shoes, Nick looks guilty and puts his hand in his pocket. Kids on the row in front turn around to watch and giggle. Then a voice from someone they can't see says, 'Talk to them in English, you ignoramus!... He's asking you to move seats. You're in a row reserved for cast members.'

Nick and James scramble over the backs of their chairs.

'Thanks,' calls James to the voice.

An hour and four pints later the show begins. The lager might be like gnat's piss but it destroys their timing on the cue cards. They give up trying to laugh and slump back in the seats. At the interval James goes in search of the lager boy. He's so pleased to get the drinks that he thanks the boy in his best and only Welsh: 'Bore-da!'

Nick is looking forward to the end, when the camera pans and zooms in on the audience. He feels in his pocket.

The programme was shown a week later and Nick watched it with his mam. The camera picked him and James out a few times as part of the crowd and Nick's mam said they both looked ill. Then as the credits rolled there was big close-up of Nick. A really close close-up of him

133

taking a pair of red satin knickers from his pocket and putting them on his head.

When he comes back Nick is happier.

'How much?' asks James.

'Seventeen.'

'Fantastic!' says Sean.

A shadow falls across James, the sun must have found a cloud. 'You lost seventeen quid?' he asks mildly.

Nick shrugs. 'I only had two to start. Then I won some... and lost some.' He is a true sportsman, it's the taking part that counts. Besides, it's not the money but the machines that he loves. The buzz.

Clang! Clatter! The door opens with an extra-zestful push, and Lenny the religious nutter disappoints expectations. Behind his back Leonard Protheroe is called Len Again because he's a born-again Christian and has a habit of repeating himself. No one can remember what he was like before being born-again so we all think he was always the same — that is, not born-again but just born like it. Behind him are Louise and Sam — Louise in vinyl and sweating like a pig on a spit, Sam cool in a summer frock. James' arse seems to tighten. Lenny, the gentleman, allows the girls to sit first.

'Sorry Len,' says Sean, 'no room at the inn.'

Lenny looks anxious. Was Sean deliberately blaspheming? He'd love to fit in, be part of the Manics' crowd. If only he could think of something cool to say. What can he compose out of page three, heavy metal, Jesus and Mam?

'Nick, you looked like a right dip-stick on the telly.'

'Why don't you piss off Jesus freak,' says Sean.

'I was joking, just a joke.' For some reason Len salutes Nick before taking Sean's advice. He opens the

134

door and shouts above the traffic, 'The fool hath said in his heart, there is no God!'

Sam salutes the closing door then gets a thick and glossy magazine from her bag.

'Look at this advert,' she skims the pages. 'What d'you think?'

Louise reads the caption: ' "Every time you sleep with a boy, you sleep with all his old girlfriends." Bloody terrible, ennit? "All his old girlfriends"? What it's saying is, amongst them must be a few slags. But it's all right for him to sleep with them of course, and he's completely innocent.'

James winces.

'Just shows what the official view is from the Department of Health.'

'Yeah,' says Nick, 'makes you suspicious about anything they say.'

'AIDS is serious though.' Louise furrows her brow and looks intelligent. 'You can get it from the toilet.'

'Not if you're a Christian,' says James, 'Lenny's safe.'

'You're talking arse backwards. It's worse for them because they trust the Lord and don't use anything.'

'In ten years' time we'll nearly all have it,' says Louise, 'and my father reckons it'll serve us right for being so workshy.'

Sam is thumbing on to other pages when Louise jabs a finger into the face of Billy Bragg. 'Don't like him! Too political. My dad says he's dangerous. Shouldn't be allowed to influence young people like he does.'

'What d'you mean?' says Nick.

'Well, like, he's famous and kids look up to him and he's a commie.'

'Yeah? Just like Cliff and Mick and all the other fascist

bastards.'

'We've always been Tory, see. Dad says.'

The man in the yellow sweatshirt steps over to our table, stands close by Sean.

'Can I fit in here?'

Sean frowns and moves up.

'Don't mind me,' the stupid grin he has gets bigger as if his words have special meaning. He sits back and we see green writing on his chest that says 'People's March For Jobs'.

Nick has been staring at him from the first. 'What happened to your foot?'

'Ah, now... you know Orgreave? Right, well. It's in Yorkshire, and the people are salt of the earth, lovely.' His finger draws circles in the sugar spilt on the table. That's it. The answer to Nick's question.

Sean tries to elbow back some seat space. 'Lovely people but they made a hole in your shoe?'

'No, I was at the front in Orgreave, smack bang against the police.'

'Orgreave?' James has just caught on to the talk, 'That was a coal mine, during the strike? I remember on telly, there was a big fight.'

'The cops joined arms like a fence. Strength in unity, see. As you say, fascists. What they'd do was stamp on your toes to start you off. I was up against this kid and I said, "Don't do anything silly because I've got bad corns." There was a sergeant behind him, from the Met, who said in an accent, "Not afraid of Taffy, are you?" Well, you can imagine. If he did... They must teach 'em not to let go. He just hung there, chin on his chest. But I was after the bugger behind. And you know what?... Those Met buggers know how to crawl, on their bellies along the ground.'

136

In the Beginning

Nick's face is screwed up in sympathy. 'Aw, horrible. They trod on your corn?'

'No. Didn't give him a chance, did I.'

'So what happened to your foot?' asks James.

'We had 'em beat but they brought out the horses. I'll tell you what, until you've faced a horse... Train 'em, they do. Me and Ronnie Morgan, Fat Ron, was trapped in a corner... '

'Who the fuck is Fat Morgan?' says Sean.

The man looks hurt. 'You never heard of Fat Ron? Part of your heritage is Fatty Morgan, he could lift a tram.'

'What's a tram?' asks Louise.

'We were trapped in a corner with this red-eyed horse, so Ron got underneath the bugger. Horse and cop went. Didn't show that on the news.'

'Big Fat Ron,' says Sean, looking at James. 'Reckon you could lift a horse, Jimmy?'

'You worked in the mines?' says Nick. 'I like the sweatshirt, what's that March For Jobs?'

'Like it says. We went to Glasgow, lovely people. And Sheffield, salt of the earth.'

'You've been about, then. A much-travelled man.' In spite of trying to fight back Sean is getting squeezed tighter against the window.

'You've heard of Holy Lock, no? On the west coast of Scotland?'

'No.'

'The nuclear submarines? Ban the bomb, must've heard of that?' When he speaks he looks directly at Louise; her vinyl is shiny with sweat.

'March For Jobs? It's a wonder you had time to work,' says Sean.

'You make time, don't you? So what d'you lot get up

137

to?'

'We're in college,' says James, 'sixth-form college.'

'Lovely. D'you get involved in things, then?'

'I was in the drama group,' says Louise.

'Really? Well, that's good.'

'We're in a band,' says Sean.

'That's wonderful! I tried to learn the cornet once, couldn't get the lips right. Not easy, is it?... Well, nice meeting you.'

Sean parts the bamboo and we all look out. The Marcher For Jobs is striding across the road, the sun beating onto his bald head.

'Boring sod.' Sam has been thumbing through her magazine.

'Yeah, I hate it when people mess up your Saturday,' says Louise.

'If you ignore 'em they go away.'

Nick has a strange face, sort of confused, puzzled.

'Some people are so flaming thick,' he says.

CHAPTER ELEVEN

There are four of us outside the Student's Union of Cardiff University, a bright red stack of bricks. It's a summer evening, and the air is damp and cold.

James taps the toe of his Doc Marten against the wall. Normally he's just nervy but tonight, for some reason, he's got the jitters. As soon as there's a gap in the conversation he fills it with stupid things he wouldn't usually say. 'Good place to play, this.' He stares up at the building. 'Not too big, the right shape.'

You'd have thought he was the act rather than the audience. He looks pathetic and cold wearing a thin motorbike jacket with sleeves that don't reach his wrists.

To someone who doesn't know that baggy biker jackets are definitely uncool, it looks like James can't afford proper clothes.

Still facing the wall and looking up, he sticks his right leg out behind himself. He straightens it and places his hands on his hips, balanced on his left leg. He could be a ballet dancer perfecting an arabesque. It looks effortless. James is flexible and double-jointed, and this strange pose is something he adopts quite often.

Samantha stares mesmerised and gormless until I dig her in the ribs and she blinks and turns away. It's obvious about her and James but in company she's coy as Doris Day.

'Cowing freezing, ennit?' Her arms are shoved tight into her Wranglers.

'I'm not so cold,' says Louise.

James turns around on the ball of his left foot. 'I noticed the tyre mark.' He points at Louise's jacket, and looks like a giant weather vane. On the sleeve of her immaculate leather is a patch of wrinkles.

'Yeah, bugger.' She grips the arm like trying to hide a disfigurement.

Appearance is everything; no one misses a detail. Even though outsiders think we look a mess, to us a new button would be noticed. Louise's dad said he was sick of seeing her like a street beggar, and dumped her clothes in the Council skip. Where's he been, we wondered? We're the only beggars around Blackwood. Sam says it's because they live in their own house, detached.

Louise ordered stuff from her aunty's catalogue, including the jacket she's wearing. It was all zips and shining new, like plastic. So she asked a friend to drive his car over it. He missed it except for one sleeve, which is

140

now flat and longer than the other one.

'So cold.' Sam's teeth are chattering.

'Let's get in the queue, might be warmer.' James lowers his right leg to the floor. Sam stares adoring, as if he's the Messiah leading us to the Promised Land.

We follow behind James, up a wide sweep of steps. He'd been insistent we get there early but didn't say why. It wasn't as if you'd have a better seat or anything. The only explanation was that he'd have more time with Sam. Couldn't be any other reason for hanging round in the cold, hours before the place has opened.

There's about twenty kids in front of us. Louise gets her ticket out though the doors are obviously locked. She squints under the light and you can see her mouth silently forming the words, 'That Petrol Emotion'. It's no wonder the piss gets taken out of her. She's not dull but it's like she can't resist acting a prat.

The kids in front are all thin. Gaunt-looking New Age with identical hair; scraggy and wild on top and not quite covering the shaved temples. Maybe one of them owns the clippers, does the lot? And they've all got the same coloured leggings and big woolly socks with muddy army boots. United anarchists.

'Why're they carrying sleeping bags? Have we got the right night?' says Louise.

Sam has been listening in to their talk. She backs away toward the steps and motions us to follow. 'From Dundee,' she whispers, 'groupies. They never miss a concert.'

'Jesus, serious groupies. Dundee! That's in Scotland.'

'They follow the band everywhere, and talk like it's their family. Obsessed, they are. They worship them. Creepy.'

James has his chin in his hand, thoughtful. 'How can anyone be so... possessed? Petrol Emotion are just ordinary, nothing special.'

There's still half an hour before the doors open. The worst part of going to see a band is the waiting, especially with a bunch of crazies for company. When U2 came to Cardiff, we queued for a whole day: a whole day, waiting to get inside a stadium. And what was inside? Some tiny specks on a distant stage and a big blurred video. If you're not out of your head, it's not worth going. And if you are really out of your head... it's not worth going. Nick told me he could imagine what the Nuremberg Rallies were like. All frenzied attention from thousands of people, focused on a few dots in the distance. Frightening, he said.

'I love it,' says Louise, 'everyone all packed together. Fantastic.'

A boy in purple tights and monkey boots comes down the queue offering posters for a quid. James pays up and opens out a giant roll that glistens black, red and white. In the centre, like a bad photocopy, is a small and fuzzy picture of the band. The rest of the sheet is little bits of writing about Love, Hate, Birth and Death. James examines every inch, 'I like that,' he says, 'nice for my bedroom wall.'

It starts to rain and though we're under cover gusts of big drippers blow in. Sam moans and complains as if she's having water torture. Usually she's tough and couldn't care less about the weather. She's acting the damsel in distress, hoping James will bundle her up in his arms.

'Wonder if we'll get to see them?' says Louise, wistful.

'Who?'

'The band, of course. Hope I touch Steve Mack, he's so gorgeous.'

142

In the Beginning

The other month Louise had seen Voice Of The Beehive and nearly pulled Mellissa off the stage. 'Worra woman!' Mellissa said into the microphone. For a while after we called Louise Worrawoman, until her dad overhead and thought we were saying Horror-woman, or worse. That's the real reason he chucked her clothes out.

Nick thinks the idol worshipping is daft, embarrassing. He says it's strange that no one believes in God but we believe all the bollocks written about rock stars. It's just entertainment, enjoying yourself, that's all.

'Have you met anyone, Jen?' asks Louise.

'My nan worked in the factory with Shirley Bassey.'

'Nah, she never, not in a factory.'

'My nan? Yes, she did. Shirley used to sing on the line, the assembly line.'

'Nah. Can't imagine her in a factory.'

'They all come from somewhere,' says James, 'think she was born in those bloody dresses!' Heads in the queue are turned our way. He lowers his voice, 'Only the shits forget where they come from.'

When the glass double doors open, a purple-haired couple cheat the queue. Ignoring the whistles and shouting, they hurry past the ticket man flashing square bits of plastic. An anarchist at the front gives a sly ankle tap, and a big cheer goes up as one of the purple heads staggers through the foyer trying to stay up.

'They've got passes,' says Louise, admiringly. 'Probably know the band.'

'Not necessarily. They could be journalists or anything.'

Inside, James rubs his red, tingling ears. 'Christ, now they're burning.'

'Someone's walking on your grave,' says Louise.

'No it's not. That means someone's talking about him. Have you been upsetting Sean again?' He looks at me, as though the thought's occurred to him that Sean is sticking pins in his effigy.

We can either turn left into the main hall or go straight on to the rows of pasting tables laid out with merchandise.

'Get a drink,' says James.

No one can afford the official fan stuff, except Louise, and you're considered flash if don't buy bootleg.

'Its all a rip-off, anyway.' James has a backward glance at the tables. 'What's it got to do with rock music?'

The stage is dark and silent. At the far end of the hall, masses of people crowd around a strip that radiates white light. By the counter, the Dundee anarchists are stomping up a fury because they can't get a drink. Behind the bar is the purple-headed couple, completely ignoring the waving and shouts.

James gets served straight away. He asks for whisky. Sam wants the same, though she's never drank it before. If he ordered triple hemlock and canker-worm, she'd have asked for one. Moving well away from the bar, we head towards the darkness by the stage.

'What's the one for walking on your grave, then?' asks Louise.

'That's when you have a shiver.'

'Oh, yeah... I wonder. Perhaps it's walking around your grave as well?'

'Why?'

'Well, the shivering outside. Can't all be walking over you. Might be people going past. You know, when we're dead we could be famous.'

Green and red lights start to flash about the room,

In the Beginning

giant speakers announce something about a DJ. 'What's New Pussycat' comes on and the volume is turned so loud it feels like Tom Jones is inside; swirling around, vibrating your bones and coming out through your ears. Talk is pointless. Suddenly everyone is doing a dance of hand signals and face mimes. Just as we are all getting into the chorus, the record is cut and The Motorcycle Boy are singing 'Big Rock Candy Mountain', which James loves. Then that's cut and a coloured spotlight dances across pretend fog on the stage. 'Naff, ennit?' says James.

Three figures come out of the fog — two guitars and a mini-keyboard. The support band do some weird stuff, and the keyboard player, who's got a cloak and a magician's hat, is booed and jeered. James says the audience is ignorant because he knows him from the recording studio, he's an excellent musician and a really nice bloke.

When they're finished the DJ plays The Undertones, 'My Perfect Cousin'. James sings along, Sam tries to do a duet. But she doesn't know the words and is not in lip-sync. We push closer to the stage. Right in front of us is a metal fence, behind it there's bouncers staring straight ahead with their arms folded.

'Don't they look stupid?' says Sam.

Louise points to one with tattoos on his neck. 'That's Debbie's dad. Fancy your father doing that? Not a proper job is it?'

'He must be hard, though.'

'I should say. He used to play rugby and got banned for biting someone's ear off. Even Debbie says he's mad.'

That Petrol Emotion run on, and we're rammed against the cage. There's a scream then quiet, and there's bodies on top of me and I can't breathe. Then the bodies are flying in the air, up into a dazzling spotlight.

145

Something pulls my arm, tugs it nearly out of the joint, and I scream into someone's face, 'You fucking bastard!'

It's James, with a terrible, terrified look. 'You're alright, you're alright.' Behind the cage the bouncers are gripping the bars, staring out like sad monkeys.

'You did well there, mate,' says one of them.

Well away from the stage, we're still wiping our faces and sniffing. James is red-eyed and the rest of us have mascara mushed all over our cheeks. You can see that Sam is fighting not to fling her arms around James. If she did, me and Louise would do the same and we'd be a blubbering mass.

The first half of the concert is brilliant, songs we all know. Then there's stuff for the die-hards, the Dundee anarchists, and it's really hard going. James looks at his watch. Nick hadn't come tonight because, he says, concerts are boring. The few he's gone to, he was relieved when they're over. He goes just for the music, and finds the big stew of emotion, with people all packed together, just a distraction. The only concert he would look forward to is with him on the stage.

Right now, his ideas seem about right. The rest of the night is like being under water, holding your breath, desperate to reach the surface. Perhaps it's the shock from being suffocated at the beginning?

The main lights flick on and we all duck. There's twelve minutes to the last train. We troop out in a daze, boots tramping over a sticky floor and cracked plastic. Jogging to the station, the rain has cleared and stars are out. Sam and James are side by side with matching strides. I'm sure their hands touch deliberately as they swing back and fore, it's too complicated a choreography to be accidental. This secrecy about their romance is

In the Beginning

mystifying. Everyone knows they must be seeing each other or at least are not just good friends. But they're so coy in public, like they are embarrassed about how they feel. I can't imagine Samantha wanting to hide it. She's not just an open book but a talking one. Perhaps James is a secret Valleys macho? Tough guys don't feel. No, that's not it; James is the anti-matter of macho. It must be something else, something deeper, more complicated.

On the train they sit together but with a decent gap so their thighs don't touch. This last transport out of the capital is always an excursion into the unknown, a bit of a safari. The great thing about it is you never see a guard, so it's free. The best way to travel is totally drunk so you don't notice all the other drunks and threats and horrors. You can tell the sober ones, sitting by themselves. They are frightened rabbits; staring out, pretending to be interested in the blackness but, really, looking in the reflection for a stray boot or head-butt. Something splashes against the window by Sam. Down the carriage there's a girl with her head out, shoulders heaving.

'Cardiff Cit-Hay! Cardiff Cit-Hay!' A gang of boys are coming down the aisle thumping seats in time to their chant. There's no need for James to feel protective, we all look handy in our biker jackets, and we stare absolutely straight back, no matter how much we're really shitting ourselves. Mind, if we had Amanda-Punk with us these boys would have some skid marks to wash off when they got home.

'Isn't the football finished?' asks Sam.

'They must be from up the valley,' replies James.

When we get off, Louise's father is there in his shiny jeep. Sam stands by the door, hesitating. 'I feel a bit sick after the train. Think I'll walk.'

'Come on then, James. Hurry!' says Louise. He's just about to get in, the silly bugger, but I say it's dangerous for Sam to go on her own. We see them in the headlights, about a yard apart.

Up in her bedroom later in the week, Sam reaches a blue shoe box from her wardrobe. 'Swear not to tell anyone you've seen them.' She takes out a bunch of little envelopes. 'Go on, swear or I won't show you.' I swear on someone, I forget who. She undoes a ribbon and hands me the top one. Her address is written neat and small in blue biro. 'Open it. Go on.'

I open a single sheet of paper with thin spidery lettering. 'No, I can't. I don't want to.'

'Read it!'

She is desperate for someone to see, to share. Maybe because her emotions are bursting, or perhaps she wants reassurance, confirmation.

'He sent you all those?' There must be twenty letters.

She nods, 'From when we first met. Three in a week sometimes.'

Sam doesn't understand that they are his, not hers. For me to read them would be seeing something that is absolutely private to James.

'Sorry... the way I was brought up, I can't.'

'Well at least look at this.' She folds a sheet and, holding it close to my eyes, points to a tiny cross under James' signature. Such a little mark, almost invisible.

Sam ties up the bundle. Putting the box onto the wardrobe, she says, 'Did you know they are cousins, Sean and James? Never have guessed, would you? Everything's a secret, isn't it?'

CHAPTER TWELVE

The next practice was in Nick's. I didn't care to ask how they moved the equipment from James'. It was just possible to imagine them lugging the stuff on a bus but I couldn't picture them sweating up the big hill to Nick's house. Well, you could imagine James and Sean struggling and cursing like Laurel and Hardy, but that kind of effort wasn't in Nick's vocabulary.

Setting everything up — the wiring and different sockets, the placings and sound checks — bored me stupid. They were 'boy things', the sort of technical role-play that boys fall gullibly into. Usually I just stood in a corner. So, in spite of the sullenness and silent treatment

I'd get from Nick, I decided to arrive at eleven instead of half-ten. Then everything would be ready, and we could get straight on without my nerves building up from the waiting.

I know something is wrong when Nick is smiling at the door before the bell chimes are finished. Maybe he's pleased with himself because he looks Princess Margarety in migraine orange shirt and red ankle socks. He puts a finger to his lips in a 'shhh' sign, then turns and tiptoes down the hallway. The front room door is open and James is sitting cross-legged on the floor with a kitchen knife and a plug.

It's as though the whole room is concentrated on what he's doing. All the tidy furniture has been heaved back against the walls, the gear is around him and Sean is looking on casually from an armchair, touching a spot on his cheek. it's obvious straight away that James is cack-handed with plugs; he holds the knife like a Neanderthal having lunch and he's sweating. Looking close, there's scratches on his thumb where the knife slipped.

'You know which goes in which?' I ask. He doesn't answer but Nick and Sean glare at me.

'Well, I don't think he does. The brown one is live and he's putting it to earth.'

'How d'you know?' This is not said like, 'how do you know?' me, personally, but how do I know because I'm a girl.

'Leave it, then. See what happens. You'll need to put an advert for a new guitarist, though.'

I haven't been in the front room before. It's bigger than the house seems from the outside. A huge green draylon sofa has left heavy dents in the carpet. Smaller marks remain from a dining table and chairs. There's a

150

In the Beginning

long sideboard, and all the wooden surfaces are shiny and smell of fresh polish. The far wall is just daylight, from a big bay window. Apart from James, the room has a comfortable, lived-in feeling.

Nick leaves me staring at James' hands, and sprawls out on the sofa. Near him is a glass-topped coffee table with a tiny radio at top volume and Credence Clearwater Revival singing 'Bad Moon Rising'.

'Goths sleep in graveyards, on top of tombstones,' says Nick.

'That's bollocks.' Sean is flicking through *Smash Hits*. 'Can you imagine Pricey or Gatehouse sleeping on a grave?'

'Me, I'm shit scared of werewolves.'

'You're in my light,' says James without looking up.

'Sorry.' I step to the side. 'Want any help?' He grips the knife handle tight in his fist, his breathing short and raspy. Sean shouts from behind his magazine, 'He can't bloody see, that's the trouble. His eyes're fucked!'

James clenches his jaw and howls at the ceiling. 'Shit! Bollocks! Buggery! Balls!'

'Got something on your mind?' says Sean.

The fair head of Nick's mother pops around the door. She is smiling, and waves her shopping bag. 'Hello, everyone.' Aitched and clipped; contrasted to our long vowels and Valleys lilt. She gets instant attention and affection.

James, embarrassed, imitates her accent. 'Hi, Mrs Jones.'

'Just popping to Blackwood. Nick, poor neighbours, keep it down love.' She is not like other mothers, there is such respect. Everyone who goes to the house says she's the perfect mam. Nick watches her closing the gate then

151

turns the volume back.

'I hope she didn't hear you swearing,' says Sean, 'don't like language in front of Mrs Jones.' A tight noise escapes James' throat, air from a balloon when you stretch the neck. He bashes the carpet.

'Fucking temper he's got!'

James throws the knife and gets to his feet. Going out, he head-butts a wall then slams the front room door. Sean and Nick look at each other. They both come across, then stare down at the plug like they've been asked to translate Egyptian.

'Are you sure about the colours,' says Nick. 'I can never remember.'

'Pretty sure.'

It's no wonder James lost his temper. The tiny screws are worn flat, and half-decent eyesight can see the knife is too thick.

'The plug's knackered.'

Nick goes into the kitchen. We hear drawers opening and shutting and James' voice. There's a strained quiet between myself and Sean. I'm the first to give in.

'Didn't know he had a temper.'

'Phew! What? Terrible temper. Keeps it in, see; bottled up and then, whoosh! You never know with him. One day he'll do some damage.'

They both come back together. James makes for an armchair by the big window. Once the plug is fixed, Nick looks over to James but he is staring out of the room.

'Right then, we better finish setting up.'

I stay sitting on the floor, and watch Nick and Sean pottering, half-hearted.

'Jen, have a go at those wires if you like,' says Nick. The tangle of cables is near where James is sitting. He watches me make it worse for a moment.

'Here, like this... ' As soon as James is involved, Nick picks up a guitar, goes to an armchair and relaxes. He strums the Animals' 'House Of The Rising Sun', the amplifier so loud it's like he's miming the words.

'Your ma said keep it down!' screams Sean.

Nick nods slowly, his eyes closed.

'Fuck off!' Sean turns it down so quick he catches Nick's voice; not as bad as he's let on. With the quiet, Sean gets on his stool and starts thumping Blondie: 'Denis'. It's hard, raucous and full of energy, exactly like the record. Even though it's just a knock about and not a song we're going to do, his head is straight and ramrod still in concentration.

James fizzes round the equipment like a firework; telescoping stands, connecting cables. Unlike changing a plug, he doesn't even need to see what he's doing. In a jiff from when he started, he's adjusting his guitar strap and telling Nick to get over. I'm having trouble putting the mic down to my level.

Sean calls from his drums, 'See, you're not that tall.'

I think about this a moment before replying, 'No, I'm not.'

He rests his sticks, stares me up and down. 'So, how tall are you?' His voice is serious, challenging. The other two scrutinise me.

'I dunno, really. About five-five.'

'Are you shit! She's not five-five. Five-five in fucking heels maybe, but not five-five.'

Nick and James glance at each other like I've lied about my height to get in the band, and been caught out.

'What's my height got to do with it? No one said you had to be a certain height.'

153

'Not as tall as you seem, not five-five anyway.'

'How tall are you, Sean?'

'You're never fuckin' five foot five.'

'Okay, whatever.'

'I'd say, five-four, four and a half,' says James.

'Well, if you can reach,' says Nick, 'give us a sound check.'

'What shall I say?'

'No, not right. Too low.'

I just check myself from speaking an octave higher.

'You're taking the piss out of me.'

'No,' says Sean, 'need more treble. And, Jenny, get closer.'

No one offers to lower the stand. I'll have to sing with my mouth reaching up like a feeding bird. Bass and rhythm start the intro to 'Dear God', a bleak and hopeless song. I have to scream the lyrics which, with the mic over my head, come out more strangled than usual. But at least I've got to the pace and can time my breathing so it's not like I'm on forty a day.

James is into it, making a face when he plays lead down the frets. Almost through the first run, Sean breaks a stick and the beat limps to a stop. James seems relieved. I get compliments, even from Sean. 'Good idea with the mic; sounds rawer, more authentic.'

'Let's get on, is it? From the beginning again.'

I've discovered why Nick is impatient between songs. If someone doesn't step in straight away, get us together, there's a tendency to lapse into individual pursuits. Each one does something different, playing a new chord, a beat, a line of song, or just drifting off with what's on your mind. The hardest part of practise is keeping together, fused on the same thing. When we are all focussed it's brilliant.

154

In the Beginning

When we are putting in ideas to change something, make it better, that's the best you can get. There's no boredom, no being fed up, no time; time just goes.

But the supreme, like a natural dose of sublime, when the body's elixir chemicals are all turned out for you, nirvana, is when you are what you're doing, it's the only thing that exists. But at the same time it couldn't be without the others. You know the others are making you, each of you make each other. When it's so tight there can't be any other way, and it can be frightening.

'Nah,' James says, picking lead and pulling a face to what might be Led Zeppelin. 'Too early, wasn't ready for that. I feel like a Jesus And Mary Chain.'

'Okay,' Nick takes it in his stride, ' "Just Like Honey?" '

The front room, already upset, is shocked with jarring guitar and crashing drums. In James' smooth delivery there is no trace of Welsh accent. He nods me in for the first chorus. Nick stops playing, waves his arms. He and James look at one another, obviously disappointed.

'Come down a bit, you're going away from James.' I pull at the mic perched above my lips. No one else seems to notice. We go again. It sounds exactly the same but they're all nodding and smiling stupid. The rhythm drops out of the last chorus, leaving a drums and bass combo. James has let go his guitar, and is blowing and shaking his fingertips. Nick points an accusing plectrum.

'I guessed, when you were doing the plug!'

'Yeah, so did I.' Sean points a stick. 'Awful suspicious.'

In this creative atmosphere emotional energy whirlygigs around the air, and crashes down on someone when it runs out of puff. Or maybe it's James' turn to be stoned to death? At any rate, it was unwise of him to have

155

just washed his hands so that now they're too soft to play.

'I've told you before,' says Nick.

'Yeah, so have I.'

James stands flapping his hands like he's drying nail varnish.

'What's he done?' I ask.

'He knows. Tell her!'

James shakes his head.

'How fuckin long're you gonna be?'

Nick unslings his bass. 'Might as well have a break.'

'But we only just started!' Funny, but there's not that charged atmosphere in the kitchen. Maybe Nick's mother left a bit of her down-to-earthness behind? Whatever, the electric has seeped away.

Sean is first in the bathroom. Nick puts bread in a toaster and opens a family pack of Golden Wonder. James' hands seem to be okay; between ramming crisps in his mouth, he points out the window to a sunny space where there's a garden shed.

'That's where we started.' It's a square of wood the size of a Wendy house, not big enough to swing a dormouse. 'We were like Lego. Just as well Sean only had two little drums.'

'Must've been a terrible noise?'

'And we had three guitars, Miles on bass. Yeah, terrible noise. But wicked.'

'Nick didn't play bass?'

'Rhythm. He was good. We made him change when Miles left. Nick is so talented, see.' James stands over the toaster waiting for the bread to pop.

'He's too modest.' Nick beats James to grab the first slice. 'By rights we should have got someone else but Jimmy boy was clever enough to play rhythm and lead.'

156

In the Beginning

'Now, now, Nicholas, don't be so ridiculous... ' They share the spreading of butter, huge dollops melt gold on thick bread, as their elbows try to nudge each other from the worktop. 'He's so clever he can play an organ.'

Nick groans, 'Oh God, that's a new one.'

'No, he can, really. It was a present for a clever-clogs, but not cool enough for Nick. Rock an' rollers play guitar... He'll get it out for you later.' James reaches down four small plates with yellow flowers. Nick gets cheese spread and honey from the fridge. They delegate me to carry the tump of toasts on a wooden chopping board, and we march our feast out of the kitchen. On the way, Nick hammers on the bathroom door.

'Grub up bog-boy!'

Seconds after the food is laid out, the coffee table is crumb-coated cheese and honey. Sean comes in, looks from mouth to crammed mouth.

'You mingy fuckers!'

'I'll do some more now, Sean.'

'Nah, fuck it. Not eating that muck.' He slouches in a sulk to the bay window.

There is something odder than usual about Sean. We all notice but Nick says first.

'What the hell've you done?'

Sean glowers over his shoulder. His face is a shock, glowing smooth like a pink balloon under a dark wig.

'It's the blackheads,' says James, 'been scrubbing in cream.'

Sean snarls 'It's the cheap fuckin' soap in your house!'

'Forget the creams,' says Nick, 'just use water, not even soap.'

'Oh, yeah? That what you feed your fuckin' spots?

What d'you use, Jenny? Like glass, her skin.'

'Water, just water. To drink and to wash... My mother said, when she was a kid in Sunday school they checked the girls' knickers. Make sure they were clean.'

'What! What the fuck's that got to do with it?' says Sean.

'They used to say, cleanliness is next to godliness.'

'Water? You been on the fuckin wacky-backy!'

'I can believe that.' Nick runs a finger over his chin. 'Valleys people must be the cleanest in Britain, scrubbing away at their sins and sense of inferiority. We're still stained with being shouted at from the pulpit, about being unworthy and imperfect.'

Sean glares. 'God, no wonder I never ask you sods for nothing. A few spots, we end up talking about fucking sin.'

'But everyone gets them,' I say, 'it's diet, tiredness, sunlight.'

'Yeah, I know. Saw it in Cosmopolitan. See, the thing I don't understand is... ' Sean points an accusing finger at James, 'how come I got 'em more than that bastard?'

Nick tries to get us going again but Sean's face and James' fingers are still stinging. So he ignores everyone and switches on the telly. All they ever seem to watch are old *Top Of The Pops*. Suzanne Vega sings 'Marlene On The Wall'.

'So effortless,' says James.

Sean is not interested. He comes from the window and sits on the arm of my chair. 'You heard about Caroline?' he asks.

'No.'

'Pregnant. Not going back to college.'

Nick and James both look from the telly.

'Good grief, she's not the type,' I say.

In the Beginning

'Yeah, she is sure,' James moves to sit closer, 'had to be. What else was there? It was like a fate.'

'Such terrible luck. Her mother's just had a kid, and there's no father. She was desperate to get out. Poor sod.' I feel really sorry for Caroline.

'Well, I can understand,' says James.

Nick turns down the telly and faces us. 'You can't understand.'

'Yeah, you're not a bloody girl.'

'I mean, you mustn't try to understand. It's patronising.'

'Don't be dull.'

'If you say you understand you put yourself above. It's worse than pity.'

'You're strange sometimes, Nick.' James rubs his fingers. 'It's all over for her, you can understand that? Imagine? She had prospects.'

'I know it's all over, but you can't say you understand what it's like. Only a god could understand a tyrant like Thatcher.'

'You never know.' Sean rubs a radiant cheek. 'Maybe the father's a rich bastard and she'll be better off.'

It puts a damper. We stare mute at *Top Of The Pops* and with the sound off even the live acts mime.

Caroline had a nightmare background; a mother who pretends to be her sister, real sisters in school and on the game, and brothers with second homes in detention centres all over the country. Caroline had such willpower, an absolute determination to escape. If she could be dragged back, there's no point in plans, hopes, dreams. We sit and watch a procession of lucky bastards, opening and closing their mouths. Some are incredibly miserable in spite of all the luck.

Jenny Watkins-Isnardi

'Bollocks to this!' James bounds flights at a time up the stairs. There's scuffling and scraping overhead then careful, deliberate steps descending.

'Why d'you bring that for?' Nick is angry.

'He hides it with his other bits of nostalgia.'

'It' is a keyboard, proper piano-length but slim as a sill. James plugs into skirting near the settee. He rests it on his lap, and, without fingering a single key, without any introduction or warm up, he blasts straight into 'Great Balls of Fire'. He's brilliant, breathless, electric; Jerry Lee Lewis without the feet up. When it's over I sit there open mouth and stunned.

'Alright. Now take it back.' Nick is deadpan unmoved.

'Leave it down,' I say, 'let's use it!'

'How? You gonna play? It's naff, keyboards are for the elderly.'

James gets from the settee, 'Jen, d'you know the words of the English anthem?'

'Yeah!' says Sean, 'Let's do it.' He hurries across to the drums.

'Miles loved this. Join in if you want.'

Nick is ducking under the bass strap. 'Not really for girls. You don't have to sing.'

James turns some dials on an amplifier.

'Neighbours,' says Nick. 'Not too much.'

At the microphone James revs the guitar then brakes suddenly. For a second there's pin-drop silence then BANG! Drums, bass, guitar; everything thrown. I'm knocked stark-staring out of my seat. Either my pupils have melted or the big bay window goes mirage shift: the room shivers like it's having a fit, and Nick, on high leaps, is touching the ceiling. Jesus! You can't think to describe; an explosion, an attack!

160

In the Beginning

I uncover one ear. Now there's some order, and James screaming 'God Save The Queen!' They make the Sex Pistols sound subtle as a chapel choir. But strange, there must be some order, it isn't total anarchic. Can't be, because somewhere beyond their rhythm is another beat. It is distant but even more incessant; a throbbing, a prodding. At first it competes then Sean gives up, and we all listen to a steady pounding from somewhere outside.

'Sweeping brush,' says Nick, 'that's what he uses. Surprised he hasn't come through before now.'

'Fuck him, stupid old cow. It'll put some blood in his veins.' Sean joins the thump with his bass pedal. Boom, boom, boom, boom...

'That's enough!' James turns down the whine of an amplifier.

The banging fades like something trapped and dying. For some reason I think of lines from a poem: 'Life remains a blessing/Though we cannot bless'. Where it's from and who wrote it, I've no idea. As I'm about to ask, Nick urges us to get up and get on with practise. I say there's a tickle in my throat. Nick starts griping but James says they can do something else. Then he looks over to me but doesn't make eye contact.

'You haven't heard this. Listen, see what you think.'

'Which one's that?' says Nick.

'The one you wrote, "Motorcycle Emptiness".'

The song is melancholy, haunting. So bloody sad, I can't associate it with Nick. How could that kid, the long streak of, write this? And James sings with raw passion yet wistful, tender. Probably it's the build up of everything, the news about Caroline... I start blubbing.

It's ended, and Nick is crisp as biscuit. 'Not perfect yet.'

161

'It's brilliant, classic.' James is usually reserved, doesn't boast his own or other people's achievements. 'Can you believe he won't go to recording studios and radio stations? Too shy.' I shake my head, not knowing what James is on about. 'It's true. Nicky sends me to try and promote, demo tapes, He just won't go.'

'You enjoy it.'

'He writes the songs, and I have to flog 'em. "Who's the mystery song-writer?" they ask. "Is it a phantom, does he exist?" '

'Didn't think you were shy, Nick?'

'I never know what to say. They talk in clichés, and ask stupid trivia about what we're doing. All so pointless. The stuff is either good or it's not, hate the bullshit. Still, that's the business — where we went nowhere.'

'Who cares!' says Sean, 'let's have a laugh and fuck the rest. Come on, we'll do the Mary Chain's "Just Like Honey" again.' As we're about to start the door bell chimes: I hadn't noticed before but it's a happy, sunny kind of sound and I have a sense of relief. The others are annoyed; Nick unplugs his lead and stamps into the passage, still wearing his bass.

The front door opens and there's Nick's voice and a woman. Footsteps tread slow and heavy on the stairs. Nick runs down the passage, his guitar glints past the front room. A tap is turned in the kitchen. James goes to look and collides with Nick holding a glass of water, some spilling onto the toe of his shoe.

'Leave all the stuff, I'll do it later.'

He turns and races up, his feet hardly seeming to touch until we hear him walking somewhere above. James comes back in; reluctant, hesitating, like he's afraid to part the air. Sean lays his sticks on the snare drum, rises

162

In the Beginning

carefully, and we stand not looking at each other. A big fly weaves between us and batters against the bay window.

A stair creaks. Nick's head pokes round the door frame. He looks surprised, as though not expecting to see the drum kit, the amplifiers, us. 'Mam couldn't find her key, she had palpitations coming from Blackwood.'

'Yeah, it's a bugger, that hill.' Sean collects his sticks and puts them in the back pocket of his jeans. 'Anyone fancy going out tonight, The Red Lion?'

'Nah,' says James. 'Cagney and Lacey are on telly.'

CHAPTER THIRTEEN

Still wearing his blue-and-white pyjamas Nick swings around the banister and down the stairs. He picks the envelope off the mat, his heart thudding. 'Mr Nicholas Jones.' It has a cold, official feel.

Today was the day but the first post hadn't delivered. He stayed in bed staring at the ceiling trying to picture how it would look. When the letter box clunked, he was too shocked to get up straight away. What if they were all bad? Stay in bed, don't think about the future. He jumped out.

Opening the envelope, he thought it was funny because his hands weren't shaking but the hairs on his fingers were sticking up. He unfolded the letter. Jesus!

Waiting for the kettle to boil, he sees a manic grin in all the kitchen's shiny surfaces. He is bursting to tell someone; both parents are at work and Patrick is in the States. He thinks of James, picks up the phone and dials. Trying to hold back the excitement, he reads out the letter.

'Fantastic, well done. I'm really pleased for you.' James can't believe he's saying these things. He feels dread and sadness, and his words are hollow. 'We'll have to celebrate,' he says. When he's put the phone down, James tries to think of Portsmouth, Nick's choice of university. It's miles away, too far.

Looking up from his tea, Nick sees his pet staring at him with melancholy eyes as though she's read either the letter or James' mind. 'Bonnie, how did I forget about you?' He grabs the golden-haired dog and ruffles her fur. 'You can come and visit. I'll meet you off the train.' He opens a tin of dog food. While Bonnie is scoffing, Nick goes back up to his bedroom. After changing, he folds his pyjamas and puts them under the pillow.

In the bathroom he discovers a few more spots around his chin. Sean would have called out the council vermin crew or Bristol Zoo. Nick says, 'Bugger it,' and reaches for his mother's hand cream. He rubs his palms vigorously in the moisturiser then puts the tube carefully back where it was on the shelf.

Going downstairs, he hears a key being turned. He reaches the front door just as his mam is pushing it open. She looks at him, a worried expression on her face. 'Okay, Mam, good news... ' he beams.

Outside, he takes a pair of sunglasses from his pocket and walks down the sunny street. On the way to

In the Beginning

Blackwood he passes a big house, grand and alone, a mansion compared to the rows of cramped terraces around it. Nick thinks of the owners, his aunty and uncle. For one delicious moment he considers hammering on the forbidding door and waving the letter under their snooty noses. They are terrible snobs; mother, father and daughter. Nick imagines them with scented hankies to hide the smell of local people. 'So stuck up, like they got shit up the nostrils,' is the common view in Nick's house. There's even the bust of some composer with a ferocious forehead, staring from a window. And though they've got a piano, it's out of tune and gathering dust. Besides, it's common knowledge they're all tone-deaf

'Pretentious bastards.'

Nick finds the place he's looking for. Rhodfa Fflurol would be a pretty road but for a stretch of wasteland; a graveyard of worn tyres and car seats where even the soil is rusting. He can't remember the number but there's only a few houses in this tree-lined cul-de-sac. A middle-aged man is pushing a mower across a daisy-covered lawn, and tiny showers of white and yellow arch toward the sun. On the kerb outside, two kids play with Barbies, so absorbed they only notice the falling daisies when picking them from the dolls' hair.

Nick stops and dodges a cascade.

'Any idea where Jenny Watkins lives?'

Before the man can answer, a little girl with masses of wild curls jumps up. 'That's my sister, she's in my house. That's my house.' She deserts her friend and swings her Barbie ahead of Nick.

I get my sister away from Nick by threatening to chuck the doll under the lawn mower. In the living room Nick sits on

167

the arm of a chair by a book shelf.

'Brilliant news, you must be thrilled to bits. All those people who said you were just wasting time, especially that horrible sociology teacher.'

'Well, I knew, and that was the main thing. Knew I was being honest with myself.'

'It's worked out perfect. You'll be a professor in a few years.'

'Yep, Portsmouth, my first choice. A full grant, filthy rich! Can you imagine? Never had more than a few quid a week.' He rubs his hands together. 'Lovely grub. Be loaded, even send some money home for Mam and Dad.'

'What did they say, about the results?'

'Mam's phoning Dad at work. They'll think the sun is shining from me. Should have said about my hi-fi being broke... Hey, I could make a list of my sins! They'd forgive 'em all today.' He goes to the window and looks at the view across the valley.

'The English think we live in slag heaps, run up and down pits all day. But it's beautiful.' Beyond the trees in front of the house, a patchwork of green fields nestles snug to a white farmhouse. Between the house and the trees is my sister, standing on a wall, making obscene faces toward the living room.

'I hate the place.'

'So did I,' says Nick. 'Never been from home more than a week, can't even boil an egg... I'll miss everyone.'

'Oh God, don't make me puke! It was your dream to get away.'

'Be hard though, by myself. Home is where your friends are.'

'Friends? Blackwood's full of deadbeats, shit-kickers! You've said often enough: small town mentality, no

In the Beginning

ambitions.' The little girl has ventured up the lawn. Just outside the window she seems to have forgotten why she's there and stands picking her nose with intense concentration. 'And you'll make new friends.'

When I knock the window, she jumps out of her skin then hurls the Barbie. 'She's got a terrible temper, really wilful.'

Nick watches her running away down the steps. 'Wilful? Not such a bad thing, if you wanna get on,' he says. He goes back to his seat by the bookshelf and scans the titles. The room is quiet except for the run of the lawn mower and, somewhere down the road, my sister's faint curses. Nick removes a book. '*Kiss Of The Spider Woman*; seen the film?'

'Film makers have such limited imagination.'

He thumbs the pages, 'This was brilliant, that Spanish actress, Sonia something. And who was the bloke, the revolutionary? From South America, I think.'

'No idea, I only read the book.'

Nick leans against a shelf with his head bowed. 'Listen to this, he's describing the way a waiter serves the food.' Nick reads quietly, as though to himself about the 'poetry' of tossing a salad: '...he caressed the lettuce leaves, and the tomatoes, but nothing softy about it — how can I put it? They were such powerful movements, and so elegant, and soft, and masculine at the same time." '

Nick looks up to see that I'm still listening then he continues reading. ' "Someone asks the question: 'What's masculine in your terms?' ".' For a moment I think Nick is asking me directly, till I realise he's still reading from the book that the nicest thing about a man is to be marvellous-looking and strong, but without making a fuss. Walking absolutely straight, like the waiter, not afraid to say

169

anything." ' Nick closes the book. 'What d'you think?'

I didn't know what to think. Was I meant to think? It was about a man, and what it's like to be a man, or what someone thinks being a man should be like. 'It's beautifully written, but I don't know what else,' I say.

'The way he mixes the salad,' says Nick, 'powerful yet elegant. The description of the waiter: tall, straight, handsome.'

'Well, he sounds something like what a gypsy might see in her crystal ball.'

'It's poetry, an essence of manliness; very tall, absolutely straight, marvellous-looking.' Nick pulls himself up to his six foot plus.

'You don't think it's a bit clichéd? Like a cardboard cut-out?' I ask.

Nick holds up the book in front of me. 'You miss the point, look: "... such powerful movements, and so elegant, and soft". It's about beauty.'

'Isn't that bad grammar, putting a comma before "and"?'

'The point is, manliness is both gentle and powerful; it's soft and strong.'

'Well, Nick, I don't need a book to tell me that.'

'No, a girl wouldn't. But you can't imagine what it's like being male in this place. You need it confirmed, that a man is more than being bandy-legged at the bar supporting your beer-gut. You need to be told it can be something... beautiful.'

'I doubt many in The Woodbine Club have read *Kiss Of The Spider Woman*.'

Again Nick holds the book up for me. ' "... nicest thing about a man is just that, to be marvellous-looking, and strong, but without making any fuss about it, and also

170

walking very tall".'

Why are all my images of stooping red-faced trolls limping for a fight? 'What's this about being tall? Just because you're tall, you think it's the definition of manliness.'

'He's not talking about height, it's not the physical. He means mentally, like, tall in his mind.'

'You said yourself, handsome and tall.'

'I meant stature, in your personality. It's metaphorical, not actual. You're not reading it right; it's poetic not fact. Where's your imagination?'

'You're too fanciful. He's talking about a tall man because he's gay and he likes big, tall men. There's nothing metaphorical about it. It's the truth.'

'The truth? Tell me about it. Anyway, you're missing the point. He says you can be a man without making a big thing of it. Being masculine around here is hard work. They make a huge fuss. It's forced, doesn't come natural.'

'Well, don't you think it's the culture? The area's so aggressive.'

'No, it's not just that. But I don't blame or look for reasons any more. When I was eighteen a relative slapped me on the back and said I'd have to start acting like a man. What does that mean: play rugby, drink more beer, have a scrap? It's primitive. I'd rather be the tall, gentle waiter.' Nick pushes his shoulders back, tilts his chin.

'You can make us tea, if you like.'

He ignores the quip and starts to read the book. After turning a page, he suddenly looks up and says, 'I'm not afraid to cry.'

'No? Well, that's good. They say you'll have less tension.'

'One day I was passing the Greyhound pub. Sitting by

the window was Miles, staring out, with such a sad look on his face. I went in and asked if he was alright. He was slouched in his seat like he had the world on his shoulders

' "Yeah, fed up that's all",' said Miles. He was wearing shiny Doc Martens and a safety pin in his ear.

' " Not that bad, is it?" '

'And he just started to cry. Pissed off with everything, he said. I felt so sorry. Put my arm round him then I started as well. Sobbing, we were.' Telling me the story, Nick's eyes become moist. 'The barmaid was pointing us out, and someone shouted, "Poofters". I knew everyone was staring but I didn't care. Just felt so sad.'

'Bet you felt stupid after?'

'No. I never do. Don't care what people say, why should I?'

'Well, most people would. Haven't you done things you look back on embarrassed?'

'Yeah, but that's different.'

'What are they, then? Give us an example.'

'Nah, too embarrassing.'

'God, I'm intrigued. What's more embarrassing than bawling in public?' I offer Nick a tissue. 'Anyway, bloody hell, it's a fantastic day. Why're you being so miserable?'

'Dunno, should get a few bob off my dad,' sniffles Nick. Out by the gate, small chippings come from behind a tree across the road. 'I can see you,' calls Nick.

A tiny body steps out, hands on hips. 'Wait till I tell Mam what you been doin'!'

*

In the evening Nick phones to say that a party has been arranged for the coming Friday. His parents must have had confidence in him getting good results, I say. No. They

In the Beginning

hadn't been optimistic. But his mother heard about someone who'd arranged a party for her daughter, and asked if she'd like to go halves, share the cost. It was lucky because you usually had to book months in advance, even for a hovel. Nick didn't know the girl but I have a sneaky female intuition.

Sam and myself walk from the bus stop by the roundabout to the Ex-Servicemen's, Pontllanfraith. It's a drizzly evening and the pavements would reflect flickering neon but there isn't any for about twelve weeks. Some smart vehicles are parked by the flaky red door of the club, not the sort you see by caravans in Porthcawl. Although, to be fair, a fortnight in Porthcawl can cost as much as a package in Spain. People get snooty about The Miners' Riviera, two weeks spent on the biggest spread in Europe. But the package in Trecco Bay makes the Costa del Sol seem like a stale sandwich.

'Who's he sharing the party with?' asks Sam.

'Looking at these cars, someone with a bit of jam.'

A short corridor takes us beyond a doorman and to the edge of a blacked-out dance floor where the spangle of ceiling lights skims slinky off the dancers. There seems to be an odd mix of off-the-shoulders gowns and stained sweatshirts.

Nick's shirt shimmers toward us over the polished parquet.

'Another of his mother's cast-offs,' hisses Sam.

'Brilliant.'

Gold, big shoulders, loose sleeves and tiger cuffs, huge buttons that threaten to sprout tea-cups.

He has a big smile. 'Thought you weren't coming.'

'Yeah, fantastic. Great music!' You have to shout or you feel you should be shouting. Most people I don't know or only by sight. Nick's good fortune seems to have infected everyone.

He leads us to a couple of low tables pushed together in a corner where there's a crowd of friends. Sam tries to greet James with a kiss but he ducks out. There's a quick, quiet conversation then she sits at one end of the layout and he takes a seat some distance.

'What's up?' I ask.

'Too many people.' Sam lights a new cigarette from the one she's smoking. 'He told me not to get heavy.'

'Saying hello is getting heavy?'

'It's our first time in public... '

'Practising already for the "just good friends"?'

Nick is going around with a crumpled piece of paper. People hold it, disbelieving. And each time, Nick looks into their faces to study the reaction.

Snug, sharing a seat, Sean and Rhian are interwoven. He unlocks an arm, smiles and waves across.

'Friendly,' says Sam, 'must be drunk already.'

Between Sam and me is a boy called Simon; nice but nuts. 'What's the difference between lager and piss?' he says. We both shake our heads. 'Two minutes.' He laughs loud, nudging my side. 'Good one, ennit? Hear about the Scotsman with a frozen kilt?'

'Excuse me, have to go to the loo.'

'No, that's not it.' He bursts out laughing.

Sam gives me a hurt look for this second desertion.

'See what I mean?' shouts Simon, 'Lager's no joke, is it?'

The dance floor is jam-packed to Whitney Houston's 'I Wanna Dance With Somebody'. Halfway across, the music moves seamless into Lloyd Cole and the Commotions' 'Rattlesnake'. And suddenly I have all the parquet to myself. James catches up and insists on guiding me to the bar. 'You don't understand, I get really shy, don't want all the fuss.' He has knocked back a Jack Daniel's and is ordering another.

'You've been going out with her for weeks. Imagine how she feels? It's like a betrayal.'

'Look Jen, tell her from me... '

'No! You bloody tell her.'

'Aye, aye, what's all this, then?' Two college friends, Elaine and Louise, push between us like they're breaking up a fight. Then Louise clinks her glass against James'.

'Just like to say thanks, for the help with the maths test.'

'Oh, good. You did alright, then?'

'Nah, did I fuck. I'm thick as shit.'

'Bad luck was it?'

'Bad genes more like. I'm fucking stupid and that's it.'

James grabs her shoulders, almost pins her against the bar. 'Listen, you're not stupid. It's the test that's stupid.'

Louise stares at the floor. 'Don't worry. No matter, anyway. I'm just an academical thicko.'

'Course it matters. Stop putting yourself down. That's these bloody tests... humiliating! Keep telling people you're stupid and you'll convince them. It's not true, Louise, you're not stupid.'

She looks up suddenly, brightly. 'I'm thinking of having a tattoo, just a little one. On my shoulder, here. What d'you think?'

Nick has shown everyone his unbelievable results, and is asking the DJ, Smiley Alan Riley, for a request. Smiley is the most miserable-looking bastard you can imagine. His long nose droops onto a grey Mexican moustache, and a huge plate of bald head is rimmed by a curtain of dyed, shoulder-length hair. Smiley shakes his head, looking at Nick like he's speaking a foreign tongue, then, suddenly, he nods energetically as though he's understood something.

The Sex Pistols' 'Pretty Vacant' comes on loud, and the floor empties. Nick has it all to himself, leaping a high pogo in tatty daps, oblivious to the watchers on the side. I sense someone tall behind my right shoulder. At first I can't tell if it's female or male, there is a slight whiff of expensive perfume, or it could be aftershave.

'Plonker, isn't he?' A girl's voice, the words clipped and sharp, not local, or maybe she's had elocution.

'He's brilliant.' I don't turn to look, perhaps a bit overawed by the accent.

'Brilliant? Apparently. Though some think he forged his results.'

'Why should it be?' I turn, intending to tell her to piss off, but she has thick black eyebrows over a fat nose, and eagle, staring eyes.

'He wasn't the most conscientious student, I'm told.'

And when she speaks, it's like the posh voice can't come from that face. She is looking down at me, mad-horse eyes, psychopath bonkers.

'Mr Cool's girlfriend, aren't you? Close your mouth, you'll get flies crawling in. Yes. Likes blondes so became one himself; the odd-ball.' She says 'thee' instead of 'th'; her accent is made up, invented.

'You don't like Nick?'

'I would cross the road to avoid the weirdo.'

I try to think of something witty or cutting. 'Why did you come, then?'

'It's my party, dear. He fucking gatecrashed.'

In the Beginning

The music finishes and she disappears soft as a shadow. Smiley shouts in the mic, 'Okay, people! This'll wake you up, let's go-go!' He sticks on Wham! to do a Lazarus; it works a miracle. The dance floor is bobbing with young guns and crazy ladies going for it. I make my way round the edge to where I'd seen Nick, passing some wise guys who stand and smirk. They probably realise the danger in emotional ties. Smiley sings along with George in the chorus, but not in the same key.

Nick seems to be keeping a distance. Sensing when I get close, he weaves away between the tables. I'm just about to drop out of his stupid game when he stops abruptly and waits for me to catch up, stern face and arms folded.

'What'd she say?'

'What?'

'Her, the one you talked to, Jade.'

'I guessed who it was. You're a plonker, she said.'

'Yeah, she's bound to run me down. And you? What did you say?'

'Well, you know, she's funny... looking.'

'What did you say?'

'Give me a break, she's a freak.'

'You told James.' Nick stares at me, hard. I'm tempted to say he's got her eyes and ask if there's madness in the family.

'What did I tell James, Nick?'

'You said about the cream.'

I laugh but he's deadly serious.

'I told you it was my mam's, remember? It's like treachery.'

I get back to find Sam scowling ferociously at the floor, and taking mighty drags on a cigarette. Across the table, three girls are sharing one seat and plaguing Sean to be drummer in their band, The Stalinist Jelly Moulds. After drunken haggling, during which one of the girls promises to learn guitar, Sean agrees. They have a deal that gives him total control over world rights, except sales in the Dominican Republic, which one of the girls has learned about in geography.

Smiley puts on the Undertones, 'Teenage Kicks'. For some reason I remember John Peel loved the song, and cried when he first heard it.

'John Peel loves this song.'

'Big fucking deal.' Sam takes a lusty pull on her fag, 'He's forgot what it's like.'

Len Again, with fat thighs and tight jeans, plonks down beside Sam. A strange scarf hangs round his neck and down to the floor. It is like those silver hologram things that reflect the light and show different pictures according to the angle you see it. Lenny has a crush on Sam.

'Good party, ennit.'

Under the scarf is a white T-shirt with a huge face of Bon Jovi printed. Sam is kind to Lenny. Only idiots take the piss out of him. She smiles.

'No, it's not bad.'

Lenny leans across and smiles at me. 'Not a bad party, is it?'

'No, not bad, not bad.'

Sam lifts a scarf end and looks at the face that bulges over Lenny's beer belly.

'Like Bon Jovi then, Len?'

'Yeah, oh yeah. Bon Jovi's ace, got every album. Only thing I don't like... ' Before Lenny can elaborate, James and Nick appear. They lean on the backs of mine and

In the Beginning

Sam's chairs.

'Alright, Lenny?'

'Alright, James?'

'Fan of Bon Jovi, Len?'

'Yeah, Nick. Big fan of Bon Jovi. Only one thing I don't like...'

'I like that scarf,' says James, 'unusual. You'll have to lend it me.'

'So you're a Big Fan of Bon Jovi, Len?'

'A big fan, Nick. He's just ace. Got every album. Only one thing though...'

'What's that, Len?'

'Ban The Bomb sign on the back of his jacket.'

'You don't like the jacket, Len?'

'Got to have bombs, otherwise the Russians and that would invade.'

Nick looks down with that scary eagle stare.

'Thought you were a Christian, Len?'

'I am a Christian, Nick, and I agree with the nuclear deterrent.'

'How can a Christian agree with that kind of weapons?'

'There's nothing in the Bible against nuclear war, Nick. What if the Argies invaded us?'

'In the football, the World Cup?'

'Remember the Falklands War, Nick. You have to be for your country. If you're not for the country, you're not for your friends.'

Nick was standing over Leonard. 'The Falklands? We were kids, Len. Ah, but you'd have been manly. That's right, isn't it Len?'

James butts in, 'Leonard, just piss off.'

'Charming!' Sam jumps up. 'Tough guy James.'

'Don't be stupid! He's nuts.'

'Can't look soft in front of your friends, can you James?'

'What're you on about?'

'Good party, Nick. C'mon, Jen.' She links her arm through mine and I allow myself to be escorted to the door.

Outside, leaning his head against the wall is a very drunk and dribbling Simon. Walking passed he sticks out a hand. 'Heard the one about... '

'Just fuck off!' Sam pushes his head hard against a brick.

We are waiting by the phone box for a taxi, and Nick and James appear, jackets zipped, serious faces.

'Getting a taxi?' asks James.

'No,' says Sam, 'waiting for a call from the Queen.'

'Never?' says Nick, 'This time of night?'

As the taxi pulls away, the two boys stand on the pavement, hands in jeans pockets, looking sorry for themselves.

'Pair of prats,' I say.

Sam doesn't even bother to look behind. 'I never saw Nick's paper. Some people said it was forged.'

'Oh no, two 'A's and a 'B', genuine.'

'Strange, for someone who's intelligent he comes so thick sometimes.'

CHAPTER FOURTEEN

Midweek in the garden of The Red Lion. The night is empty, except for us; me, Nick, Sean and James. Our table is one of two set on a concrete patch. The rest of the ground is neglected. The grass is long and weedy, and a gleaming red slide lies on its side. Above our heads are two clothes lines. The higher one holds a few coloured bulbs. The lower, some black underwear, moving with the slight breeze.

The evening is muggy. We all wear T-shirts, uniform white except for Nick who wears red. We've been talking about Nick going away to university. Sean and James are not at all surprised he did well in his A levels.

'He was the swot.' It's Sean's dole day, and he's drinking rum and cokes.

'So you were all in the same school, then?'

'Nick always did his homework, read a lot. And he worked really fast, always rushed to finish first.'

'Don't talk crap.'

'Yeah, you did. Even took books home from school, and brought 'em back. Wanted the teacher to like him.' I don't know whether Sean is just teasing. But Nick doesn't protest too much so I guess there's truth in what he says.

'And him...' Sean nods at his cousin, 'we called him the Pirate.'

James squirms, runs a hand through his hair, looks down at the concrete.

'Should have seen him!'

Nick stands up. 'My round, who wants what?'

'No, it's mine,' says Sean, 'just let me finish telling Jenny.'

'Come on Sean, give him a break.'

'What's wrong, there's nothing to it! He had a pink patch over his lazy eye. Which was it James, left or right?'

'I'll get the drinks,' says James.

'Had a lazy eye, didn't you? Not like Nick, he had two good eyes, bright an' quick. Remember that song, "Bright Eyes"? I fucking hated it.'

'What's a lazy eye?' I ask James.

'Nothing, lots of kids have it.' James walks slowly along the path to the pub.

'The muscle is weak,' says Sean, 'the other word for it is a turn, a turn in the eye. it's when your one eyeball is always pointed at your nose. The Pirate! A little pink patch, it was. He looked cute. Had to wear it for two

182

In the Beginning

years, never complained. I used to feel sorry for him. When he took it off in the bath he was like a one-eyed, cross-eyed panda, this pale ring round on his face. Poor sod, that patch used to, I don't know, attract the bullies. We had to protect him, didn't we Nick?'

'Did we? I can't recall.'

'Yeah, for sure. Remember, playing soccer, the cruel things they used to say? "He's playing a blinder"... "watch him on the blind-side"... "he can be the ref, they're all one-eyed"... That sort of thing.'

'Well, kids weren't we? All cruel then.'

'You can tell he's posh, can't you? So responsible, is Nick.'

'Posh?' Nick puts his feet on the table, ripped daps showing a hole in each sole. 'My father's a manual worker.'

'Yeah, but you live in a house on a hill, and you went on school trips.'

James arrives back with a tray.

'Where's my rum 'n' coke?' asks Sean.

'Can't afford it, got you half a lager.'

'Fucking skinflint. I was telling Jenny, Nick is posh, school trips abroad and that.'

'Compared with us, yeah.' He winks at Nick. 'A bloody posh one, he was.'

'Where did you live, Sean, when you were young?' I ask. He pauses, looks first at James then at Nick. There's a moment of silence in the garden.

'My mam's house... wasn't far from James'.'

The question sobers him, he's wary. It feels like I've touched a taboo, something unmentionable. I want to crawl among the weeds. For a while there is just the sway of the coloured lights and the underwear above our heads. I gulp my drink and the swallow seems deafening.

James breaks into the quiet.

'Remember that time with the pigeons?'

Sean frowns. 'Bloke in my street, madman. He wanted to kill us.'

'Yeah,' says Nick, 'the first fags we tried. We were in junior school, or was it first year Comp?'

Sean shakes his head, sullen. 'No, I wasn't there.'

James forgets his shyness, looks direct at me. 'You know my house? Well at the back there's a lane, the other side of the lane there's allotments. The end one had all these rows of cabbages, straight and perfect. The man's fanatic. Down the bottom was this shed with pigeons.'

'They stank,' says Sean, 'and flapped about. We used to go there to frighten ourselves; the scraping and the cooing scared us shitless.'

'Only birds,' says Nick, 'why'd they scare us?'

'We were nippers. James had that imagination, wound us up. Said monsters were hatching.'

James takes a long swig of his lager. 'Anyway, we hid behind the shed and Sean got out ten Regal. Put three in his mouth at the same time. Then he lit up, one by one, and passed them.' James screws up his face at the memory. 'My first and last.'

'Like a bunch of girls, they were. He took one puff and threw it. At least Nick had a go.'

'Coughed my guts up. Churning stomach, gob down my chin. And you said I wasn't inhaling. "Come on, you're not taking it down!" you said.'

'He turned every shade of Laura Ashley,' Sean laughs, 'I didn't have a clue what inhaling was. Then he threw up and James ran away. Just jumped up and

184

bolted. What I didn't shout after him!'

There was quiet again. Was that the end of the story? I thought I'd better be polite, show my appreciation.

'So, you learned your lesson, Nick?'

'Hang on, Jen, this is the best.'

'Nick was out of it, tears, spit, sick and moaning. He couldn't move. Someone was bound to hear, and I'd get the blame. I was pulling him under the pigeon cot when James came back. He had a big key in his hand and climbed up the steps to the shed. The door opened and there was hell to pay; squawking, feathers and shit all over the place. Nick came round in no time.'

'Yeah,' Nick nods agreement, 'should use pigeons in these detox clinics.'

'They were all over, must have been hundreds; hopping and fluttering. Then footsteps came running down the path and shouting.'

'We got out, and all the birds were flopping into the lane.'

'Running my fastest, I couldn't catch Nick. He had whirlwind legs when he was little. You could hear the man chasing, shouting what he'd do to us.'

'Yeah, I remember being shocked with his language, didn't think grown-ups knew such words.'

'We ran down to the river. The old bugger kept with us, you'd never guess he'd been years on the sick. But we knew all the hiding places, secret paths and where the bank overhangs.'

'And this old bastard knew 'em too.'

'Lucky it was summer and the river was low. Well, it's called a river but you're more likely to get a splinter than a sopper.'

'He chased us across and up to the main road on the other side. Then we were running along the pavement beside the big park.'

'By now it was a jog, a marathon. Measuring your steps, and controlling your breath.'

'For some reason, Nick turned sharp left into the sports field entrance. There was a car park, then a cricket pitch and a game of cricket was going on.'

'And Nick went in and out the cars and straight across the pitch, right between the wickets. We all followed.'

'There were people shouting "Owzat!" and a cricket bat whizzed past.'

'We didn't slow, carried on back across the river and up toward the lane. God, we must've been fit.'

'It was adrenaline, terror. Got halfway up the slope and we heard a shout.'

'No, it was a little cry, a shock.'

'Anyway, we looked round and the bloke was lying flat on the river bed, must have slipped.'

'Heart attack.'

'Sean said not to stop, it was a trick.'

'So we were halfway to Blackwood before we slowed.'

'First thing was, dump the fags.'

'Evidence.'

'Crushed 'em with a stone and covered 'em in grass.'

'We were murderers if he was dead.'

'There was a big argument between Nick and Sean about who was older. The oldest would come off worst. Be in jail longest.'

'Nick said he didn't do anything and it didn't matter.'

'So James and Sean said they'd be in prison together

and put their arms round each other's shoulders. They left me out till I agreed to share the blame. Then we walked back to James', arms around necks like a walking scrum. We swore to stick together.'

'My dad was reading the paper. The three of us sat on the settee, waiting. Only Nick's feet could reach the floor.'

' "What's wrong with you lot? Looks like you've seen a ghost. Haven't been frightening yourselves down by the pigeons, have you?" '

' "I haven't done anything, Mr Bradfield".'

' "Well, that's alright, then." He smiled at Nick and picked up the paper.'

'We went upstairs. From my window you could see the pigeon shed. The door was open. In the dusk it looked deserted.'

'Emptied.'

'Freed, like the spirits and monsters had gone with the birds.'

I feel a chill on the back of my neck, but there seems to be no breeze. Above my head, black lace winks seductively at the bulb on the next line up.

'That's a good story,' I say, 'but I'm not fussy on the end.'

'That's not it,' says Sean. 'The door bell rings and Nick is done; down the stairs and out the house.'

'Didn't stop till I was in bed, under the blankets, clothes an' all.'

I feel like a novice in a concert who doesn't know when to clap. I wait. Was that the punch line?

'Right, my round.' Sean gathers up the glasses.

'Nick was always sporty,' says James, 'cricket, football, the skateboard. Always nagging us to ride; me and Sean couldn't even stand on it. Yeah, really into sport, funny he had those spindle legs.' Nick sits there with a stupid grin, James is paying him a compliment.

'You was the only one, Nick, who couldn't wear Doc Martens, still can't. Matchsticks in spuds, Mr Potato-feet, Herman Munster's diving boots.'

Nick looks hurt. 'Too heavy, my legs ached. Every step was a dead weight.'

'Could've persevered, run 'em in, done some joggin'. They'd have built you up. Too late now.'

Sean returns with the drinks. He's bought himself a big, ice-clinking rum and coke. Once settled, he tilts his chair and gazes up.

'Which one's Orion, then?'

The night sky is thick with stars since the pits have gone. Smeared above the frilly knickers and coloured bulbs is the Milky Way. Nick has a dap off, and is massaging his foot through a luminous green sock. 'On one of those stars, my father's not born yet.'

James points to a lone speck on the horizon. 'Maybe the earth's not even formed on that one. Hard to believe, ennit?'

'No, not hard to believe.' Sean swirls the ice in his glass. 'Does my fucking head in.'

Nick pulls his shoe on. 'All that distance, and time. Nothing in between except dark and cold. Makes you feel so small.'

'Gotta be life there,' says James, 'must be. Exciting.'

Sean puts his glass on the table, 'Thing that gets me is, how d'they stay up? Nothing holding them, is there?'

'Might be a God?' says James.

'Jesus! Imagine the kind of weirdo who makes all this empty space, just for us to look at.'

'Yeah, that's right, that is. Load of bollocks, the sky's just a big fucking bunch of ditty lights. Nothing.'

I feel a resentment, a need to spite. 'They say we've all got a lucky star.'

'Oh yeah.' Sean sweeps an arm from horizon to horizon. 'Which one is it, then? Fucking good choice, ennit?'

'What about fate, that sort of thing? How come some do better than others?'

He looks at me with his mouth dropped open, 'Hey? Haven't you heard of fucking Darwin and why some people are thick? It's called Natural Selection.'

'That's not what I meant. Why do people have advantages, get the breaks?'

'Fucking luck.'

'Makes you wonder, though. Why's it like that?'

'Because it fucking is! Like the sky... it's like that. Fuck all else, fuck all to it.'

'So you don't believe in conjunctions of planets?' Nick is unlacing the dap of his other foot.

'Whatever the fuck that is. No, I don't.'

'I dunno,' says James, 'they must have some effect. Full moon, the tides. P'raps they affect the future?'

'The past is for wishing and the future's just regrets.' There is a hole in this sock, and the big toe gleams white.

'What the fuck's that mean?'

'Don't know. No idea.'

'Makes more sense the other way round; the past is regrets.'

'You have to write like that,' says Nick, 'fast, without thinking. Get the moment, the mood.'

'Oh, yeah? What if you get it in the bog or on a bus?'

'Working-class culture's written on the back of fag

packets and envelopes.'

'Who writes letters? Not the working fucking class.'

A man comes out of the pub, and passes our table. He walks unsteady; wears a Welsh rugby shirt. At the sprawl of hedging alongside the garden, he kneels down and looks into the shadows. Then he straightens up and treads the length of the hedge, calling someone's name. After he's returned where he started, he shouts over to us.

'Where'd she go?'

When there's no reply, he comes to the table and stands; arms folded, sleeves rolled for business, swaying. He looks from face to face.

'Simple question, where's my missus?'

'Only us here,' says Nick.

'I can see that, mun, where is she?'

'Beamed up, p'raps,' Sean points to a bright star directly above, 'might be looking down right now or in a hundred years' time.'

The man wavers an unsteady finger. 'Watch it son. Don't give me lip. We're going for a Paki, see, me and the missus.'

'Oy!' James stands up. 'Watch your language!'

The man blinks, confused. 'What happened? Haven't used language.'

'Paki? I don't like that, don't like people using it.'

'No? Well, no. Bad, is it, that one? Love their food, see. I love it.'

'I don't like racists.' James speaks quietly, matter of fact.

'I agree.' He puts his arm round James' shoulder, 'Fucking bastard English, all racist. Hate us, don't they? We'll show em, we'll show the bastards how to play.'

190

In the Beginning

'LIE-NULL!' A woman stands by the pub door, hands on hips, 'What the bloody hell you doing now? If you wanna Indian, you better move!'

'Got it wrong.' Lionel gives a timid smile before heading down the path. 'It's Indian, it is. Indian, not Paki.'

'Makes you despair,' says James, 'so soaked in, they don't even realise.'

'Right,' agrees Nick, 'you have to wonder.'

'I hate it.' James looks downcast. 'With every bone and every sinew, I hate it.'

His head jerks up suddenly. 'Christ Sean, I didn't notice them!'

'Thought you'd gone blind.' Sean puts his feet on the table. The usual Docs have been replaced by a brand new pair of red baseball daps.

'Something less sweaty for the summer,' says Sean.

'Gives me the shits just looking at them,' says Nick.

'Not that bad, are they?'

'We were in Newport, some sports shop. There's rows of top-price trainers but he's got his eye on a wire basket full of these plimsolls, all paired and bagged. Two kids are working, and Sean asks the price of T-shirts, feeling the material like he's making up his mind. One of the kids goes out the back. Sean tells me to keep the other talking. I'm shaking like a leaf.'

Sean licks a finger and rubs a scuff from his toe. 'Nick asks to see a pair of trainers. The kid says they're forty-five quid, we haven't got forty-five pence. When I finished I stood by Nick and asked if he was ready. He's undoing laces on the trainer, shaking so much he fucking drops it. Says sorry and runs.'

'My legs were like jelly. Him, stupid sod, unzips his

jacket outside the shop. Can't wait to give me a peep. I nearly had a heart attack.' Nick clamps a hand to his chest. 'I'd rather have paid for 'em myself.'

Sean bursts out laughing. 'With what? You're fuckin' skinter than me.'

'Don't do that again, I'm not cut out for thieving.'

James and Sean glance at each other, raised eyebrows.

'Nice though, no?' Sean clacks the sides of the shoes together. 'Fucking bargain.'

'My round.' Nick scoops up the glasses.

'Here.' Sean throws a fiver on the table.

Nick looks, hesitates. 'No, it's alright.' He stuffs the money in his pocket.

'Upright Nicholas Jones,' says James as Nick disappears to the pub, 'too honest to tell a fib.'

'Honest Nicholas Jones. Who's he trying to fuckin' kid?'

'What d'you think, Jen?'

'What do I think, James?... Why d'you release the pigeons?'

He looks up at the light bulbs, arms behind his head. 'I don't know. To this day, I don't know.'

Nick returns with the drinks and the drummer of their rivals, Funeral In Berlin. His name is Gatehouse. No imagination needed to guess the affectionate nickname the Manics have for him, behind his back. He's a thin-armed boy with regulation blond hair and his mother's see-through pac-a-mac. In spite of the heat, Gatehouse has the plastic hood up and the string pulled tight under his chin. His moon face pokes out pale and sweaty like an anaemic Red Riding Hood in need of a shave. He's a brilliant storyteller, at his best talking about his band. He continually taps out a light beat on the chair, between his legs.

On stage, he is probably Goth but off duty he'd agree with the description of weirdo-slob. He has just dropped his girlfriend off. Ruth is evidence of the incestuous nature of Welsh cosiness; an ex of Nick's and Sean's fantasy girl. There is tension between Sean and Gatehouse because they are rival drummers, and Sean can't understand why his fantasy girl likes someone who's not idol handsome.

'Went to see the Alarm in Cardiff last week. Fucking wicked.'

Nick leans back, adopts a pose of languid boredom. 'Oh, yeah.' He affects a yawn.

'Rock solid,' says Gatehouse, 'best to come out of Wales. What else is there?'

'Gene loves Jezebel.'

James groans, 'Oh, for God's sake! They're not a band.'

'Were you with Pricey?' asks Sean.

Gatehouse nods vigorously, a big grin on his face. 'You heard about it? It's true, every word, all true.'

'Tell us,' says Sean, 'tell us the details.'

Pricey is a guitarist with Funeral In Berlin, and a close friend of Gatehouse. He is debonair Goth with ornamental hair and a fanatical fussy dress sense. Even his friends call him Joan Collins because they're sure he wears his make-up to bed. He makes the most of his fame from playing in the band; thinks he has a reputation with 'the chicks', as he calls us.

'He's got a lot of luck,' begins Gatehouse, 'and after the Alarm gig we went to a club. He thinks he's the kiddie in white Levi's and patent black Docs. This girl, fabulous looks, is introduced to us; long black hair and a body, Christ, makes me sweat to think about. She's impressed with Pricey.'

Nick and Sean look at each other. Sean smirks, Nick coughs; they are a bit sceptical.

'Pricey's luck was in. On the dance floor she's all over him. By the early hours she's pissed and he's going to her flat.

'We all leave together. On the way to the taxi rank a friend of hers comes running up. We find out the girl's got a boyfriend, not far up the evolutionary chain. Word has reached him that some bloke has his girlfriend drunk, kidnapping her for sex. He's dragging his knuckles our way, very unpleased. Pricey tries to laugh it off: "No need to make up stories if you don't fancy me, love." But the friend says we'll be in Cardiff Infirmary, very infirm. What? Nothing to do with me, I'm not his pimp.

'Around a corner comes a bloke, not so much dragging knuckles as ducking lampposts. He's fucking huge. I mean huge; his shadow is boxing us halfway down the block. Pricey doesn't wait for a goodnight kiss. But what's it got to do with me? Then again, he don't look particularly discriminating.

'Behind us there's a noise; a scuffle. They're trying to stop him. We're going so fast down St Mary Street my feet don't touch the ground, it's a floating dream. Then there's a loud crack, like the scenery split, and Pricey is stopped dead, just in front. Stopped absolutely, non-skid, dead. I stop too, instinctive like, right behind. And the arse of his Levi's is a growing stain. HP sauce? That's what I thought, a sachet of HP in his back pocket had burst.

'Pricey turns around, a fucking stupid grin. Turns

194

his lacquered hair; the rest of his body is, like, stiff, caught in mid-stride. And this stain is spreading, slowly, down his leg like melting rust. "I think we lost him," says Pricey, "but he had me scared there for a minute." '

Gatehouse rocks back in his chair. ' "Had me scared for a minute." True, every word of it, all true.'

Sean and Nick are round-eyed delighted. James has his head down, staring at the floor. He looks up, his forehead furrowed, serious. 'I've read about that, people shit scared: the Rosenbergs being electrocuted. Hard to believe, so scared there's no control. For me that's the most terrible, because no matter what you think you might be thinking or feeling, your body is saying something else. And you don't even know... Does that make sense?'

'Oh fuck,' says Gatehouse, 'heavy stuff.'

'Sounded runny to me,' Sean fingers out ice from his rum and coke, 'What happened to his kecks?'

'Posted through a letter box in Howells store. Imagine those toffee-nosed bastards opening up next day. Watch out for the summer sale!'

'Cheer up, for Christ's sake,' Nick gives James' chair a kick.

Gatehouse pulls down his hood, revealing a hack of self-mutilated hair.

James bursts out laughing. 'Bollocking Bill! Cover it, quick!'

Gatehouse sits grinning, glowing with the attention.

'Finished college, then?' asks Sean.

'Got a test tomorrow on fucking *Emma*?'

'Fucking Emma? What's that, biology?'

'No, English.' Gatehouse, like a lot of wits, sometimes missed the most blatant sarcasm.

'Jane Austen?' Sean spits her name. 'English class, hey? Snob writing. Why d'you have to read that crap? What's the relevance to scum-bag kids like us? It's propaganda, middle-class brainwashing.'

'Not fussy on her, then, Sean?' Gatehouse looks slyly around the table. 'Still, you're the English expert. Third time lucky with your O level?'

'Listen, you don't read that shit to enjoy or learn anything; you do it because you have to, for passing exams.'

'So what d'you read for pleasure? The *Sun*?'

'Ginsberg.'

'Bullshitter! Never heard of it. Who's the writer?'

'Ginsberg is a writer,' says James, 'a poet.'

A friend of mine, in photography class, had the portrait of a boy stood in front of a blackboard with the words HOWL written huge. 'That was you, in the photograph?' I ask.

James replies proudly for his cousin. 'None other, he knows all the words. Come on, Sean.'

I expected Sean to say 'fuck off!' Instead he closed his eyes to concentrate: 'I saw the best minds of my generation destroyed by madness, starving hysterical naked...' He recites the Ginsberg without a pause, right through without a hesitation.

He stops and there's silence. The four listeners are looking up at the stars, perhaps trying to hear this 'dynamo ... Machinery of night'.

'Go on,' says James.

Sean opens his eyes, 'I can feel that bastard smirkin' '.

Gatehouse gawps in wide-eyed innocence. 'Me!'

'Yeah, you. Cynical cunt.'

'Me, cynical? You can bloody talk. Mind, I had no

idea you were a hippie.'

'He's norra hippie!' shouts James.

'Said in the poem, "Hippie angels, on fire, in a fix".'

'You're so fucking thick! What does she see in you?'

Gatehouse yanks up his hood, pulls the string so tight his face swells. He sticks out his tongue, and gags. 'Sthee thinkth I'm gorgeouth.' He rises and staggers backward down the path, as though he's been lassoed round the neck.

'Fuck off,' shouts Sean. No one else says anything.

Sean seems to be looking to the heavens, except there's a slight, tell-tale, movement of his eyes as he follows the sway of the washing line. The other two follow his stare.

'The slip,' says Nick, 'black and silky.'

'No, the knickers. The lacy knickers,' says Sean.

James glances at me, embarrassed.

'Wonder what she's like?' says Nick. Then after a while he says, 'Gatehouse is funny though, not a bad drummer.'

'Yeah, funny as a fucking amputation.'

'Underneath he's sad like all clowns.'

'For Christ's sake.' Nick gives James' leg another kick. 'Why can't you cheer up?'

'He's in love,' says Sean. 'Miserable in love.'

'Are you, James?' Nick asks accusingly as if inquiring about a crime. James shrugs.

'James-In-Love.' Nick recites it like a song title. 'James-Is-In-Love... Who is it, Jimmy?'

'Who d'you bloody think?' says Sean.

'Have you told her?'

'I'd rather not.'

'Oh, I say: he would rather not. Wanna sit this one

out, do you, James?' James' face is glowing, embarrassed.

'Doesn't it make you happy?' Nick turns to me and talks like a doctor explaining to a nurse. 'Trouble is, when you're shy, emotions are a pain in the arse. You can't share; can't... unburden. People in love are usually happy. Dangerous, bottling things up.'

'Shy? He's no fucking choir boy. Remember the camping? Like a rat up a drain-pipe.'

'Oh, no.' James looks agonised. 'Don't say.'

'Why not? You should be proud.'

James gets up and plods down the path.

'Call him back.'

'Rum 'n' coke!' shouts Sean. 'It was Nick's idea: borrow a tent, camp down Swansea. That Easter was fucking freezing. He got so excited waiting for the train, started jumping up and down, and James joined in. They're like that African tribe, leaping fucking miles, standing still.'

'The Watusi,' says Nick, 'or is it the Masai?'

'Yeah, them. I'm wondering, how can they do that and my back is bent with all this stuff? I give it a go, one jump. There's a racket of tins and fucking saucepans, feels like the bottom's ripping out of the bag. And they're up and down on their toes, nice and dainty.'

'He packed half the kitchen, all we took was sleeping bags.'

'That was a good start. They didn't tell me there's a shop on the site.'

'He had tins of Happy Shopper beans. Actually, why d'you want to tell this story, Sean? You're a right prat in it.'

'Actually, am I?' Sean points a finger at James who is coming back along the path. 'At least I didn't split us up.'

'We had a big argument about the camp site. It was on a slope, and I said to go higher in case of floods. Sean had a tantrum, too far to the beach every day. We only booked two nights.'

'Yeah, but it didn't fucking rain. And who wouldn't complain? The tent was a one-man; room for Nick to curl round the pole like a fucking grub, and I'm wrapped under the fly-sheet.'

'Well, it was cold outside,' says James, 'freezing.'

'He kept us awake. Teeth like fucking castanets. At least you had something to lie on!'

'The Happy Shopper carrier bag? In the morning I was under fog. Thought I'd died and was floating in cloud. Then I saw the top of the tent. When I unzipped the door, the stink knocked me back. I swear, the mist turned yellow.'

'And James wanted to pack up and go after breakfast, until he met the girl. Sean brought all those beans and no tin opener. The nearest tent was a field away. Give James his due, he volunteered to go and ask. Gone for ages, he was, and didn't... '

'Remember!' James interrupts, 'We played soccer on the sand! Marked out a pitch for three an' in. Then I went to the shop, bought pop and crisps. When it was dark we lit a fire.'

'Eerie, really eerie. The flames made those, like, jagged shadows. There was just the noise of the sea. And that seagull swept through the light, with white wing tips. We both ducked, Sean ran back to the tent.'

'Hardly sur-fucking-prising! You was winding us up about giant waves, and saying it was the worst place to be for lightning. Shipwrecks on that fucking bay, you said, and drowned sailors' ghosts. I wasn't going to sit around. Anyway, you're forgetting what this is about... '

'Nah,' says James, 'You pretend to be tough, but... '

'Well I don't pretend to be a fucking boy scout. Next morning he's bright as a button, not feeling the cold, wants to stay another night. We had one towel, mine; shared after a swim in the bastard freezing sea, and put it over our heads when we got caught in the rain. Then James took it, sopping, to have a shower. Should've guessed something was up. He told us there was a club on the site. They wouldn't let us in till Nick flattened his hair and took his dog collar off.

'Couldn't understand why James was so keen. There was a man playing waltzes on a Bontempi, little kids sliding across the floor, and people round the sides staring into deep space. Like the waiting room for hell, it was. After a couple of pints James disappeared.'

'A bloke was playing the organ, and they had karaoke going the same time. It was just a noise, a racket. So I put 'Sonic Boom Boy' on the juke box, Westworld.

'And they kicked us out.'

'Went back to the tent and cooked some beans.'

'I guessed where he was. The dark horse.'

'Lucky sod.'

James looks at me. 'It wasn't like they thought. A dry tent, a ground sheet... That's what it was.'

'You romantic,' says Nick.

A plump, short woman comes tramping along the path with a wicker basket. She lowers the clothes prop and the line falls, skimming our heads.

'Oops, sorry.'

She unpegs the underwear efficiently, dropping each

200

In the Beginning

item into the basket.

'Getting damp, ennit?'

The boys stare beyond her into the black corners of the garden. She stretches close by James and undoes the black slip.

'Not too dark for you, is it? Some of them bulbs have gone.'

She looks at me and smiles. 'Chopsy lot, you got here. Cat's got their tongues, has it?'

CHAPTER FIFTEEN

Giro day. The line in the post office is from the door to the counter, turning right at a sign that says 'Do not go to cubicle until free'. On the lino are some small pools of water from a couple of umbrellas. The windows are closed and misted.

Nick and myself are with Sean. At the start of the queuing there was subdued excitement as we shuffled by posters for saving schemes and investment bonds. 'That's what you ought to do, stick some in savings,' says Nick.

Sean is famous for not saving. Without friends, the money would be gone before he was out on the pavement. He always wears the same smart top to cash his giro: navy striped fisherman's shirt with long sleeves and slashed neck. He's extremely, shiningly, well scrubbed, and his hair is lacquer-perfect in spite of the rain. That's his dole paranoia: everything has to be right or he won't get paid. They'll claim his signature's forged or something. Perhaps he can't believe his fortune getting benefit when the rest of us rely on scraps from parents?

Getting close to the counter, Sean is fidgeting and sweaty. The way Nick's dressed could bring bad luck. I can't imagine luck being so stupid. There's so many witnesses, every single one gawking at six foot plus of lime green jeans, turquoise shirt with purple zigzags, and a halo of fizzy peroxide. Luck has nothing to do with those colours.

Sean thinks the post office people are gone mad from giving away money. That's why they never smile or talk, and they can sit on a stool for days at a time. They hate the dolites, resent their freedom: a few minutes queuing then out to sing and dance in the rain, while they have to work through the dreary day. Behind the glass screens they are planning deaths and torture.

By the time he slides the giro under, Sean's hand is trembling, maybe expecting a sawn-off shotgun to poke from the counter. There's a quick stab of the stamper then a fan of fivers, two weeks' money, is pushed through the gap.

Some kids are so desperate hard-up they can smell dole. They come slinking out of doorways and sidle along, stepping over the puddles. You know he'll be broke before the day is out but Nick makes sure Sean gets to the pet store, a few shops down. The notes still folded in his back pocket.

'They've got new pups, tiny red ones.' Nick holds the

door open.

'Nah. I'll wait outside.'

'Come on, you'll get soaked.'

It's narrow like a tunnel, dim-lit from the wavering light of fish tanks. Sean hesitates on the step. For a pet shop it's quiet, a few genteel tweets and a stifled meow. But the smells are powerful: blood, pee, flesh; smells you could imagine in damp, primitive caves. Sean tries to back out. Nick lets the door close and breathes deep.

'They're at the end.'

There's cardboard boxes on the floor, one is labelled 'Boiled Snouts' and inside are blackened shapes like frizzled mushrooms.

'Thought it said Boy Scouts.'

Sean trips against another box. This one has big cow bones flecked with greasy meat. Nick nudges him forward.

Further in, the stench catches raw down your throat. Lidless glass cartons with ingredients for soil: Elements, nutritions, orange, yellow, sulphurous and vile; blood, bone, ground. Both Sean and I try to turn around.

'It's one-way.' Nick points to an arrow on the wall drawn in blue felt-tip. 'Come on, nearly there.' He steps ahead. When we catch up, he's crouched with a finger waggling through the wires.

'Gorgeous, aren't you? You little, little beauties.'

A heap of brown spawn pulses shapeless in a bed of hay. Nick coos and coochies and wiggles his finger.

'Wouldn't you like one?'

Sean shakes his head, face buried in a sleeve.

'There's three. You want to see them with their eyes open... '

Sean's eyes brim and he seems to sway in the strange light.

'He wants fresh air.'

A slimy nose pokes from the mess and sniffs at Nick's hand.

'Aw. Look!'

There's a gentle thump on the floor. I turn round to see Sean sitting, legs straight, staring dumb at the cage.

One of the puppies wobbles to its feet.

'You gorgeous little beast.'

'HELLO GORGEOUS! HIYA DARLIN'!' A woman calls from the boxes of hoof 'n' horn. 'WHERE'S THAT BLOODY TEA!'

Sean supports himself on an outstretched arm, a trickle of spit dangles from his lip to his chin. The puppy sticks out a red tongue, sucks on the end of the finger. Nick is in a swoon.

An army voice shouts, 'GOOD MORNIN'! GOOD MORNIN'! WHAT THOSE WASTERS UP TO?'

I try to stop Sean from lying out flat. 'Nick!'

'NICK! NICK!... THE TEACHER'S A BASTARD!'

Footsteps creak on the floorboards.

'Drunk izzee? This time a day.'

Dragging Sean down the aisle we pass a glossy black bird, it's head cocked on the side. A bright yellow eye follows us out.

'DRUNK IZZEE? DRUNK IZZEE?... '

In The Dorothy there's a few concerned looks before people get on with supping tea and having a fag. We slide Sean along the wet seat. Nick sits on the outside and pours a tump of sugar into Sean's coffee.

'I said... ' Sean's damp face is pressed against the window. The odd old biddy looking in hurries to the far side of the pavement pulling up her headscarf, otherwise

In the Beginning

Blackwood passes without taking much notice. '... You had us going there.' Nick steadies the cup in Sean's hand. 'No breakfast?'

'Not on dole day.'

'It was that smell,' I say.

'No.' Sean swallows the coffee in one gulp. '... There's a thing to them places.'

'My parents used to buy me goldfish.' I glance at Nick. He looks from me to Sean like we're both gone. 'They bought dozens. And, I don't know, they always flushed them in the toilet. I remember asking why, and they said... they're gone to be with the mam and dad fish.'

'Yeah,' says Sean, 'Why? Why keep fish?'

'Is your blood alright?' asks Nick. 'People faint from pressure.'

Sean stares out the window following the walk of pregnant girls, their swells blown tight in the wind, and teenagers fighting prams along the pavement. 'That stink... must be like when you're dead and your body's sorted.'

'I wouldn't know,' says Nick.

'Yeah. It's earth... compounds. The chemicals... decay.' Sean turns away from the window, squeezes by Nick. He calls from the counter: 'I love the sound of cappuccino.' He gets a tray and has it piled with things wrapped in clingfilm. The coffee machine bubbles and froths as it fills the cups.

Nick bollocks him for the money thrown away and all the food. It stays untouched while we stare out, and a shower with slanting wind gobs rain on the glass.

'YTS is the bastard,' says Sean, 'slave labour... they put a vegetarian in a slaughter house.'

'At school,' I say, 'we went on strike against YTS. Well, a few of us.'

'Strike?' asks Nick.

'A demo. We sat on a kerb and the Echo took pictures. Neil Kinnock said we were a bunch of dafties.'

'Dafties? Daffodil lefties. Bet his kids are nerds. Remember the video with Tracy Ullman?'

Sean picks at some clingfilm. 'Anyway, we can all vote in the next election.'

Nick looks up at the ceiling. 'That'll make a difference. Apathy in the UK... I'll vote for a dog.'

'The problem is the English: they're all Tories.'

'The problem is: it doesn't make a blind bit of difference. What about the North England? Is Sheffield Tory? Is some great Welsh redeemer coming on a dragon? Knock the valleys down and send everyone to Bethnal Green, we'll all be English.'

'My mother said we're in shock since the election.'

'Shock? We're in shit. Prostitutes or politicians? I know what I'd vote. The mistake we make is, we think they're human so they get elected. But they're still perverts, wasters. Remember those types in school? They don't change; the biggest buggers you can imagine running your life.'

'No,' says Sean, 'it's all colonial. England wants to keep control so they hold us down.'

'Control? Of what? Once there were pits.'

The sound of a zither follows a man crossing the street. His coat is undone, a bald head bowed into the weather. Without slowing he bangs open the glass door of The Dorothy: 'Go and breed, you bastards! Breed and eat yourselves.' A few near the door look up, most continue blowing smoke or sipping their tea. He lets the door go gently and marches close passed our window, arms swinging. In one hand is something small that looks like a

In the Beginning

bible but is a transistor radio.

'I need some air,' says Sean.

Half-eleven and the pub is already sticky and packed; can't be just from dole day. A bloke shifts up on a wall seat for me and Nick. He looks a bit girlish and out of the crowd with a grey ponytail and his legs crossed. Most other heads are cropped or shaved. There's a lot of suits and jackets; nearly all the wrong size, either too tight or too big. It's like a misfit convention.

We don't usually come to this place. But Sean is out of sorts and fancied a change. He's at the bar and a ginger-headed kid is cadging off him. The pub has a lot of styles; on the ceiling there's bunches of hops, on a shelf are Davy lamps and figures carved from coal. The walls have brass lights over pictures of Welsh castles.

When Sean brings our drinks he's got his colour back. 'Hell getting served. Not this many usually, is there?'

The man smiles and squeezes up even tighter.

'Don't stare,' says Nick, 'some real hard knocks here, bottlers and stabbers in this lot.'

The man leans over Sean, his legs still crossed. 'Watch your pockets if I was you. Magistrates today, place is full of robbers.'

Nick shifts the green bag onto his lap. 'What magistrates?'

'Court, you know. Some've been... some're going. Always meets up here. Say who's on the bench. What they got... what's expected.'

'A pub full of criminals?'

'You what? Don't wear laces on Friday. Mind you, get anything you want. This is where it ends, off the back of lorries and that.' He gets out a tin of tobacco and rolls with

209

one hand. It's a thin, mean-looking cigarette. As an afterthought he offers the tin before putting the lid on. With one drag, half the fag disappears. He looks around. 'Yeah, fair bit of private property passed through them hands.'

'Property?' Nick obviously doesn't like him, and he's on the side of the robbers. 'It's all theft anyway.'

'You can say that again, they wouldn't know how else to get it.'

'I mean owning, possessions. How do people own things?'

'Don't say you don't own nothing.'

'Not really. This is my mam's shirt... '

'You look after that bag well enough,' says Sean, 'must have a fair bit of property in it?' Nick puts the bag on the table and lifts the flap so that it shields him when he dips his head to look in. He pokes a hand amongst the contents. 'Show us.' says Sean.

'Nah, there's nothing interesting...'

'Come on.'

'It's private.'

We all look at the bag.

'Come on, show us.'

Nick starts taking things out and putting them on the table: An old bus pass, a paperback, a creased photo of Bonnie, another old bus pass, chewing gum, two biros, a strip of paracetamol...

'Told you, it's nothing. Nothing interesting.'

The man tries to look over Nick's shoulder. 'It's still half full, come on. He's probably hiding the best stuff.'

A Marks & Spencer carrier, neatly folded, a spearmint lip salve, bus tickets. The last thing on the table is a Blondie single, the cardboard cover battered and faded.

In the Beginning

' "Union City Blues", a classic. Got it from a record fair in Cardiff. Cost me seven quid, but... ' As he's talking, he starts to put things back in.

'It's not empty.' Sean prods a finger against the bottom of the bag, pressing something soft and plump. 'What's this?'

'Nothing.' Nick scoops the rest of the stuff off the table.

'See,' the man sits back, his arms and legs folded, 'everyone owns something, we all have possessions.'

'Hardly. A few bus tickets, a second-hand record?'

'Yeah, but they're yours. You own 'em.'

Nick looks around the room, like he's searching for a witness to the man's ignorance.

'That's owning something!' He points at a photo of Caerphilly Castle in a big gilt frame. 'Those forts, that's ownership. Symbols of authority from when Wales was first subjected.'

'That's crap,' says the man, 'I been there, place is falling down.'

'And the coal mines? That was owning. Above and under; the land, the people!'

'Why're you shouting, sonny?'

'Now they've had everything, and we're no use. We can get stuffed far as they're concerned.'

'I remember the pits, good days they were. Sense of community, people did things for each other and you could leave your back door open. Honest it was.'

'I bet it wasn't like that. Hate that golden view of the past.'

'Wasn't gold, no. All a bit sprinkled in coal dust, and the river was black but they were good times.'

'How, good times? It was slavery. They died coughing

211

their guts up.'

The man glances at the faces close by. He speaks quietly. 'You had a different class of criminal, not like these scumbags. There were rules. It's all drugs and cars these days.'

'You a policeman?'

'Trouble is, today's too soft, too lenient.' His voice drops and he leans closer. 'What they need is some of that Islamic Law. Know what I mean? No messing. Cut your hand off or your head. And that's what they should do. No second chance, no first... Bang,' he chops down on his knee, 'away to go. Soon sort 'em out.'

Sean nods agreement. 'Yeah, it is bad. I've noticed the difference from when I was young.'

The man spreads his hands and looks up like asking God if He heard.

'Well, I don't follow that,' says Nick, 'The old days seem better but it must've been like a military occupation. Nostalgia crap. When you get a bit of freedom, have a bit of fun, it's against the law.'

'Fun? Fun? I don't call it fun, do you? Kicking people's brains in. Raping, robbing; not my idea of fun. All the abuse and violence... Can't walk through Blackwood after six o'clock.' He looks from Sean to me, me to Sean like he's making a bid for our friendship; discredit Nick, put himself in place.

'My mother said you always got a fight in Blackwood. There was a beer keller, after chucking out they battled the length of the street.'

The man picks up his pint and sits back like he's given up on us, disgusted. He stares at me through slitty eyes.

'Yeah? Your mother had experience, did she?'

In the Beginning

'I don't understand you,' says Nick, casually. 'Experience of what?'

'You're deliberately bugging me, kid.'

He stands, much taller than he seemed folded up. Nick giggles. The bloke hitches his belt, a John Wayne caricature. 'Here or outside?'

Nick tries to stop laughing with a hand over his mouth, eyes dancing like loose marbles.

'Where d'you want it, son?'

A tight rim of spectators has built up. Beyond the front row they are straining over shoulders or jumping up and down for a view, and there's encouraging shouts to get stuck in, give it a go, sort it out.

'Come on. Get up, be a man.'

Nick is hysterical, cheeks wet with laughing. Sean waves to someone; a ginger head stuck through legs like it's in a scrum or the stocks. The legs buckle and the head pulls a short body after it. He reaches up and gives the man's ponytail a tug. 'Dad. Don't wanna fight, do you? Not on top of what you got.'

'No respect, look at him.'

The ginger kid turns to Sean. 'Why's he laughing?'

'Thinks it's funny I suppose.'

The wall of spectators is closing in tighter.

'Get him out, if I was you.'

I grab Nick's arm and pull him after me. There's jeering, and a few pats on the head.

'Why're you such a prat?' asks Sean.

'Bit of an anticlimax, wasn't it? Bet I could've dabbed him.' Nick dances off the pavement, snorting down his nose. 'The old one-two-three. I've shadow-boxed the best, boy.'

We walk in fine drizzle back to Blackwood and The Dorothy where Sean is meeting his girlfriend.

'You're just bloody stupid! Could've been killed.'

'You got no sense of adventure. Anyway, he was just a hippie.'

'Hippie? He was a bloody nutter, obvious.'

'That why you agreed with him? I didn't realise you were a Fundamentalist. Put 'em in irons, string 'em up, bring back boiling oil and thumbscrews! I tell you, scratch the surface of Valley boys and you find bloodthirsty bloody tyrants. Isn't that right, Jen?'

'You're lucky Sean knew that kid.'

'Not luck. If you talk the talk, you gotta walk the walk.' He balances tiptoe along the kerb; hyped up, excited. 'Life on the edge, can't beat it... You didn't know that was his father, then?'

'Didn't know the kid till he asked me at the bar for a fiver.'

'I'd have talked myself out of it, usually do.'

Nick is kicking a tin along the gutter, keeping it skilfully out the way of cars.

Sean has his hands in his pockets. 'Rhian's dying her hair.'

'Like mine?' Nick daintily fingers a white spike.

'More strawberry blonde.'

'Yeah, like mine. Ennit Jen?'

'Yours is more bleach.'

Nick is quiet for a while. 'Strawberry? That must be red?'

'Just the name that is, not the colour. What'd you use on yours?'

'Dunno, peroxide I think.'

'That's like putting Domestos, strips it.'

In the Beginning

'Does a good job, look.' He bends for us to see: distemper-white hair, scalded scalp, dark seeds at the root.

'Don't go on to me about wasting money,' says Sean. 'Seven quid for that Blondie single, plus the fare to Cardiff.'

'Worth it though; classic.'

'Been a funny morning, hasn't it?' I say.

'Dole days are always the same. Nothing's ever really free.'

'You're a fatalist, Sean.' Nick gives the can a kick into rusting waste ground.

'Well, you should be looking forward to it, giro. But you know something's bound to happen.'

I snatch a flower growing tall amongst bed springs and car seats, 'Good film on last night. Anyone see it, *My Beautiful Laundrette*?'

'All them poofters!' says Sean, '... Yeah, wasn't bad.'

'Now, he's got nice hair, that Daniel Day Lewis,' says Nick.

'Must be Welsh with a name like that?' Sean spits on the pavement, not a practised gob, more a drooping trickle. 'Anyone got chewing gum? I can still taste that pet shop.'

'Yeah, somewhere.' Nick rummages in the green bag.

'What was that you kept hid?' Sean tries to peep in. 'Gonna show us?'

'No. Some things are secret.'

The rain has cleared up. In the cafe there's a sweat on, everyone's been caught out by the sun. We are still waiting for Rhian.

'Taking her shopping, are you?' Nick has fought off all Sean's offers of pies, pasties, chocolate.

215

'Just to get a record.'

'Don't, let me guess. Echo and the Bunnymen? Thought you had 'em all?'

'After this one.'

'They're heading for a split, you know that? Going in different directions.'

Sean is upset, agitated. 'No they're fu... flippin' not... '

A girl with pasty hair slides into the seat. She looks roasted in a thick orange jacket.

'Rhian! Didn't recognise you. There's nice your hair looks.'

She ignores me, snuggles up to Sean and whispers something that makes him laugh out loud.

'Got you a present.' She puts a string bag on the table.

Sean grins, coy like teacher's pet. 'Show us then.'

Rhian reaches out something loose in Christmas wrapping. She peels back the paper and holds up a blue checked shirt. It's got a faint stain on an armpit like sauce or gravy, and a frumpy, waiting-room smell.

'Aw, brilliant!' says Sean.

'Yeah, it's nice,' says Nick. 'Bit conservative, though.'

Sean gives Nick a pitying smile. 'By your standards... Be right as rain after a good boil-up.' He smoothes the collar, then folds the shirt and lays it carefully in the Christmas paper.

'Where'd you get it?' asks Sean.

'Newport Oxfam. Knew you'd like it.'

He kisses the tip of her nose, 'Right. Let's be off.' Walking out they hold on desperate to each other, afraid a Siamese-twin surgeon might sneak up, slit them apart. At the door they half turn and wave a limp goodbye.

I wait until they're across the street. 'How cringy. That lovey-dovey stuff makes you puke.'

In the Beginning

'Bit suspicious, ennit?... Maybe you've never been in love?' says Nick.

'Maybe. If love's oily, clingy... smug.'

'You don't feel sorry then?' asks Nick.

'For them? Think they'd notice? The world's about half an inch big when they're together, no room for anyone else.'

'God, you're bitchy today. Thought you liked them?'

'Course I do, separate. Together though... you feel you're barging in on their personal paradise.'

'You're hard. Nothing ever lasts, never ever. Dying sees to that. Why begrudge?'

'I don't know because it's... so self-satisfied: "We got something no on else has!" '

'Notice anything about Sean today, his language?'

I shake my head. 'No idea. Never says that much, does he?'

'Didn't swear. Didn't swear, all day,' says Nick.

'Never?' I try to recall. There's not even a little shit or bloody. 'Don't say he's got religious?'

'No, because of dole day. Part of the ritual, not to have bad luck. Makes no bloody sense, does it? But that's what we're like. Sort of cling on to things, afraid.'

CHAPTER SIXTEEN

We are listening to tapes in my bedroom. The rest of the house is quiet. Mam and Dad have taken my little sister to the seaside in the warm weather. She wanted to stay, fascinated by the tall man with painted hair, and was dragged bawling into the car.

Nick asked for the curtains to stay closed. The sun is small and vague through the material but the room is hot and stuffy.

'I love those curtains,' he says, 'so Picasso.' He touches the black cotton patterned with blue, grey and orange triangles. His forehead is beaded in sweat and his skin, usually very pale, is pink.

'Why have you got that jacket on in this weather?' He's wearing a thick motorbike leather, coated with a humid sheen.

'Oh no, can't take this off. Don't like running round in just a T-shirt. I feel naked.'

'And you don't want to sit in the garden?'

'Too hot.'

'It feels like you're not stopping, just popping in to say hello.'

'What's the big deal?' He reluctantly slips the jacket from his shoulders and drapes it on the back of a chair. Then he sits on the bed rubbing his bare arms as though there's a chill. 'Feel awful, all exposed.' He looks thin and vulnerable, and stares affectionately at the jacket. 'Love that leather. Had it on when they arrested me. Kept me company in the cell. Funny, you'd never think, but it was like a friend. Especially when I got sober and miserable.'

'Like a comforter,' I tease, 'a teddy bear.'

'Just hope you don't spend a night in jail. It's the worse experience, you feel such an outcast. Still, how many kids can say they've been inside?'

'Few hours in a cell? Nearly everyone around here.'

'Tell you what, it was freezing! I'd 'ave died without that jacket. Warm in here though... Get us a glass of pop, Jen.'

'We don't drink rubbish in this house, have to be water.'

'Hate water. Is there squash in it?' he asks.

'Just water.'

'I'm parched. Nearly passed out walking here.' He leans against the wall and closes his eyes.

When I come back he's almost asleep. I touch his arm.

In the Beginning

'Oh thanks. No ice, then?'

'No ice.'

He sips and pulls a face. 'Ugh! You can tell it's from the tap. Funny tang. Just can't drink the stuff.'

After putting the glass on the book shelf, he lifts up a bulky art book and takes it back to the bed. 'These're well thumbed. You like Picasso? His Blue Period was best. All those poor people he painted. A bit depressing, though. Guernica is the masterpiece. It's absolutely massive.'

'You've seen it?'

'Not yet, but I know it's big. Sad pictures have the most impact, don't you think?'

'No, not really. Abstract painting isn't happy or sad, but you can't say it doesn't have impact, can you?'

'Hm, not sure really. Jackson Pollock is sort of happy.' Nick skims through the pages for evidence to back his theory.

'What about... Ah! Van Gogh, some of his stuff looks really gloomy. It's not the terrible subject matter like Guernica, but his paintings are so lonely. See.'

He holds up the heavy book. 'See. Starry Night. One of my favourites. Makes you feel lonely, doesn't it?' I study the picture; first from close up and then standing against a far wall. Does it make me lonely? I try close up again. The painting begins to tremble.

'For Christ sake, get a move on. My arm's killing me.' Nick lets the book down with a thump.

'Well,' I say, 'the feeling I get is, it's like a whizz of energy, like the heavens spinning round.'

'That's right! All these whirling, whipping spirals; nothing's stable. Everything's in a crazy motion. Really scary... See, he was mad as a hatter. Spent ages in a mental asylum. Even painted there. You can tell, his swirling got even madder as he got worse.'

'But what's that got to do with it being sad or happy?' I ask. 'Just because he was nuts doesn't mean his art is sad. What about Gauguin or Modigliani? They weren't smiley and happy but their paintings are full of colour and life.'

'There's a thin line, I reckon, between being mad and creative. Not just with painters — anyone.' He seems to have conveniently forgotten what he was looking for, or perhaps he's placing himself somewhere on those borders between genius and insanity, and for a moment has lost his way. Suddenly he smooths out a two-page spread of ballet dancers. 'Look, Impressionists! Absolutely love Degas. Those sketches he done in pastels, beautiful they are. My absolute favourite though is... ' He licks a finger and flicks quickly through the pages. Then the book is held up triumphantly, showing Monet's famous and utterly boring, Water Lilies.

'Massive, these paintings.'

'You've seen 'em?'

'No, but I can read. Used buckets of paint! Buckets. They were so generous with their paint, the Impressionists.'

'Generous?'

'Layered it on like cement, plastered the canvas. Don't you just feel that richness, the texture? It's sculptured.' Then he closes the book; snaps, or rather bangs it shut. 'I used to paint,' he grins like it's a confession, 'did something every night.'

'Sounds intriguing. What did you get up to?'

He holds out his hands as though they show the answer. The long, sensitive fingers of an artist. I imagined them after a few years on a pick and shovel; thick and

222

In the Beginning

callused.

'Usually pastels or charcoals. I loved it. Shut myself in the bedroom, closed the curtains, just the lamp on. So snug and alone.'

'I know. Used to spend ages in my bedroom. They thought I was cracking up. Don't realise do they, parents? Sometimes you just can't be bothered.'

'No!' Nick shakes his head in vigorous disagreement, 'Wasn't like that with mine, never. Always loved my mam and dad.'

'Oh, sorry. Mine are okay, in a sense. We call my dad Hitler.'

'Christ!' Nick hides his hands between his knees. He is shocked, as though I've said a terrible obscenity.

'No, Hitler. We got it from a Sylvia Plath poem, "Daddy You Bastard", or something.'

'Is he that bad?'

'Victorian Dad is another name, behind his back of course. All fathers are hypocrites, aren't they? He was a delinquent as a kid, apparently.' This kind of talk made Nicholas uneasy. He sits uncomfortably on the edge of the bed.

'Yeah, I suppose,' he agrees reluctantly. 'Mothers are better, generally. Not such hypocrites.'

'So, what did you paint?'

He brightens. 'Oh, anything. Still life. A bit boring but good for practising textures and stuff. Tried water colours, never got to grips with it though. Because I don't like water, I guess, too runny. Love oils, just love 'em! Used to feel like spreading it on toast.'

'Interesting,' I say. 'I had an aunty who couldn't resist licking things she liked the smell of. She was in hospital a few times to get her stomach pumped. Had lead poisoning

223

when she was a kid from sucking pencils. They say it affected her brain but because she's from Ponty you can't tell if she's mad or criminal. Did you have anything displayed?'

'Oh, no. It wasn't for that. Just personal. Started experimenting, designing posters. Things for the band... ' I wait for him to continue but he seems to be thinking about something else.

'You working on anything now?'

'God, no. Can't be arsed. Still got all the stuff, paints and everything. Strange, nothing's an effort when you're young, if you want to do it. When you're older it becomes a chore.'

'Oh, good grief! Old Father Time, come in your age is up. Wait till you're twenty or something!'

'I'll never get there. Have no intention.'

It's oppressive in the room, stuffy hot.

'Fancy some fresh air, sit on the yard?'

'Nah, it's baking. I'll burn up.' He holds out his knobbly arms. 'Look, they'll frazzle.' If Nick has beautiful hands, what they are stuck on are touched by the ugly stick. His arms are like those robot things that do the welding on assembly lines, except his are bone white.

'We'll have to open a window, then. I'm nearly passing out.'

'I'll do it.' He turns around and kneels on the bed. When he opens the curtains a dead moth flutters off the sill. He stands up suddenly. 'What have you done? All these moths!'

'All? There's only a few.'

'Why did you?'

'Samantha stayed last night. She swatted them with *Cosmopolitan*, rolled up.'

224

'Oh, the poor things.' He leans to look close.

'The light was on and we had the window open. They just flew in.'

'Of course, you've got a bare light bulb.' He extends a finger, gently touches a furry body then the fragile, silvery wings.

'How can you kill these beautiful creatures?'

'Because she's shit scared of 'em. They gave her the creeps.'

'Sacrilegious. Moths are sacred.' He is so upset I think he's going to cry. "Life is fragile as a moth".'

'I beg your pardon?'

'It's from a poem. The moth symbolises life.' He picks up a tiny body by the filigree of a wing-tip, holds it close to his eyes. 'They are drawn to the light, which they love. Light has heat, and they die when they touch.' He lets go and it spirals light as a snowflake. 'We should go out. It feels like a graveyard in here.' Nick takes the cassette player and tapes, I carry the two dishes of salad my mother left for us.

It's nearly midday and the only bit of shadow is a narrow triangle by the shed. We sit on the steps squinting over the white china plates. Nick has his coat back on to protect his arms.

'Tour de France tonight, gonna watch it?' He's sifting the food with his fork, picking.

'I don't think so.'

'The 74th. Starts today in Berlin.'

'Would you believe it?'

'It's brilliant, fantastically exciting... You won't be watching, then?'

'Not a priority. Is there any sport you don't like?'

'There may be. I can't think of one. You don't like any,

225

do you?'

'It's the whole thing I don't like. The macho, aggressive, gotta take sides, gotta win. Our team's better than yours, and some thicko who's hero-worshipped wins first prize, gets all the cash.'

'Wow!'

'Hate it, all of it.'

'What about cricket?' says Nick, 'The rhythm, beauty... excitement. Supreme drama, better than anything that can be written. So unpredictable, so emotional. I love it, sublime.' His eyes are moist.

'You sound like a white supremacist.' I say. He looks puzzled.

'Isn't it the game of reactionaries?'

'I don't know, never thought of it like that.'

There's a newspaper on the top step. Nick picks it up and turns to the back pages.

'What sort of shite is this?'

'My mam reads it.'

'Don't have any sport.'

'Dad's probably taken that.'

Nick puts the paper on the yard and thumbs the pages quickly. 'Heavy going this, bloody rubbish.'

'Thought it'd be right up your street — arty, liberal.'

'Me, liberal? Cheeky bugger! This paper stinks of public school. The writers are like naughty kids being bolshy, really they're pathetic little nerds in love with each other and the headmaster. I hate it.'

'Mam says it's the best of a bad lot.'

'Used to be called the *Manchester Guardian*, know that? They reckon it was genuine then.'

'Well, I know what they read in your house.'

'So? You snob. My dad's a manual worker, the *Sun*'s a

worker's paper.'

'A worker's paper? Why is it always smashing the workers then? We won't have it in this house.'

'A worker's paper! I mean when you come home from work, too knackered to read this airy bollocks.' He scrunches the *Guardian* into a ball and throws it onto the yard.

'Yeah? Great during the Miners' Strike, wasn't it?' I counter.

'The Miners' Strike? You were too young.'

'A year younger than you; my father took food parcels round.'

'Well, I don't remember much, except it was boring and on the news all the time. Anyway, all papers are crap, they just confirm your prejudice. Who gives a shit, let people read the *Sun*.'

'And what d'you think of salads?'

'Alright, yeah. Why?'

'My mam's famous for her salads.'

Nick's meal has been swept by a minute hurricane: bits smashed all over the plate; a vegetable wreckage.

'She made it pretty.'

'But you don't like the taste?'

'Not used to weird food.' he sniffs a piece of garlic bread. 'We have good, plain stuff.'

'Like what?'

'I dunno, normal things; cooked dinner, ham and chips. My mam does lovely home-made pie.' He picks up a lank lettuce leaf, nibbles along its edge. 'We have tuna sometimes but not these smelly things. Sorry.' He puts the plate down, and starts to unlace a shoe. 'Do you mind turning round?'

'What for?'

'My feet are throbbing, want to take my socks off.' He pulls a trouser leg up to show the thick red towelling round his ankles. 'My toes are on fire.'

'Why should I turn round?'

'You'll stare at my feet.'

'What the hell for?'

'Because... People do, don't they? Feet are horrible, ugly. They're, like, deformed. You can't help looking.'

'Don't be absurd. In this house we hardly wear shoes in summer.'

'Oh, suit yourself. I was only thinking of you.' He yanks off a shoe and peels down the sock. His foot is long and X-ray skeletal, the white skin seems sprayed to the bones, and it is shining with bright sweat. I just stop myself from gasping out loud.

'See, I told you,' he quickly slips the foot into a shoe. The laces are tied into a neat bow. When the other foot is finished, the socks are rolled into a tight ball and he has a crafty sniff before it's stuffed in his pocket.

Up on the guttering sparrows chirp like mad. For a few minutes this is the only sound on the yard. Nick is in a sulk. If I don't speak we'll sit silent all afternoon.

'I've still got the tape you gave me.'

'The tape?'

'I played it for Sam. She thought it was a bit strange.'

'What tape?'

'The one with you talking. Did you want it back?'

'What blinking tape are you on about, please?'

'It's here, somewhere,' I rummage amongst the cassettes piled by the player. 'This is it, I think.' Nick looks puzzled as the speakers crackle. An acoustic guitar twangs and he groans.

'Oh God, no.'

In the Beginning

I stop the tape. 'You gave it me to sing along with.'

'Must have been drunk. You played it for Sam?'

'She said it sounded strange. We had a laugh.'

'For Christ's sake, it's personal. No, don't put it on... ' I keep his hand from the stop button. The guitar strums monotonous in the background, like a metronome for the deadpan voice: '... and my brother's not here. He's away. Far away. Miss my brother. Lovely day. Two lovers in a park. Sunny-sunshine. Lovers are men. Two men. Two lovers in a park... ' He knocks my hand away and hits eject.

'I'll have it back, if you don't mind.' He gets up and shoves the tape in his jeans pocket.

'Why did you play it for Sam? That's like... betrayal.'

'She found it, amongst a stack of tapes. Just, by luck. I didn't do it on purpose.'

'Yeah, but you sniggered with her, didn't you? That's worse.'

'I'm sorry. Didn't realise.'

'Personal, that was. For myself.' Nick looks at me accusing. 'I shared it with you.'

'I didn't even understand, still don't. What's it supposed to be?'

'A technique. Something I was into. Don't think I should tell you.'

'Come on Nick, you're being silly. I promise I won't tell.'

'You have to say the first thing that comes into your head, and you speak along to guitar music.'

'Sounds interesting... Why d'you do it?'

He looks at me despairing. 'Oh, I'll tell you some other time. Listen, what's the time? Christ! I have to go.'

'Hey? Look, I'm sorry, right. If I'd known what that

tape meant... '

'Now you're being silly,' says Nick, 'Dad's arranged a job for me.'

'On Saturday afternoon?'

'Cutting the neighbour's grass. Imagine? Be hell in this heat. Can't go back on a promise, even though my dad made it.' We start to walk around the side of the house.

'My dad's got one of them push mowers,' I say, 'thinks the electric ones are for wimps.'

'Bad enough with a fly-mo! Wouldn't do it otherwise. They don't pay much, anyway.'

'Oh? Not doing it for nothing, then?' He glances at me like I've asked if a bear shits in the woods.

'Have to trim round the edges as well, with clippers. Last time I had bloody blisters and my poor hands looked terrible; ruddy wrecked they were.' He slides his palms together as if rubbing imaginary cream.

'So, you got bloody hands to look forward to?'

'Like hell. I'll take a pair of Mam's gloves.'

'What kind of gloves?'

'Gloves! Like, you know, the sort you put your fingers in.'

Samantha is breezing up the steps looking cool and summery in a sleeveless yellow dress and sunglasses. Nick stands to the side, letting her pass; his leather jacket limp in the sun.

'You've got company, Jen, the moth killer... Sorry I can't stop,' Nicholas stretches his arms like a crucifix, 'have to get my hands bloody, too.' He hurries down the steps and away up the street.

Sam removes her sunglasses. 'He is a weirdo, isn't he?'

'Off to cut grass for a neighbour.'

In the Beginning

'What's all this bloody hands, then?'

'Last time he got terrible blisters.'

'Really? Ah, how sweet. He's so kind underneath. She's probably old, can't manage herself. Gonna be hot in that jacket, though.'

On the back steps, a slice of shade has appeared from the overhang of the roof. 'Been having a feast, have you?' Sam picks up a piece of stiffening bread.

'Not Nick. He'd die of hunger if he had to eat garlic.'

'What!... Don't mind, do you?' She scoops up forkfuls of melting salad. 'Mam's in work. Hm, you can taste the chives. He missed a treat. So Welsh, isn't it? I mean, dull food. James' parents are the same, boring meals. I'm lucky my mam's a fantastic cook... yours ent bad either.' Funny, just one habit changes your whole impression of someone. Nick was so artistic and flamboyant, broad-minded in every respect. Yet there must be some kind of flaw if he only liked fish 'n' chips.

'What makes people that way?' I asked. 'It's like they're afraid. How can you hate garlic?'

Sam munches loudly on some celery and looks pensively up to the chirping sparrows. 'Know what I think? It's where they live. Dead conservative in that valley, they are. Mind you, James will try anything. Taught himself to cook, he did. Follows the recipes. Loves onions, shoves 'em in everything. Mind you, did I say about the time with the quiche?

'His parents were out for the night and he managed to persuade Sean to stay in Rhian's. There would be just us two, a romantic night.

'In the morning, early, he puts the Hoover around his room before hurrying up to Blackwood with a shopping list. Most of the stuff he gets from Tesco's; a bottle of white wine, some long green candles and paper napkins, plus the stuff for an onion quiche. He wants to make a gateaux but can't find the ingredients so instead he buys a frozen chocolate cake from Kwiksave. Then he rushes home to do the quiche.

'He whips the eggs, chops the onions and rolls out the pastry with a milk bottle. Unfortunately he forgets to wear an apron and his black T-shirt is dusted with flour. So he changes into a navy shirt with polka-dots. I think the sprinkled flour gave him the idea because I'd never seen that shirt before.

'After I knock, I hear him belting up the stairs. He opens the door, turns, and runs back along the passage, shouting over his shoulder for me to follow. When I get down to the kitchen, he is pouring out wine while Frank Sinatra is singing "New York, New York" from a little cassette player on the table.

' "You like Liebfraumilch?"

' "Why not?"

'His hand is shaking slightly and, as he puts it down, some wine spills from the brimming glass. The liquid fizzes on the surface, cleans the wood. I take a sip and cough to hide my grimace. It's like malt vinegar.

'James gulps a mouthful. "Hm, lovely ennit?"

'Frank croons, the clock ticks on the kitchen wall, and the wine is working on my fillings.

'James, on his second glass, tries to top me up. I put my hand over the glass. "No, thanks, I like to... savour it?"

' "Yeah, of course. Hungry?"

' "You told me not to eat, remember? Only have breakfast, you said."

' "Won't be long, been in the oven a while."

'Forty minutes later I check my watch; starving,

232

bored with old blue eyes, and a nervous wreck from James diving up every five minutes to check the cooker.

' "Perhaps we could get some chips?"

' "The recipe said twenty minutes."

'A stomach rumbles. We look at each other. Whose is it? We both apologise.

' "Won't be long now."

'He spins away again. "At last! Ready!" Heat blasts out of the red-hot oven, flushing his face and burning his throat.

' "Go on up," he croaks, "to my room. No, take your wine, take the bottle." As he lifts out the baking tin with an oven glove, the quiche flows over the side.

' "I'll bring the food up. Nothing to do, just relax."

'James' room is on the third floor from the kitchen. You have to pass through the living room. On the way I'm tempted to tip some wine in a plastic plant pot. But it would be like acid rain.

'The door to his bedroom swings both ways and can't be locked. It has the privacy of a cowboy saloon. Inside it is almost dark except for an orangey glow in one corner where a red checked tea towel has been thrown over a little lamp. There's a wicker chair and he's carried up the coffee table from downstairs. I put the wine on the table next to the unlit green candles and serviettes which have been folded into two neat triangles. Then I sit on the chair and wait, and wait. My stomach makes all kinds of noise: growls, howls, bellows, barks. It's unbearable, and I decide to make a break for it, run up the chip shop. As I'm creeping along the landing, a floorboard creaks, loud.

' "Just coming! Be there now." I don't know whether to bolt down the stairs or go back in the room. And suddenly I'm feeling trapped, held against my will. I freeze, waiting for something horrible to happen.

'Then there's the sound of him bounding up. A bowl of salad comes into view and an oven glove and a steaming quiche. And gleaming Doc Martens jumping two steps at a time. I want to run but there's no room to pass. Nearly at the top, he trips over a fold of carpet. The food flies up; the quiche erupts, the salad explodes. James just makes the landing in time to catch the falling food all over his shirt. He closes his eyes. I tiptoe round him.'

Samantha flicks bread crumbs from her dress. 'Terrible it was.'

'Poor James.'

'Poor James? Tell you what, he gets on my wick sometimes. Got a knack of winding me up. A saint would lose patience with his hang-ups, always worrying about his clothes.'

'Strange, he looks so casual.'

'Scruffy, you mean, like he doesn't give a damn? Really, he's so fussy. Spends ages deciding what to wear. The chair in his room is always piled with things he tries on and throws off.' Sam and James are a pair well matched, I can't help thinking.

'Remember when I got my hair cut?' I nod, though I can't recall.

'Well, at first James said it was brilliant, really liked it. Then he wouldn't speak to me, just sulked. When I asked, he said I looked better than him. Can you believe?'

'No, I don't. It sounds far-fetched.'

'What do you make of this then? He's always complaining he doesn't have enough clothes. When he buys new, which is pretty often, he won't wear them because he feels stupid! So they end up on the wicker chair.'

In the Beginning

'Well, you know what it's like. See something in a shop and think it's great, and when you get home you look like a prat.'

'It's worse than that. Deeper, psychological. He feels conspicuous, like everyone's watching. That's paranoia.'

'Don't you feel that sometimes?'

'Yeah, but it's different. I've really seen people looking... Anyway, he loves jeans but hates buying 'em. Imagine? That's bound to cause problems. Hates having to take up the bottoms, says he cuts yards off. And it reminds him of Nick.'

'Wow. Cutting trousers reminds him of Nick! That is psychological.'

'Because Nick wears them off the peg. James has got a thing about tall men. I tell him, he's not that short. Unless I wear heels.' She laughs.

'I don't think Nick is that vain,' I say.

'Oh no! You heard about his bad hair dye?'

'You mean day, bad hair day.'

'I mean bad hair dye.'

I scratch my head. 'Don't think he's mentioned it.'

'They arranged to meet in Cardiff, James and Nick, to see a band. Well James was waiting but Nick didn't go.'

'Can I guess why?'

'Took him hours to spike and colour his hair but it all went wrong. So he didn't bother. Stood James up.'

'Bet James was mad?'

'Went on his own. Rang Nick later but he wouldn't go to the phone.'

'Why?'

'Stayed in his room all night, would not come out.'

'Weird. Wonder if it's why she finished with him, the last girlfriend?'

Jenny Watkins-Isnardi

'Nah, he was too moody, I heard. Nick likes his own company, James said. Needs to switch off, recharge his batteries.'

'Sounds like he should be kept in a garage.'

'He gets fed up of people. Does his head in. Have you noticed on Saturdays, he sometimes stays in when everyone's going out?'

'Not so much this summer.'

'Winter he goes to bed early, really early. Puts on U2's *Unforgettable Fire*. Brilliant in the dark, he says. From bed there's only the red dot on the hi-fi. If it's raining, even better. Pulls the quilt up to his chin; lies still.'

'You know a lot about Nick in bed.'

'James certainly does. I don't think they've got any secrets. They're so close it's frightening. I had a row with James once, and saw Nick later in Tesco's. He could barely open his mouth to say hello, dead unfriendly. It was like, a row with James is a row with us all. When I challenged Nick, he said he didn't know about any row. Scary, ennit? They're in touch through, what d'you call it?'

'Telepathy?'

'They were like the three musketeers, went everywhere together. James told me about this party they went to... ' The shade had moved further along the back yard, and the skin on Sam's arms was rough with goose bumps.

'Fancy a cuppa?' I asked.

She collects up the plates and follows me in. While I lay out the tea things on a tray, she leans against a worktop, her arms folded. 'Where was I? Oh yeah. Well, it was a working man's club, an eighteenth birthday. You know Karen Lewis from Six Bells?

'They were late because it took so long to get ready.

236

In the Beginning

By the time they arrive, the drinks have loosed everyone, and there's a huge noise coming from inside this big hall.

' "Got your invitations?" asks the man on the door.

' "Yeah, here they are." Sean pushes his cousin forward. James searches inside his motorbike jacket then unzips a side pocket.

' "For fuck's sake," snaps Sean, "can't trust him with anything."

' "Trousers?" suggests Nick.

' "Can't come in without tickets," says the doorman.

' "I was sure I put them here." James shows his inside pocket, hanging out like a tongue.

' "Well, it just goes to show," says Sean, viciously, "you can't be sure of anything."

' "Can't we just slip in?" asks Nick.

' " 'Fraid not, son," says the man, with relish. "Do it for one, do it for all."

' "Right, that's it then." Sean is in a fury, he looks around for something to kick.

' "Come all this bastard way, and we can't fuckin' gerrin! And why? Because prick ears can't even look after a few tickets!" Meantime James is looking puzzled at the inside pocket. Sean thinks he's still searching. "Are you retarded? Think they've magicked into the seams? You've lost 'em, idiot."

' "Never noticed that before." James holds out the pocket for Nick to see.

' "Don't say," Sean scoffs, "you've found a big hole."

' "No, look. I swear, never saw this red-felt mark before."

' "What red mark?... How're you wearin' my fuckin' coat? I put that mark, in case it was nicked!"

' "Check your pocket, Sean," says Nick.

' "There we are," the man holds the tickets up to the light. "All's well that ends well."

'The double doors open to a big Bee Gees sound. On the top trestle table, is the birthday girl's family. Aunty Pam nudges the woman next to her. "Kah-rist!" says Pam's sister, "What the hell is that?" The nudge travels the table like a Mexican wave. The whole family watch as the boys walk to the bar. "How does our Karen know wasters like that?"

'They are identical down to the buckles on black belts: the same white T-shirts, combat jeans, silver chains, motorbike leathers and Doc Martens. The sides of their heads are shaved, and the mohican spikes are the same shade of green, and height. Replicas.

'The barman is a bit of a comedian and a film buff. "Where'd you park the spaceship, amigos?"

'Back at the top table, Aunty Pam turns to Uncle Ky: "Go and chuck 'em out."

' "Oh, no. Don't," says Pam's other sister, Pat. "They're so cute, especially the smallest, like those little gremlin things."

'James gets the drinks, pints of lager and lime.

' "Beer's crap," whinges Sean.

' "Music's good, though. Here, hold my glass." Nick strolls to the dance floor. Aunty Pat feels sorry for the other two.

' "Aw, love 'em, like lost twins without the big one." She finishes her cider, and makes her way toward the bar. 'Good party, ennit? Enjoying it, yeah?" She squints closely at their faces. "Identical, then? Swear to God, like two peas in a pod."

'Sean snarls under his breath: "Like fuck."

' "So, who wants a dance? Your big brother ent bad, is

he? Bit jerky, like. But you can see he got rhythm." Nick had begun well. Then he got throbbing ankles and shooting pains up his shins. He's sorry now he choose Mental As Anything singing "Live It Up". It's going on forever.

'Sean and James are staring into their pints. Aunty Pat looks from one to the other. "Not shy are you? Come on, good one, this."

' "I'm holding the drinks," says Sean.

' "Give em here," offers James.

' "Now, now boys, no fightin'. Aw, I don't know which to choose, you're both so cute."

' "Have him," says Sean, "he's older."

' "Only a few months."

'Nick is hobbling off when he sees James headed for the door.

' "Awful shy, that little brother of yours. And this one's a bit grumpy."

' "My brother's in the States."

' "Aye, terrible. You're alright, though. Come on, I like this song."

' "No, please," says Nick, "my feet are killing me. Can't lift my legs, honest. And they cost a fortune, these boots. Dad'll go mad."

' "You'll have to flog 'em," says Sean.

' "Don't wanna buy 'em, do you missus?"

' "Awright, are you? Fuckin' boats! Too big for me." '

We take our tea into the living room. Years ago, according to my parents, this used to be called the front room. You'd think it was called the front because another room was called the back. But if there was another room, that was called the sitting room or the parlour. People argued whether the front room was in fact the best room where the china cabinet and three-piece suite were kept. There used to be heated disputes, said my mother, whether the front room should be the best room.

I'm bored with Sam's story and interrupt her. 'Didn't know James was so shy.'

'Privately. Very,' says Sam, emphatically.

'What does that mean?'

'Well, he's extrovert when he's performing. And he's a brilliant mimic. Should hear him doing accents. I swear there's no one better. Better than anyone on telly. In Burger King, he ordered in a Scouse accent. The waiter said he knew Toxteth and asked which street James was from. Even wanted to know if James was Everton or Liverpool.'

'Oh, God. Not sport, please! But that's not a performance, is it? It's with friends, so he's not really shy in private.'

'That's a performance for James. A group of friends can be an audience. That's when to avoid him, when he's at his worst, when he can't see the difference between private and public. Not nice to be with because you're just a member of the audience. I hate it. All performers are selfish gits.'

'Nick's not like that. Always the same, what you see is what you get.'

There is a big mirror over the fireplace. Sam stands on tiptoe and tilts the sunglasses to see which angle suits her best.

'What you see is what you get? James locks himself in the bathroom, practises in the mirror above the hand-basin: "Hey punk, you talkin' to me?" and all that. Gives him a rush of adrenaline, he says.' She turns away from the big mirror, holding the sunglasses; her face frowning, serious. 'That's strange, isn't it? Most people get depressed looking at themselves.'

'James obviously thinks you're pretty neat.'

'Know what I think? Apart from Susan, I'm the only girlfriend he's had.'

'Susan? I don't think I know her.'

'Course you do. Drives a yellow beetle with a blue daisy on the door. Friendly, bubbly; really nice girl.'

'She packed James in?'

'As if! She was nuts on him. James hates hippies.'

'Oh? I don't recall any hippies.'

'She had flouncy dresses and a few bangles. To James that's hippie uniform. Don't go with his image.'

'What's his image, then?'

'Well, sort of... military, I suppose. You know, everything pressed, clean, sharp; tight and matching. Closer to military than hippie, anyway.'

'Hey? You said yourself, he's a scruff.'

'I told you he works hard at it. Like he works at being relaxed around girls. Really he's shy and uptight, worried what they'll think. Maybe that's why he does all those stupid voices?'

'Different to Nick then... '

Sam put a hand on my arm. 'Sorry to interrupt... did they leave you something for dinner?'

'I think we've had it.'

'That wasn't lunch? Only, as I said, Mam's in work, and I'm not cooking for my lousy brother.' We went through to the kitchen and Sam hung on the fridge door, examining what's inside, not too impressed.

'Spoilt see, with Mam being a cook. What's in the freezer?'

241

Jenny Watkins-Isnardi

She settles for oven chips, grilled. And watches the burner as though it can't be trusted. 'What were you saying? Something about Nick being a crap impressionist?'

'You remember his last girlfriend, Rachel?'

'Now, if Nick has a fault, that's it. Something of a snob. That's why he takes up with snooty girls. Rachel was, wasn't she? Looked down her nose.'

'What does that make me?'

'Well, come on Jen, you put on airs and graces. And you're the first to laugh at yourself when you've had a skinful, Princess Hoity Toity.'

'Anyway, where was I?... '

'Where d'you get it from? Your dad's a bit of a roughneck, your mam's from Bargoed, and your sister's a thug!' Sam turned quickly, grabbed my head in both arms and rubbed my hair vigorously. 'Oh, but I love 'er and she's my best friend! Come on, then. What's this story?'

I stare at her, trembling, my scalp in a tingle, 'Bloodiest of cows! You know I hate my hair being touched.'

'It's brilliant when you're mad, you look really mental.' She gets down two dishes from a wall cabinet and forks out the chips. 'Tomato sauce?'

We take our plates into the front room or living room. Sam says she'd wash the breakfast things if I'll tell the story.

Rachel finished with Nick on the Friday. On Saturday he is dying, stays in bed with his arms round Bonny, listening to A-Ha's 'Hunting High And Low'. There's a phone call from someone called Kate that he tells his mother he's too ill to answer.

Sunday evening. *Songs Of Praise* coming from the telly downstairs when his mother shouts to say there's a

242

In the Beginning

Jackie on the phone. Jackie. Jackie? He remembers from school: blonde, slim, tall. He hurries down.

'Okay, yeah. Eh, no, sorry, can't pick you up.'

They meet outside a pub in Blackwood. She wears an off the shoulder mini and stilettos, with pink lipstick and hoop earrings that match her tinsel-silver hair. This pub is packed on Saturday but on Sundays there's a stale after-party feel. The carpet is worn smooth as lino, and still soggy from spilt beer.

'I'll have a packet of salt 'n' vinegar an' ... cider and black.' Jackie settles herself in an alcove, touches her hair and looks at the sad Sunday night drinkers, mostly men on their own.

'Ooh, ta, lovely... Quiet, ennit?'

'It's surprising there's any jobs left to get up for on Monday.'

'Hey? Yeah, half-seven. Been working there since I left school.'

'Where's that, then?'

'AIWA, you know, by the pond.' She crunches down crisps between gulps of purple cider. 'Good money.'

'I wouldn't mind some bad money, to be honest. What d'you do there?'

'On the line. Production.'

'D'you find it boring, the same thing all day?'

'Nah, have a laugh. Get your breaks for a fag.'

She reaches into her handbag, brings out a lighter and a pack of fags.

'Want one?'

'No. I don't.'

After a deep drag, she speaks with the smoke. 'Jap factories. Have to ask for a piss. Christ knows what'd happen if you wanted a shit!' Nick moves slightly away. He doesn't like girls swearing or talking about body fluids, or solids.

'Anyway, going for promotion. Better money, be rakin' it in; double-time Sundays. Gerrin an XR2.'

'You've got the one already?'

'Which one?'

'Before the two.'

Jackie tries to recall Nick in school. Was he in remedials?

'You ever had wheels?'

'On a skateboard.'

They don't get in touch after this one date. On Tuesday Nick is miserable and telephones Kate. 'Okay, yeah, great... The Red Lion.'

He looks through the window. She's at the bar reading a book.

'Oh, hi.' She puts the book in a brown leather satchel and gets down from the stool. 'We'll sit over there. No, I've already got a drink.' He joins her in her corner. She smiles and crosses her legs, black lace tights and red winkle-pickers.

'What were you reading?'

'Kafka, "Metamorphosis".' She picks up her lager, long fingernails painted scarlet. 'Where a man wakes up as an insect.'

'An insect?'

'A giant cockroach, actually.'

'Radiation, I expect. He mutated. I love science fiction. They say cockroaches will survive a nuclear war. He eats all the family, or something, yeah?'

'You don't know the story?'

'Yeah, of course I know Kafka. But I'm a bit fuzzy about that one. Is it where he thinks he wakes up but it's a

244

In the Beginning

dream and then the dream turns out to be sort of real?'

'No, it's about alienation, being an outsider. Finding yourself displaced. Like you, in a way, Nick. You're different.'

'Ah, right. Now I remember, in the end he goes to live with, eh... '

'No. He dies... Have you read any Castaneda?'

'Let me think. Costanada? Costa-nada? No.'

'The Rings of Power series?'

'Ring of Power? No.'

'Carlos Castaneda deals with the idea of otherness, challenging our preconceptions, our cultural reality.'

'You know James, James Bradfield? He swears he saw something going low over Pont, about six nights ago. A big triangle of lights. Flying saucer, he said. But no one else saw it. They say some people have special powers.'

Kate cups her chin in her hands and sighs. 'Had to see the principal, me and Amanda, Amanda-Punk.'

'Well, I know Amanda, that's for sure.'

'Is she over the top?'

'How d'you mean? Hair's a bit tall.'

'The principal said you make a statement by the way you dress. How you look defines you. The fucking prick.'

Nick recoils.

'There he is, in a three-piece suit, lecturing us about the way we look! Hey? What does he define? Who does he represent? The Czarist pig!'

Heads turn toward their corner, Nick checks the legs on the table.

'Didn't have the balls to say outright; he just beat around the bush. "How do you people feel about yourselves? Clothes create emotions," he says, "anger, aggression, submission, hate". Too right! He's wearing a

Mickey Mouse tie, and a waistcoat like a corset.'

Nick is thinking hard for an excuse. If only the walls would burst into flame or the cellars flood.

'He can't tell Rambo from bimbo and he says we're trying to draw attention!' The barmaid, pretending to gaze into the distance, is deciding when to kick this pair of druggies out.

'Yeah,' says Nick, 'makes you sick. Try to talk quieter.'

She whispers: 'So what d'you do? Say, yes sir? What colour lipstick would be appropriate, sir?' Nick shakes his head and Kate bangs her fist on the table. 'Like shit! Stormed straight out, I did, slammed the fucking door!'

The hatch lifts on the bar top. 'Alright you two, hop it!'

Next day Kate phones and talks to Nick's mother. She rants on about the fascist barmaid then tells her about a new, cool club in Newport. 'It's alternative sounds on Wednesday. Tell him to give me a ring. Goth all night. It'll be crazy.'

Nick stays in, watches *Coronation Street* with his parents. Next day he rings Sean. 'Have you got Keri's number?' He can feel the smirk on the end of the line.

'You asking her out? Not a hope in hell, not with you.' Sean is right. He looks at the figures on the scrap of paper. Even her phone number is classy. He screws the paper into a ball and aims at the yellow bin.

Late afternoon, Nick is bored to death. James is in bed with the flu and Sean is with his girlfriend, Rhian. Or was it the other way around? He kneels over the bin and fishes out the paper, soggy and stained with tea bags. The ink has run, is that a seven or a one? Not knowing makes it easier to call.

'Hi... Yes, of course I remember you. The friend of

In the Beginning

Rhian's boyfriend, Sean... Why not? I'll pick you up about 8 o'clock.'

Just before eight, a pretty girl with red, nape length hair and a thick fringe, calls at the house. She wears a pale blue, summery dress that shows a small eagle tattoo on her shoulder. Nick follows her out to the car, she looks lovely. Keri puts a Voice Of The Beehive tape in the cassette player, and they drive out to the country.

The pub is posh: low ceilings with wooden beams, black and white photos, polished tables. There is a faint smell of cooking. Nick has only a few quid and hopes Keri isn't hungry. She takes out her purse and tells him to find them a seat. The barman obviously knows her. They laugh about something, and Nick feels uncomfortable, out of place.

She returns with two lagers, hands one to Nick and takes a gulp of her own. Then she chats away; relaxed, confident. She tells him about the history of the pub, the age of the beams, how coaches used to stop here two hundred years before.

Nick tries to think of something interesting to say.

'That's a funny tattoo.'

She explains about the eagle, its symbolism. When Nick becomes quiet, she asks his opinion of the programme on telly last night about the Women's Movement.

'Watched *Coronation Street*,' he says guiltily.

'But you know about the Suffragettes?'

He nods his head, indifferent.

They stay for one more drink but before it's half-finished Keri gets up. 'C'mon, I'll drive you home.'

Outside his house, Nick walks round to the driver's side. He waits for her to roll the window down. Even though the night was a washout, he still fancies Keri.

'Like to come out to Blackwood one night?'

'Tell you what, Nick, I'll give you a call.'

'And?' says Sam, soaking up sauce and vinegar with her bread.

'She never did.'

'No, she wouldn't. Much too nice for Nick.'

'I can't believe you. You're so thick-skinned! I suppose I'm alright though?'

'Most girls like tall blokes.' She leans across and picks at my leftover chips. 'He's a bit girlie for me.'

'Girlie?'

'Not exactly rugged, is he? I prefer more... well, manly.'

'Like James?'

She bursts out laughing, 'What d'you think of him, then?'

'If he wore platforms... '

Sam gasps, almost choking. 'That's not funny. He'd never speak to you, and he'd kill me for listening.' There's silence while she mops my plate.

'Would he really be mad?'

'I'll find out tonight when I see the short-arse.'

'Where you going?'

'Erehwon. He's putting a new song together, wants to go over some chords. Boring as hell watching him strum that guitar, same tune over and over. Drives me nuts.'

'Take it serious, don't they? I wonder if it'll come to anything?'

A butterfly has flitted in through the open window and Sam reaches into the magazine rack.

'It's a load of crap. Anything good on telly tonight?'

248

CHAPTER SEVENTEEN

Friday evening. Louise and myself press under Sam's umbrella. She curses us for pushing her out. We are under the sign of Fred's Fish Bar. The 'h' in 'Fish' is broken and makes a 't' Which is appropriate because there's usually a fight at weekends from nudges at the counter.

It's muggy and the drizzle is warm. It would be hot to walk, we'd get soaked with sweat and rain. A car with foggy windows speeds deliberately close to the kerb sending a wave from an oily puddle.

'Bastards!' yells Louise.

A window rolls down. 'Slags!'

Dirty water drips off Sam's eyelashes. 'The fucking

wasters.' By some odd luck, one flimsy pump is clean and the other only specked; she wets a finger, and smears it worse.

'Bastards!'

'What's the time again?' asks Louise.

'Twenty minutes past.'

'Would've been fucking drier to walk!'

Dennis and Pricey had arranged a lift. The Dog was only half a mile but Pricey insisted because the weather said rain. Not much of a forecast to make in Wales.

I've got the first sniffles of a cold. 'If they're not here soon I'm going home.'

Louise panics. 'No. We can't do that, Richey will be waiting.' Richard Edwards, home from university, was meeting us outside the post office, just along the road.

'That's them!' Sam jerks the umbrella. 'Useless farts.' Two boys are hurrying in our direction; one is big and striding, the other hopping to keep up.

Dennis, the smaller boy, wipes sweat from his forehead. 'Car broke down.'

'Didn't even start,' says Pricey.

Within sight of the post office Louise gets a limp. In the doorway is a thin figure, head bent over something. He has a wisp of a body, and a strong gust would blow him away as easily as the book he is holding. He looks up and slips what he was reading inside his jacket.

'Sorry we're late,' says Louise, 'all Dennis' fault.'

Richey's short brown hair is plastered wet, and a pearl dropper hangs from the tip of his nose.

'Don't worry.' He smiles.

The rest of the way to the Dog, Richey walks with his head slightly bowed. Not because of the rain — the wind is blowing from behind. The car park is full. Richey pulls the

250

In the Beginning

door open and stands aside.

Pricey rubs his hands. 'Lets get at it then, make a talent check.' Richey nods, solemn. Louise waits to be last, and limps into the foyer. Sam shakes her umbrella then pokes it into a black metal bin of wet brollies.

'Won't be there after,' warns Richey.

'Have to take a chance, won't I?'

'A good one, isn't it?' He touches the curved wooden handle.

'Yeah, my mother's. Cost a bit.'

'Seems a shame.'

When the rest of us go through to the bar, he lingers and looks at the umbrella bin.

'Fucking weird,' says Pricey. 'Brolly fetish?'

'He's just concerned,' says Louise.

Unless you get in before eight, the only tables are by the dartboard. We curse Dennis again. When a game is played, you're ducking elbows and dodging bouncing darts.

'Bad choice,' says Pricey, 'can't see the dance floor.'

'So small,' says Dennis, 'only see the fucking thing if you're on it.'

'Language!' Louise glances at Richey.

'What d'you think, Rich?'

'It's fine.'

Two separate gangs of women gather under the dartboard, inspecting their flights and sipping lager.

'Didn't know women played darts.' Richey seems genuinely surprised.

'Dykes,' whispers Dennis.

One of the gangs wear baggy yellow sweatshirts with a car on the back and the words 'Fordrace Tyres'.

'My father plays for them,' I say.

251

Jenny Watkins-Isnardi

'Really!' Richey scrutinises the faces and chests.

'They got a football team as well; bottom of the fourth division, North Gwent Sunday League.'

Sam nods vigorous agreement. 'I've seen him, he's really crap. D'you like soccer, Rich?'

'Eh, yeah, it's okay.'

Someone from a darts gang shouts something about hockey. The women form a queue, pressing close by Louise. While Richey and Sam were talking, she was strained across the table trying to listen. Now she has an excuse to squeeze in by Richey. But when Sam asks me to help with drinks, Richey jumps up.

A blond boy and a blonde woman are busy behind the bar.

'They're a bit crude, Dennis and Pricey,' says Sam.

Richey looks about the pub. 'There's loads like that.'

'Is it a shock, coming back?'

'Only been a few months, and Swansea's not exactly...' Richey recognises someone further along the bar. 'Excuse me a minute.'

Pricey is trying to see who's on the dance floor. Louise is hunched, forlorn. 'Thought you were never coming back.'

Dennis spots a likely girl. 'There's Marge from up the caravans.'

'Her with a face like a soggy fuckin' dap? You must be joking. Bollocks to it, just as well get rat-arsed. What d'you say, Rich?'

Richey stares at him, blinking, uncomprehending.

'Oh well, please your fuckin' self.'

The DJ racks up Bon Jovi's 'Living On A Prayer'. It booms off the walls around the dartboard. The women turn to each other, mouthing the words of the song and
252

In the Beginning

moving their shoulders. The dance floor seems to writhe higher and thicker.

'Shit music.' Dennis has a false tooth that he flicks out now and then on his tongue. It seems to be a habit and he's not aware of doing it.

'I like it,' says Sam.

'His voice is great,' agrees Richey, 'and the guitar, brilliant.'

'Oh, pardon me.' Dennis folds his arms and sits back. 'Learn you good in university, do they?' Louise fidgets, shifting the weight on her backside.

'What's up with you,' asks Pricey, 'got a flea in your arse?

'She was shot,' Sam giggles.

Dennis sits forward. 'Shot? In the bum?'

Richey is dumbfounded. 'Shot?'

'As if... ' says Pricey.

'Wasn't I?' Louise looks to Sam.

'Near Jenny's. This kid comes from a house with, like, a silver gun. Aimed at me and Jen. We legged it down the street.'

'That's all I saw was them running. Then... whoosh, took my breath away.' Dennis has his mouth open; Pricey sits back with a cynical smirk.

Richey stares at Louise. 'What did the police say?'

'Police? I got a terrible bruise.'

'Prove it,' says Pricey.

'Wasn't a bullet, then.' Dennis is disappointed.

'Stuck this gun against the cheek of my bum. Shot a blank, thank Christ. Could hardly walk let alone run.'

Richey looks away, no longer interested. He stares at a framed picture on a nearby wall. It shows a fisherman holding up a big fish by the hook in its mouth. The fish is

253

contorting, not yet dead, and the man is smiling with twinkly eyes.

'Big fish, ennit?' says Dennis. 'Wonder where from? Foreign, I expect.'

Richey gets up and heads for the toilet.

'Who asked him along?' Pricey looks accusingly at Sam.

'He was in college, the canteen, on his own.'

'Shy,' says Louise, 'but really intelligent. Always got his head in a book, knows something about everything. Told me, he loves reading. Know what he said? "With books you're never alone." Brilliant, ennit?'

Pricey tuts. 'He didn't say that.'

'Yeah, he did, honest.'

'Nah, Marlene Dietrich. See, you think I'm thick because I don't act it.'

'I remember now, that's right. He said she said it. Not just books, though. He loves films as well, even black-and-white. Knows all the actors' names, and women. Don't know what he sees in Clare Grogan. Just an actress, not a real person.'

'Fuckin' hell,' says Pricey, 'what would an angel want with a real person?'

'Well, he can't play the harp, that's for sure.' Sam takes a drag on her cigarette. 'Can't even a toot a recorder, and he loves music, all sorts.'

'Does he like girls, like?'

'Dennis, just because your brain's never seen above your belly... '

'Oh yeah, he definitely likes girls,' Louise gives a quick, coy smile.

When Richey returns he stays standing up. After a bit he asks me if I'll give him a hand with getting drinks. It

254

In the Beginning

surprises everyone because I hardly know him and it's common knowledge I'm going out with Nick. On the way to the bar, it's obvious he wants to say something. It seems a big effort and he gets agitated. When he speaks, he lets out the words like an asthma attack.

'So, you're in with the Manics?'

'How d'you mean, "in"?'

'They're changing the name?'

'That's right, Betty Blue.'

'Shame. So original, Manics.'

It's like being accused of stealing something. 'It was Sean's idea.'

'Ah, Sean,' he sighs, as though to say, 'I might have guessed.'

'You know them? Nick?... James?'

He looks at me accusing, 'Not as well as you... Not much, really. Done some fliers. I see Nick about.'

'You like the music?'

'Yeah. Brilliant. They've got it; special, unique.' He speaks like they deserve reverence.

'Yeah, we're not bad. Need some practice, though. Still a bit raw.'

There's a sort of gasp. Maybe he does have asthma? He gets the drinks with a pristine tenner that has to be from a cash machine.

'Do you want to go back?' he asks.

'Where?'

He's obviously richer than Nick.

'I thought we might talk... about what it's like, playing with the band?' He speaks hushed, almost in a whisper; as if we're sharing a conspiracy.

'No, I can't leave my friends. And there's nothing to say, the Manics are just ordinary.'

255

Jenny Watkins-Isnardi

'I don't agree. it's special.' He stares hard, like confronting an impostor. 'Raw? The drive, the energy. I'm not sure you understand. They can't lose that.'

'Okay, I'll tell Nick. Might see him tomorrow, if he's not washing his hair. Oh no, that's tonight.'

'You're taking the piss out of me.' He'd be a crap poker player, wears emotions like a blush. He looks desperately hurt; someone who's confided a secret and had it laughed in his face.

'Oh God. Look, this is stupid. I can only afford to go out once a week, and I've got a cowing cold coming on... '

There's a commotion by the dartboard. A big, Germanic blonde woman is squaring to a little opponent from the Tyres.

'I was not a foot over the line!' The Fordrace holds her darts in a bony fist, close to her tight tits. Sleeves rolled up, her forearms are veined and sinewy. 'How can I be a foot? I only take size two.' She has a gravely smoker's voice.

'You was a fuckin foot!' The blonde's features are screwed to a grimace and pushed close.

Richey stares like a little kid watching big boys face up. There's a movement. The sinewy woman staggers back with a trickle of blood from her nose. All the noise, except the record, stops. The music plays incredibly loud. Far away, the bar flap slams.

'She started it.' Wiping her nose, there's red smeared over a thick vein.

'Come on, bugger off if you can't behave.'

The woman from the bar jerks her thumb and the Fordrace sweatshirts open a gangway for their team-mate to leave. Voices start to climb until the music is a blur in the background.

256

In the Beginning

'That was quick,' says Dennis.

'Women can't fuckin' fight. Don't have the stamina for a slog.'

'I've seen that blonde around. She's handy.' Dennis tips his glass to drain the pint. 'Now, her nan could handle herself. Mauve. Mountain fighter, she was. Used to battle up Mynyddislwyn, by the church. Ganks said he won a lot a money on Mauve.'

'Lucky punch.' Pricey lifts a cheek off his seat and farts like it's ripping his arse. They both look at Richey, and laugh. Richey smiles back, a choked and utterly stupid smile.

'God, you're dis-GUST-ing!' Louise.

'Where's Nick, then, Jenny?' Pricey asks. They think Richey wants to get off with me. In their dumb way they are being loyal, chivalrous, trying to put him off.

'Washing his hair, I think.'

Richey stares brooding at his pint glass. He seems to shrink into himself, becoming unnoticeable. After a while people are laughing and joking, getting drunk around him as though he's not there. And Richey has withdrawn to somewhere else, without even a reflex to screaming laughter, or to a nudge or a reference to his name. His body is there but not his mind. Any moment you expect him to simply get up and leave. Leave without goodbyes, as though he was always just a stranger sharing a table. It's easy to feel sorry. But you wonder whether he would treat you with contempt if you showed pity. Even Louise has given up, shied away. When he reaches into his jacket and takes out a book, no one pays any attention.

We are discussing violent vomits. Pricey and Dennis compete, trying to top each other's adventures with an auction of tall stories.

'In Benidorm. On that stuff, what's it now? Chucked up so hard, blew my contact lenses out. True. Public bog, it was. Been in one a them? Couldn't see a fuckin' thing. On my hands and knees, I was; feelin' all down this...'

Richey tugs at Dennis' shirt, 'Listen to this, "... Boy, it began to rain like a bastard. In buckets, I swear to God. All the parents and mothers and everybody went over and stood right under the roof of the carrousel, so they wouldn't get soaked to the skin or anything, but I stuck around on the bench for quite a while. I got pretty soaking wet, especially my neck and pants... ".' When he stops he doesn't take his eyes from the page. The rest of us are gawping, not quite open-mouthed, but unbelieving.

'Genius,' says Richey, 'genius.'

'What is it?'

Richey lifts his head slowly. Although he looks direct at Dennis you wonder what he's seeing. '*The Catcher In The Rye*. J.D. Salinger.'

'Oh yeah, course. The guy who shot Lennon? Nothing special though, is it? Just a stupid cunt who wouldn't get outta the rain. And how can it rain like a bastard? Doesn't make sense.'

'I've read it so many times, always fresh. Never get fed up of reading it.'

'Yeah, that's right.' Pricey strokes his chin and squints into the distance as though he's thinking. 'I'm the same with my books. Never get fed up. Pages are a bit sticky, mind.'

Sam blows smoke in his face, 'You just don't have the timing, do you? I like *The Catchit* too. Everyone should read it. Brilliant.' A slip of paper, perhaps a bookmark, has dropped from one of the pages. Louise picks it up. There's writing on it that she first reads to herself. 'Listen to this:

In the Beginning

A creel of eels, all ripples.
Jumpy as a Mexican bean.

Right, like a well-done sum.
A clean slate, with your own face on it.'

She looks at Richey. 'Is that a riddle?'
Richey takes the paper. 'Sort of, it's from a poem.'
'What's beans got to do with sums?'
'A baby, a newborn baby. In a well-done sum everything fits, nothing is left. Like the baby, perfect. Pure, uncontaminated by society, man. A new start.' Hmm... Clever chap, this Richey. There are invisible nods, an inaudible chorus of approval. 'I've read everything she's done. The baby really represents new life for her. A chance to wipe the slate clean. Start again. I like that: a pure, new beginning.' Hmm... We murmur sage agreement.

'Does anyone know her stuff?' Who's the secret egg-head? We glance at each other. No one owns up.

' "A creel of eels, all ripples." Fantastic imagery, isn't it?'

' "A creel of eels",' Dennis repeats slowly, ' "A creeeel... of... eeeels". Yeah! Sounds, like... the same.' Wow. Wow, Wow. So perceptive, bright, intelligent. We're struck dumb by Dennis' newly discovered literary ears.

T-Rex. Get it on. The pub pants to the opening bars. Even before the drum slaps in, the guitar is pulling everyone to the dance floor.

'Aw, I love this! Who's gonna dance?' Sam gets up and we all follow.

'This is a classic,' says Richey.

'Classic!' shouts Dennis.

'Marc Bolan was... ' Richey starts to bellow, thinks

better of it. Dennis' denture flicks out in split-second timing with the bass, even doing little double flicks to the ba-booms. Sam closes her eyes; enraptured, overtaken. Only Louise is not quite there. She cups a hand, screams in my ear: 'Must've have been great then, in those days.'

'When?'

'You know — then, when he sang live.'

The record finishes and we all stay, waiting for more.

'Bollocks!' Dennis is the first to recognise the next song's opening. 'Why d'they always do that?'

The floor clears like a dismissal. We troop off to leave A-Ha do their crying in the rain alone.

'Listen to the words,' says Richey, 'beautiful, really sad.'

'They are fuckin' sad!' Pricey plonks himself down by Louise who gets up straight away and squeezes in by Richey.

'You were saying? About Marc Bolan?'

Richey thinks for a moment. 'Well, he hit a tree, really young. People still put flowers there; on the tree.'

Louise looks perplexed. 'Why do they feel sorry for a tree?'

'He crashed. His car crashed into that tree.'

'Was he killed in America?' Sam is doubtful.

'What I find amazing is, after all these years people still pay homage. Pop music is supposed to be ephemeral,' says Richey.

Pricey gags on his beer. 'Fuckin' hell! What kinda word's that?'

'Ephemeral? It means not permanent, insubstantial, lasting only... '

'Okay!' Sam puffs her fag impatiently. 'I think we got the drift.'

260

In the Beginning

'Isn't it strange? They sell poppies and have services to remember the ones killed in wars but people still put flowers on that tree, after all this time. And all he was was a pop singer.'

'Even stranger though,' says Louise, 'the tree, in a way, killed him. And they treat it, like, special.'

'Chop the fucker down!' Dennis slices air with the side of his hand. 'Who was that one, used to spit at people? Died of something, what was it now?'

'Drugs. They all died of drugs: Jimi Hendrix, Keith Moon, Keith Richards.'

'He's never dead?'

'Sure to be. Imagine when they get to heaven, first thing they ask for's a fuckin' fix. Or maybe they cold turkey? No, that would that be hell. Makes you wonder. Perhaps God's got a rehab place. If hell's evil, they'll fuckin' take everything. But you're supposed to suffer in hell. Makes you wonder, doesn't it?'

Dennis is looking agonised toward the ceiling. 'That one... used to gob on people,' he clears his throat, 'big green ones, I expect. What was his bloody name?... Jim! Jim something. I can see his face now.'

'Davidson! Jim Davidson!'

'Jimmy Saville!'

'Jimmy Hill?'

'He was a fucking singer. Famous, really famous. Died... Where was it? Somewhere. Oh God, I can see him now... '

Pricey looks slyly at Louise. 'Much talent in Uni, Rich?'

'Talent?'

'Things with skirts, tits 'n' bums, females.'

Richey shrugs. 'Lots of girls in the city, Swansea.'

'What's the nightlife like?'

'There's the Cinders Club in Mumbles. I mainly go in the university bar.'

'Have bands there?'

'Port Talbot's the place for gigs. Don't go much, too expensive.'

Louise nods agreement, 'I'm not going to Uni, sick of being skint. Get a job when I finish col.'

'Wouldn't rush into it, if I were you. Should try something you like first. You'll lose ambition working nine to five.' Louise stares in awe at Rich — awed with his wisdom, awed that he thinks she has ambition.

'What are they like, the other students?' Pricey eases his bum up for a sly fart.

'Scum.'

'No friends there?'

Richey shakes his head.

'So, what d'you do, stay in?' Pricey sounds accusing, the nearest he can get to being sympathetic. There's a heaviness around the table. Shoulders slump as Richey's misery is shared. Drunk and half-drunk, any one of us would reach across and give him a cwch, but you know it would make him freeze, recoil. Even Louise sits intact, arms folded.

Only Dennis is completely without sympathy. 'You live on your own, then?'

'Got a place in the Uplands.' You can almost hear synaptic gaps fizzing, see the picture building in our minds: Richey on a bleak and windswept hill.

'Don't you get lonely?'

'Fed up sometimes.'

It's going down, down. Slow descent to the dark basement, where you sit with your head in your hands and between your knees.

'I suppose there's a lot of studying?' Sam is going up, bright, no-nonsense.

'Not that much. There's Yanks on the course, they work all the time, have to. They still get crap grades because they're thick as shit. Can't cope. Don't have the background, I mean, like our A levels. They must have the worst education in the world. Certainly creates the stupidest students.' Richey doesn't mention his own achievement. Everyone knew about his brilliant A level results: straight 'A's. They'd put him on telly because of it.

'Its all right for clever-clogs.' Louise is back in the cellar of misery. 'You and your sister. You could share a brain, still have ten times more than me.'

'Rachel?' Richey cheers. 'She loves studying, actually likes it! But she takes it serious.'

It's Sam's turn to gag on her drink. 'More serious than you? That, I'd like to see.'

'Get on okay with your sister, then?' Pricey is back to normal — cynical, disbelieving.

'Yeah, she's a friend.'

'They even go out together,' says Louise.

'Sad,' says Sam. 'Don't even talk to my brother, he likes Rick Astley.'

'I know the feeling, Rachel likes Deep Purple, Bob Marley... the Doors.'

'The Doors,' mutters Dennis to himself, 'I've heard of them. The Doors.'

'So, you're not identical, then? Least, not with music.' Pricey senses an imperfection.

'Let's say, there's room for improvement.'

'Yes, let's. How though? How can she improve, Uni-boy?'

'By liking the Godfathers or Wedding Present, now that would be quality.'

'Quality shit. Can't do anything with shit except flush it. Sisters of Mercy, the Mission; now that's quality... '

'No comparison! They're miles apart. Sisters and the Mission are just crap, simply crap. Can't even call it music.'

'It's all shit and crap, then, ennit?'

'Not Punk. Punk is sublime.'

'Punk is fuckin' constipated!'

'You don't understand. It's brilliant! It's Isaac Newton!'

'It's fuckin' what? Don't give me that pretentious crap!'

Richey smiles. 'Yeah, it's all crap and shit, ennit?'

I stand up, slip my arms into my denim jacket. 'Yeah, it is. And bloody boring.' The cold is getting worse, I feel it dulling my hearing, clogging the back of my throat.

In the foyer, the umbrella bin is empty. Sam waits for Richey to say something. But he just glances and shrugs.

Outside, the clouds are clearing and stars tinker. It's warm, sultry.

'Who'd nick an umbrella on a night like this?'

We decide on chips. During the walk, I sweat, feverish. Climbing the last hill, a big and battered car stops. We all pile in, though no one seems to know who it is or where it's going. Then Richey says 'Hi'. And that's all that's said.

She drops us off outside the Wishing Tree chip shop at the bottom of Blackwood. And no one has said a thing, not even Dennis. Across the road is a low wall by the

264

In the Beginning

library. Sitting on the wall are a few boys. Sam immediately recognises someone. She screams: 'James!' He raises his arm, a pathetic little wave. Sam turns to me, speaks quietly: 'I'm not having this.' Staring straight ahead, she big-strides across the road, ignoring the beeps and braking cars.

Louise shouts after her: 'Invite him back, the old uns are in Cardiff.'

Sam goes up close to James and pulls him to his feet. She puts her arms tight around his neck and clamps her mouth on his mouth. The other kids on the wall look up and down the street, embarrassed.

'Christ, that's shameful,' says Pricey, 'a girl should never do that.'

We are lucky in the chip shop. There's a few minutes before shut tap, that means there's no queue, no violence, and the chips won't be floppy with fat. Dennis can't wait the short walk to Louise's house, so he buys two bags and two potato fritters. One lot for on the way, with a pickled egg. They all offer to treat me, not believing I don't want anything because I feel rotten. When Richey asks only for a diet drink they ask if he's ill as well.

James crosses over the road as we leave. No, says Louise, the others on the wall are not allowed. What do they think her house is, a bloody hotel? She tries to be in heel with Richey but he always seems a stride behind. A few times he checks if James and Sam are lagging too far back, then stops, and we all wait for them to catch up. It's a stop-start walk.

Richey and James don't seem to know each other, at least that's how it appears. There's no greetings, no acknowledgments, nothing. Then again, James hasn't spoken to anyone else, not even to Sam much. The others just treat James the same, like one of them, familiar, equal. Richey, though, is over-aware. You can see he's preoccupied, and, in a subtle way, wants James to notice him back. If Sam says something quiet to James that hardly anyone can hear, and if it's something general, you can tell that Richey is dying to reply, make a comment. But he holds himself in check. And all the time, poor Louise is tagging along like a whipped dog. Even Pricey feels sorry. He walks in step and leans close: 'Give it up, if I were you.' Said with his trademark impatience.

Louise lives in a big house with an alarm on the white front wall. The gate has a metal arch with climbing flowers. By the gate is a speak-phone box that you talk into and that buzzes when they open the gate from somewhere inside. But Louise has a key. We file through on to the crunchy gravel, everyone except Richey. He stands on an imaginary border, under the arch. I'm beginning to feel a chill; the sweat is drying cold. We wait as he looks the house over, stares down at the floor.

'What's wrong Rich?'

He puts a foot across onto the drive and scuffs the gravel.

'I'll be getting back.'

'Don't be stupid, you've just come!' Louise is desperate.

The boys are trailing off into the shadows around the side of the house.

'I don't think James wants me to.'

'What d'you mean? Why not?'

'I think he's annoyed with me.'

'What?' Sam covers a yawn with the back of her hand. 'He hasn't even noticed, can barely bloody see.'

'Please Rich. There's loads of drink.'

In the Beginning

He is looking to where the boys have disappeared and is not listening. I have a kind of convulsion of sneezes, rapid; one after the other, close to him. Louise shouts, 'James. You like Richey to come in, don't you?' There's giggles and coughing from the shadows, then whispering. Dennis shouts back.

'Tell him he can please himself.'

'James! Please! Say or he'll go home.' It sounds like someone's fallen over. There's more giggling and a scuffle.

'Tell him to fuck off, then.' This time it's Pricey. Someone else laughs out loud.

The kitchen is spacious, shiny white, bright and shadowless; perfect for Louise's misery. She sits on a high chrome stool, elbows on the breakfast bar, her meal cold in the wrapping.

'I'll make you a nice cuppa,' says James.

'Yeah, forget him. Fucking weirdo.' Dennis reaches across to steal some chips.

Louise is left-handed. Using the right hand to wipe her eye makes her look a bit backward. 'All you had to do was say. Why couldn't you say?' James rests his hand lightly on her shoulder. He is fond of Louise.

'You shouldn't beg, it's humiliating and they're not worth that.'

'But he likes you, he's your friend.'

Pricey is wandering round the kitchen cabinets with a pint of brandy. He clicks open doors and, if they are big enough, sticks his head in for a look. 'Fucking cool stuff, hey?' Sometimes he takes out strange gadgets and presses buttons or turns handles to figure what they do.

I start to shiver and go over to the big stove that they keep burning all through the year. I'm hoping Louise will ask me to stay.

Pricey stops at the collage of photos on the huge fridge. They are mainly Louise's parents on holiday in different parts of the world; invariably with the sun in their eyes, invariably smiling and invariably toasting the photo-taker.

'Where they now then, your folks; abroad again?'

'Concert in Cardiff. Shirley Bassey or something.'

'Shrilly Fucking Bassey! That's fucking diamonds and furs.' He takes a long swig of the brandy. 'They got anything else, your mam an' dad?'

'What d'you want to see? Dad keeps his room locked.'

'Nah, come on. They must have a fuckin' stash somewhere, some coke or something?'

Hot water splashes over the worktop.

'Are you fucking mad! Where d'you think you are?' James holds his finger under the cold tap.

'Well, they do, rich fuckers... They can afford it.'

James tears off tissue towelling to dry his hand. 'Pricey, it's difficult. But can you imagine someone saying your parents take drugs?'

Sam drags a chair to the stove. In sympathy, she rubs her hands; holds them to the warmth, though she's sweating.

'Weird night.'

'Getting a habit.'

'That was just an excuse with Richey. He don't like this house.' Louise is the only one whose parents don't buy from the catalogue. Round here, you only see kitchens like this on the telly.

'He's jealous, you think?'

'He sensed it. The gate, the security light. Dead give-away.'

In the Beginning

She is staring at the door of the stove as though there's a fire with flickering flames.

'Sam, are you are pissed?'

'I respect Richey, he's straight. Reads all that crap and talks depressing, but he's dead straight.' She leans close, her mouth almost touching my cheek. 'James adores Louise, really. But he said... ' she breaks away to eye Louise; making sure, perhaps, she's not lip-reading. '... if you get rich with Thatcher, you're a crook. Before that fuckin' bastard her parents had nothing. Know why all the security? Her father had a taxi during the Miners', got a fortune taking scabs. James' dad said the men hate his guts.'

'Poor Louise... Think she'll let me stay? The night, I mean.'

'God, where's your principles? You're coming with me in a taxi.' She digs me in the side. 'We'll ask Louise for a discount.'

'Who was the fucker died from his drugs?' Dennis screws his head around from the front seat. 'First name was Jim or Jimmy. But not Hendrix.'

'Is this from a quiz?' asks the taxi driver.

'No. It's just buggin' me. Can't think of it.'

'Morrison, Jim Morrison,' says the driver, 'he died in France.'

'I knew it! The man's a fucking genius!'

'Nearly clever as Sam,' I sniff. 'She reads those weird books that only Richey understands.'

James is sceptical. 'Reads, does he? What sort of books?'

'What's it called now?' Sam looks along the faces in the back.

Jenny Watkins-Isnardi

'Catshit something?' suggests Pricey.

'That's it, The Catshit On The Lime.'

'Funny title,' says Dennis.

'I think you mean *The Catcher In The Rye*,' says the taxi driver.

CHAPTER EIGHTEEN

Nick gets up from my dressing table, takes a few strides and crouches on the floor by the tiny speaker. 'No idea what it means but I can see it!'

The lyrics are about some weirdo little girl scrabbling in the earth, threading worms on a string and spiders in her pocket.

The song ends. Nick squints up into the weak autumn sun, thin arms folded round his knees. 'Brilliant, or a pile of pretentious crap. Can't decide. They're a bit weird, especially Björk. Too hairy-fairy for my liking.'

'James adores the Sugarcubes.' I am sitting on my bed, leaning against the wall. There's a large pad on my lap and I'm trying to do a sketch of Nick. I've given up telling him to sit still or even stay in one place. For the last two weeks my mother has kept everyone away because she said I needed complete rest. My room is only just getting out of the feel of an isolation ward, but the dose of flu is still hanging around with a gruff-sounding catarrh cough. Nick is my second visitor, after Sam.

He shields a hand to his eyes. 'Well, James would. What'll he be like when I'm gone?' He smiles to himself. 'Still likes the teeny-bop groups. Notice Sam looks like that dark one in Bananarama? Dresses the same. Getting serious are they, James and Sam?'

'Like super-glue.'

'God almighty, James hated all that kissing with Sean and Rhian. He was suspicious of cuddling in public. And he was old-fashioned about showing feelings. Should've given him a talking to, bit late now.'

There's a faint tapping outside the bedroom door.

Nick gets up and goes back to the chair by the dressing table. He looks closely at his face in the mirror, pulls the skin tight over a cheekbone; maybe checking for old age? His interest in the Sugarcubes and the concern about James are not convincing; just small talk. He has come to say a last goodbye before he leaves for Portsmouth. We both act cool as though we'll see each other next week, like the way we've been for the past few months will just carry on. And on this particular day, for our final moments, my parents have gone out and left my sister.

The tapping, still faint, becomes more urgent. Although there's a lock, I've lost the key and the door is secured with a small bolt.

'Why don't you let her in?' Nick bends to wipe a tiny

speck of mud off the bottom of his jeans.

From the landing comes a little voice. 'Jenny, I'm afraid on my own. Mam said you got to look after me.'

Nick scrubs furiously at the blemish.

'You'll rub a hole in it.'

'Can't stand dirty clothes.'

'Jenny! The sky looks funny, come an' see, quick!'

'You'll be wearing stay-pressed next.'

'Will not. Only like clothes when they get old and scruffed. Like yours, real cool.'

'That's a lovely compliment. Thanks ever so much.'

'No, I mean... when your clothes look tidy but close up they're sort of sewn.' He stands and turns his back to me. There's a neat little square of paler blue on the bum of his jeans. He runs a finger along a precise rectangle of stitching. 'I keep needle and cotton in a matchbox I painted purple. And there's spare buttons. Taught myself.'

'Is there no end to this boy's talent? You could make your own clothes.'

Nick gives it a thought. 'Nah, I'm not that good. Only do small things, patches... underpants.'

'Patch your pants?'

'When they need it; just stitches mostly.'

'Most people buy new ones.'

'Done a survey, have you? What if you can't afford it? Not dirty because they're old.' He sits in front of the mirror and studies his face again. Pushing out his chin, he fingers a spot. 'Christ! I'm a dog. What do girls see in me? Too thin, spotty face and hairy legs.' Reaching down, he struggles with a tight trouser leg. The hair is so thick it's like the back of a head stuffed in a sock. He shudders and quickly covers the thatch. 'Look at me. I'm repulsive, sick.'

'You're not that bad.'

'Girls think I'm attractive.' He gazes at the mirror in disbelief. 'They come knocking on my door.' He is dumbfounded, stupefied. 'Can't understand. Don't find myself handsome, pretty, nothing.'

'Is this anything to do with going away?'

He stares hard at himself, as though trying to see through the skin and the flesh, to see what others might have seen. Then he grabs a T-shirt off the dresser and throws it over the glass.

The tapping starts on the door again. Gentle, soft little knuckles on tough wood.

'Jenny... Jen. Can I talk to you a minute?'

Dejected, Nick leaves the chair for the edge of the bed. On the radio is a Colourfield song. Nick listens to the lyrics about wishing to love the human race and wanting a pretty face. Does he identify with those words? He slumps, head on his chest.

'You all packed, then?' I ask.

He nods without looking up. 'Well, Mam's done it.' He talks into his orange shirt, fiddles with the sleeve cuff. 'Good as gold, she is. And worried sick, thinks I won't eat properly or have friends. Upsets me, worrying about her worrying. But she's right, I won't have friends.'

'Of course you will! You're really nice. Course you'll have friends.'

'No I won't.' He looks like a stubborn kid. 'Hate all that crappy chit-chat you have to do. Trivial, waste of time. I get nervous... '

The tapping comes again. This time like a code, as if there's a special knock to open the door. Nick snaps from his melancholy. 'My first week in Crosskeys, I had a twitch in the left eye.'

'What about Sean and James, weren't they there?'

In the Beginning

'Started earlier, didn't I. It was embarrassing, like a nervous tick.'

'It was.'

His chin falls back to his chest. 'Yeah, suppose so. Kept myself apart, tried to avoid people. This bloke sort of felt sorry, asked me to a meeting.'

'Don't tell me. They look for the sad and loonies... Jehovahs, was it? Or the Born Again ones?'

The tapping is like Morse code. Maybe she learnt it in brownies?

'We went to a massive hall. Me, the bloke and another chap. There was three of us and a speaker with a megaphone. The other chap sat at the back, so the speaker had to shout. We had to arm ourselves, he said. Get yourselves armed! Frightened the shit out of me.'

'Funny message, that. Not New Testament, it was all love and strumming in Sunday school. Was he American? They have far right nutters in the pulpits.'

'Far right? No.' Nick is pensive. 'There'll be loads like that in Portsmouth. Uni will be swarming with 'em.'

'No, that's Plymouth, not Portsmouth; the Plymouth Brethren. We had them in our family, they went to America.'

'Plymouth? Is there a university in Plymouth?'

'I'm not sure. But that's where the Brethren come from.'

Nick looks at me like he's searching for the split in my head. 'What brethren you on about?'

'Religious nuts. You said they'll be swarming over Portsmouth. But that's Plymouth not Portsmouth.'

'I was talking about socialist revolutionaries, militants... Jesus! Middle-class pricks who'll patronise me because I'm Welsh Valleys trash. I'll shut myself in my

275

room, lock the door.'

'Well, you'll make a lot of friends like that.'

'Don't need 'em. Got friends here.'

It's gone quiet outside the door. She's probably spying through the keyhole. I creep up to it, pointing the rubber end of my pencil. Nick jumps across and covers the hole with his hand.

'That's stupid, you'll have her eye out.'

'Wasn't going to push hard, just a little tickle.'

I feel trapped in this room. Trapped with bunged-up feelings. But open the door and it'll be worse, even more nerve jangling. I get back to the bed and pick up the pad. Nick sits by the dresser, uncovers the mirror.

'Is James going with you tomorrow?' I ask.

'Off to Barry Island or somewhere, with his dad. We said goodbye already.' He stares gloomily at the grey carpet. 'Was horrible. Been my best friend for... ' Nick looks at me as though I should explain the injustice, the cruelty of his having to leave, 'forever'. 'I called at his house before coming here,' he continues. 'He was terrible, never seen him like it. His mam said James was in his room. Went up, and the bedroom was empty, no one there. Thought, maybe gone out the window. But it was locked inside.'

'You said you saw him?'

'Yeah, well, I haven't finished. If you can just wait... As I walked out, he called me, called me back: "Nick, I'm here." A funny little voice, muffled: "Nick, I'm here." Jumped out of my skin. Freaked me out.'

'Spooky. Think I'd've run.'

'I called his name, "James. Where are you James?" He was under the bed. I knelt down but he was facing the wall, wouldn't turn round.' I can imagine my little sister

In the Beginning

hiding under a bed but I can't picture James. Perhaps my mouth dropped or my eyebrows lifted. 'Yeah, it's true,' says Nick, 'lying flat, turned to the wall. He knew I'd be there, couldn't bear it. He was sort of sniffing. I asked if he was okay. Said it was dust on the floor. Then he didn't say another thing. When I left he was crying, open like.' Nick looks on the verge of tears.

Maybe I felt jealous of James. Does Nick feel the same about me? 'Never heard anything like it, he must be demented.'

Nick is straight to James' defence. 'It's the way he is, can't deal with heavy feelings. Doesn't cry like me and Sean.'

'Cry special, do you? Different to everyone else?'

'I mean, we're not afraid to cry. It's no big deal. When we watched *One Flew Over The Cuckoo's Nest*, me and Sean cried buckets. You know that bit at the end, with the pipe music and the Indian running over the fields? James did a runner as well, hid in the toilet and kept flushing the chain. Couldn't admit he was bawling.'

'Oh well, he's too manly.'

Nick stares at me as though I've made a discovery, said something profound. 'You're dead right! James is the only macho in the band.' He pushes his hair back like an affected actress. 'One of us has to be, can't all be wimps.' He's taking the piss.

TWANGGGGG! Nick dives onto the bed and grips the windowsill. He scans back and for along the rows of gardens. TWANG-TAWAWA-TWANGGGGGG! Sparrows scatter for the rooftops, swallows on the telephone line make an early start.

'What the hell is it?'

'A neighbour's son, he's barred from the house.' I

point out a small hut in a garden behind ours. Nick cups both hands to the glass but the shed is in deep shadow from a tall tree. The guitar starts again, this time so loud you think the shed must blow. Nick covers his ears, screws his face. As the noise continues, he removes his hands one at a time; squinting, listening, trying to make sense. Suddenly his expression brightens.

'Got it! "Apache". The Chinese version.'

A woman is screaming through the racket. Her voice drifts in between twangs, as though the kid is using it as an echo or fade.

'JOHN-A-THAN... ATHAN.'

'Christ! How d'you put up with it?' As he is speaking, the noise drops like it's fallen down a drain.

'She's got the plug.'

'Jenny, Jen, is it time for tea?'

The room is now so quiet you can hear electric hum in the wiring, or maybe its the afterburn of the twanging.

'He should be banned.' Nick is rubbing an ear with the heel of his hand. 'Can he play anything else?' I shake my head. 'God, that's wild. Not in a group or anything, is he? That would be terrible.'

'You had to start somewhere.'

'How long's he been on that one?'

'Month, two months.'

'What? I had "Apache" in a week!' Nick fingers an imaginary guitar, pressing strings with his left hand, plucking with his right. 'Less than a week. He's crap.'

'I heard you weren't so hot when you started.'

'Yeah? Who said that, then?'

'A little bird.'

'You know that kid, do you? Friends, like?'

'No.'

In the Beginning

'Why're you sticking up for him, then? He's crap.'

'And just a bit older than my sister; he's got a while to learn.'

'Good for him. It's all a bloody waste, anyway. What's he want to learn guitar for? Never comes to anything.' Nothing had really been said about the band or me. It was like an illness you didn't mention or musicians playing while the ship sank. We carried on as normal, like nothing would happen. And here it was. Nick read my mind. 'Kiss goodbye to it now, anyway.'

'What d'you mean? Does that include me?'

'Portsmouth is too far, impossible. James will be off next year, then you. And Sean? It's gone.' There's a tiny spasm at the corner of his mouth. I hope to God he's not going to cry. Then he looks angry. 'Shit ennit? Everything turns out crap. Few years' time, we'll be watching telly, some Welsh gits making it big. Maybe that kid in the shed? So bloody unfair. Thing is, we could've done it.' He seems determined to make our last time together bleak and final. When the tapping starts on the door again, I clench my fists. If that little sod only knew what she was on the edge of.

'Jenny, Jen. I'm a bit hungry. Mam said you'd do me something.'

'It's all my fault.' says Nick. I feel like giving him a kick up the arse. 'I know deep down, university's not gonna work. Not as important as the band, that's what I've always wanted. But... gone too far now. Can't let your parents down.'

At last he notices I'm pissed off, steaming. If he hadn't spoken next, I'd have maybe just let him go. 'Anyway, that's all over now. What about you, Jen? Gonna finish college an' all that?' Before I can answer he gets nostalgic about the place he was desperate to leave. 'Loved that library in Crosskeys. Wrote all my essays, I could really work there. At home I'd be watching telly or talk to Bonnie. Yeah, I'll miss that... '

I cut him off. 'Well, I've got a real job.'

'Course you have, only part-time though, like James. He's always moaning as well. I couldn't handle a job.'

'It's not the work, nothing to it except boredom.'

'You still on fruit and veg?'

'Just about. Keri the supervisor, I'll never forget that name long as I live. "You can't work here with peroxide hair", she said. Figure that out.'

'You figure it. Mean little lives, it makes them bitter... Really, when you think, there's no difference what I'll be doing and your work in Leo's. Both soulless, dead. And what's the future? Strange, ennit? Study like fuck to get out, and where d'you go?' He combs his fingers roughly through his hair. 'Oh God, I dunno.'

'You never worked, though?'

'Mowed some lawns... No I haven't worked. Couldn't take orders from shit-thick morons.'

'We all have to some day.'

He smiles, patronising. 'I don't think so.'

Heavy footsteps tramp down the stairs. She'll look for revenge, probably in the kitchen.

'You better get going.'

Nick stands up, stretches, pressing his fingertips against the low ceiling. Then he looks around the room as though seeing it the first time. He goes close to a wallboard and prizes a card from hardened Blue Tac. 'Didn't notice that before.' He holds it just in front of his eyes, looking at the detail. The card shows a can of Campbell's soup.

'Keep it if you want.'

In the Beginning

'Nah, it's alright. Not exactly rare, is it?'

'I suppose the original is.'

'Died last February, the 23rd. Two days after James' birthday... The original? Didn't believe in it, did he? Everything is manufactured; everyone gets fifteen minutes' fame.' Nick stamps the card on to the Blue Tac. 'Not much, is it, fifteen minutes?' He sits back down on the edge of the bed. 'Wanna cup of tea?' I shake my head. 'Well then, that's it. Definitely time to be going.' He gets up and wraps his skinny chest with bone-thin arms. Only then I notice he's without a jacket, looking half-dressed, vulnerable. I wait for him to speak. 'Lovely.'

I slip the bolt.

On the landing, I say I'll write. At the bottom of the stairs, a pair of eyes are peering up from the gloom.

'Are you two gonna kiss?'

I mean to say something, like good luck. But there's maybe dust in my throat. He steps forward, gives me a hug. Then he seems to fall away, and I hear the front door slam.

CHAPTER NINETEEN

Change is wonderful, if you're not excluded from it. Nick had gone away to university and I was left behind. By the third week back in sixth-form college I was fed up and numb. Summer seemed to change straight to winter and the valley was a corridor of grey and drizzle.

Nick had promised to write but he didn't. In my imagination Portsmouth became the sun capital of enjoyment. I'd forgotten Nick had gone there to study. Now I really begrudged his going even though we all knew you had to get out, that here was only slag heaps and the dole.

Since Nick had gone, James had been morose,

annoyed, impatient. It was as though he went though a character change, and his forehead started to get lines. I had to pluck up the courage to ask if he knew anything about Nick. If he did, he wasn't going to share it.

A couple of nights before his letter arrived I'd ripped Nick's name from my address book. He wrote to say he was very bored: the lectures were dull and didn't stimulate or challenge his intelligence, and he hadn't made any friends; in fact he hadn't met anyone. Worst of all, Portsmouth was a Gothic university. He was the one and only punk! It was more of an SOS than a letter; a plea for someone to get him out of the place. I felt happier straight away.

I showed Sam the letter and she wasn't surprised, from what James had told her. She was in her dressing gown with a hangover and wanted me to make coffee.

'Why wouldn't James tell me anything?' I asked.

'Because... it's his best mate. You're just a girlfriend... Know what I call 'em, Nick, Sean and James? "The little family". Like a Mafia.' I got the impression she saw herself as a sort of gangster's moll, an always outsider. 'One thing for sure,' Sam added. 'Nick hates the university. Just stays in his room watching telly, won't even go to the canteen. And he can't cook, can he?' Nick was so thin before he went, I had a visions of his body wasting to bones on the bed. 'But he's not starving,' she continued, 'lives on chips. Won't do his spots much good, will it?' I wrote back to Nick and my doubts were well-founded. He never replied.

A wet afternoon in Blackwood. I'm in the paper shop, soaking wet and thumbing through a magazine article titled, 'Fifty Ways To Improve Your Life'. There's a tap on my shoulder and Nick's mother is smiling down on me. God knows what she sees in people but for sure it's not just the obvious, the skin deep. I know I'm wrecked,

In the Beginning

confirmed by the sneering and snooty shop girls. But Nick's mam looks like she wants to put her arms round me. I nearly start to cry.

We moan about the weather, then there's nothing much to be said. Out of the blue she tells me she's worried about Nick. 'Do you think he seems down, depressed?'

What can I say? Surely to God he's written to his mother? Honesty is the best policy, I don't think. Yeah, I think he's depressed.

'Knew it!' she's distraught, 'I knew it wasn't right.' He has written and phoned but managed to spare his parents the burden of how he really felt. Though upset, she looks in through the window with a wonderful smile, and waves goodbye. Then I start to bawl my eyes out.

'You buying that, love?' asks the shop girl. 'Only you're getting drippers on it, see.'

Nick doesn't ever write again to me. After the encounter with his mother there's no one with either information or interest in what he's up to. The news is always stale: from Sam, via James, through Nick's mother or brother. And most of it is pure gaga, like he's joined the Hare Krishna or the Moonies. But that's the nature of Valleys gossip, it makes Chinese whispers seem like the Ten Commandments. The only certainty, perhaps, is that Nick hates Portsmouth but loves pie and chips.

It must have been around Christmas that Sam called to say Nick had fallen off his pedestal. This 'falling off' had a lot of interpretations. At first he'd been kicked out of university for failing exams, then he'd dropped out, left. The final, correct, version was he'd changed for a university nearer home.

'He's coming back to Wales,' said Sam, 'the great explorer will be just down the road from where he lives.'

Just down the road turned out to be sixty miles away, in Swansea. I'd misunderstood Sam. She wasn't pleased or gloating that Nick messed up, she was disappointed in him. If the best, the cleverest, the most determined couldn't hack it, what hope for the rest of us? In her darker moments Sam saw herself as a spinster of Wales; stuck in her town, never going anywhere or doing anything. 'At least he'll know someone in this other university,' she added. 'Remember Richey? Richey Edwards?'

Sean's giro luck ran out, or rather the strings attached to it were pulled tight. At the same time, his musical career was channelled into a different direction.

Called to Interview Room 4 at the DHSS, Sean was introduced to his personal career advisor and asked to consider the benefit of a Youth Training Scheme. He was told that the YTS had a huge range of opportunities to improve job and career and life prospects. In theory, there was almost no limit to what he could train to be. For practical purposes, at that very moment, he was offered carpentry, plumbing or welding. The welding was a 'sandwich course': some days in college and other days getting work experience. A local firm had just got a big order to make metal frames for Land Rovers. With luck, they'd take Sean on.

'Doesn't sound very appetising to me,' said Sean. If the man got the joke he preferred to ignore it.

'The work experience is invaluable, makes you attractive on the job market. We're very fortunate the firm are willing to take on trainees.' Did their taking trainees have anything to do with the big order? Wouldn't it be cheap labour? wondered Sean. As if! It was a fantastic scheme, surely he could see that?

Sean saw quickly that he wouldn't get out of Room 4 without being signed up on a YTS. From the peak of welding, the training opportunities slipped down rapidly to shelf stacking in Safeways.

'I'm a musician.'

'Got just the thing, then.'

The next day Sean was working in Our Price record store and was given a nice blue waistcoat to wear for free. The manager was just a little older, and when he discovered that Sean had a good knowledge of music he put him moving boxes, seemingly from one place to another then back again. When he had time, Sean improved his boss's knowledge of music and before long the manager was answering customers' questions with a lot more authority. But Sean hated every second in the place. The extra ten quid on his dole couldn't compensate for the terrible disorder in the shop. There was a continual mixing up of the LPs: Frank Zappa next to Whitney Houston. And Sean is a very organised, well-ordered person. If he had his way, customers would look but not touch.

Towards the end of the week the manager took Sean on one side. 'See him in the stonewashed shirt? He's got a Bros tape down his trousers.'

'Best place, too.'

'When you nab him, make sure it's outside.' Sean recalled his own exploits. It made perfect sense to shoplift if you couldn't afford something. The only consideration to make was whether you'd get away. It was a game of cold logic.

'Get ready,' said the manager, 'he looks a tricky bugger.'

'To be honest, I don't really want to.'

'Oh, you really don't? Well, every bit of stock that goes from this shop unpaid for lowers your bonus.'

'Bonus?'

'Depends on how much we sell.'

What kind of prat would nick a Bros tape, anyway? But the boy had enough sense to know plans were being made for him. The store entrance gave on to a shopping mall. After walking quickly to the door he bolted, and Sean instinctively chased. The boy was years younger than Sean, skinny and tall.

'What's wrong tub, can't keep up?' He even had time to reach in his pants and wave the tape at Sean. But, as luck would have it, he ran into a posse of young mothers with pushchairs. He looked up from the floor. 'Come on, give us a break. Don't say you never did this?'

'Not for a Bros tape, no.'

That night Sean was in a foul mood, suffering the day's events. In the living room, James was sprawled out on the sofa. Sean ignored him. He slumped down in the old chair. He glared over at James. 'Don't say any thing to me James. I've had a fuckin' nuff.'

Sam thought James was cracking up. Nick's leaving was supposed to bring her and James closer but it just made his behaviour increasingly bizarre. He became obsessed with the idea of selling out.

When Sam had said she wanted to be a professional photographer, James was thrilled she'd found something she felt passionate about. He was like a mentor, encouraging and advising. Then Sam discovered she liked portraiture and wanted to become a fashion photographer. James didn't like the idea. He thought he could reason her out of it. She would be exploiting her own kind; it was waste of her talent. When Sam said she loved it and was good at it, he replied there were all sorts of things you could be good at and liked but it didn't mean you should do.

'Maybe you're good at shooting guns... '

He bought her a copy of *The Bell Jar*, and inside he wrote, 'Don't give it all up for commercialism. Don't sell your soul'. It was getting out of hand; James was trying to rule her life. How could he equate photographing people with selling your soul to commercialism? He was going nuts.

And he did. Sam related how, in her bedroom, he ranted and raved about her being whorish and an exploiter of her own sex. When she said everyone was exploited by someone, he went berserk and Sam's mother had to bang on the ceiling with a brush handle. He was banned from the house but even when he phoned he couldn't shut up. If she did this for a career she would lose her soul, he guaranteed it. Sam tried to joke that it was those photographed who lost their soul, maybe he'd got it the wrong way round. But he just kept on about selling souls, like there was big sale coming at the supermarket in the sky. As she was about to hang up, James confessed to a dream. Samantha had been photographing male models who were extremely stupid but handsome. And Sam had been more impressed with the looks. It was an omen, said James. Sam told James he was stupid and tiresome, and broke off with him.

James wrote. In the letter he said he was fed up and couldn't stand another year in Blackwood. It was dead and he was forever waiting for something to happen. He'd end up waiting for the undertaker. Really, it's not waiting, he says, but always looking forward. You start when you're young — Christmas, weekends, birthdays... always anticipating. And what did he have to look forward to now? Marriage, mortgage, promotion, if he had a job? Sam wrote back and said if it was any consolation he wouldn't have to wait for her, because she thought he was mad.

The next I knew they were back together, and Sam told me there was a thin divide between madness and genius. There probably is. And James didn't waste any time jumping back across onto the nutter's side. It was coming up for Christmas and Sam told me she was going to a party without James. He couldn't understand. Those plans were made when they were apart. Now they are back, she must see it's different? No, said Sam. James went through his repertoire of reasons, seasons, excuses and threats, finishing up with 'If you go, you'll be sorry'. He convinced himself but Sam was beyond caring.

On the afternoon of Sam's party he borrowed a tenner from his dad and went to Newport by himself. By ten o'clock James was drunk and looking for a fight. In a trendy pub, his anger focussed on a group of rugby boys. At first they ignored his snide remarks. His luck ran out when the biggest objected to being called a 'Fucking fat faggot.'

James spent the next few months with his jaw wired up, a bolt sticking out of each cheek.

Easter 1988, and Nick has been back in Wales for a couple of months but not got in touch. A late Friday afternoon I bump into Richey in the college canteen. He's on his own at a table reading a poem. It's on a big sheet of paper with big writing. It's a poem I don't recognise, about how buying a rocket ship and being rich will be no fun if it's not

In the Beginning

'action-packed'. It means nothing to me.

I've been sat down ten minutes and he's still staring at the words. He's shy rather than unsociable. When he didn't look up I knew he wasn't simply ignoring me. Anyway, this is my college, he'd left it a long time ago. Why the hell does he keep returning? Most people can't wait to see the back of it. He looks out of place, you can tell he's not a sixth-form student. Too intense, too studious.

I glance at what he's reading. With a felt pen he's written 'KAPOW!' in huge capitals across the poem.

'Alright Jen?'

'Yeah, fine.'

'Fancy a... coffee or something?'

At the counter he asks for hot water and lemon. The woman says it's a popular drink with skinny girls who think they're fat, and Richey shouldn't have it. He tells her it's detoxifying, cleanses the body.

'There's not much of you to clean,' she says. They're like a double act.

He sips his hot water, picks up his pen and circles some words: origin, beginning. Be pure, disappear. Vanish, reality. Good heart, hate. Antisocial. After staring at the page, he draws thick black lines, over and over again through the writing. Over this he writes with a coloured marker, 'WHITE TRASH ON SPEED THRILLS.'

'What's that?' I ask.

'I'm giving them a hand.' He doesn't look up. 'Doing flyers and posters.' He shows me a piece of paper. The band's name is written boldly in the middle: MANIC STREET PREACHERS.

Sam comes in and straightaway bends over to look at what Richey is doing. 'Opposites,' he says, 'clashes. Most are obvious, but there are grey areas. Some words don't have an opposite.'

'It looks like a something James has in his bedroom,' says Sam. 'Are you working with the Manics?'

'I don't play,' says Richey, 'just design posters, and give them a hand. I lug equipment, do whatever, heavy stuff.'

Sam looks doubtful at Richey's skeletal, X-ray wrist. 'Like a roadie, yeah?'

'Yes,' says Rich, 'I'm a roadie.'

'You were never part of it,' I say, 'how'd you get involved?'

'Well,' Richey says, 'I see Nick in university, all he talks about is the band. It's hard work carting the stuff around so I offered to give a hand.'

'Are you going home, Jen?' asks Sam. I grab my bag and haul the strap over my shoulder. Richey is left by himself in the empty canteen.

At the bus stop I ask Sam about Richey's involvement with the band.

'I don't really know,' she replies. Perhaps she's embarrassed because the Manics have just cut me off, not been in touch. James and Sean still speak to me, they're friendly enough, but it's like I was never part of the set-up. I get snippets of news about the band the same as everyone else, gossip and rumours.

Band practice was easier with Nick back in Wales. James thought they were good enough to go professional, and he arranged to make a demo tape at a recording studio. He had always sworn to go up to London, walk into John Peel's studio and slap the tape on his desk. He was the organiser, though. He and Sean put every penny they could spare into the band. Nick was enthusiastic and

In the Beginning

convinced they would make it. But any money he had went on gambling. James never made the trip to John Peel's studio; instead he posted the demo tape to Cardiff's Red Dragon radio station.

Mad Mark was a local kid who knew everything about bands and music, so he said. After hearing the demo on a radio, he persuaded the Manics to let him be their manager promising to get them some juicy venues. Sean was sceptical; James was doubtful; Nick said they had nothing to lose.

Mad Mark got himself a swivel chair and arranged some bookings. He liked the chair so much that he couldn't leave it to check out the places he'd booked. They were usually cramped and cobwebbed; often the band outnumbered the audience, and what they paid didn't cover the cost of transport.

One Saturday they were at the Square Club in Cardiff, playing a small back room downstairs. In the half a dozen audience was a bloke about forty years old who went up to them when they were packing away their stuff and told them they were good. The man had a foreign accent — he was from London and said he had connections. Sean thought he was putting it on, winding them up. They could be big, the man said, and then asked about the beautiful kid with thin wrists struggling to carry the amps. He should be part of the line-up, suggested the man. But the others pointed out that the kid couldn't play a note and, far as they could tell, was tone deaf. 'So what? He looks the part... give him a go,' the man is reputed to have said. And that was the incident that made Richey a Manic.

EPILOGUE

After finishing sixth-form college I studied photography in Swansea then I had the luck to visit South America.

The visit turned into a stay of nearly five years. During the summers I lived on a remote farm on the Uruguayan pampas, a very different way of life to the cramped streets around Blackwood.

When the Manics were struggling to make it in Thatcher's Britain, I was photographing a huge and dwarfing landscape where tough individuals literally held their own fate in their hands. That's just to say you got about by horse and had to hold tight on the reins.

I escaped, I guess, from the terrible oppressiveness

and depression that choked the Valleys after the mines shut. The same feelings nudged away a lot of my friends: Amanda-Punk studied for her degree in Birmingham then did social work in London; Sam took the train to a nice English town just over the border.

Mostly it was the blokes who stayed, and suffered. Born-Again Len slogged in a local Pot Noodle factory, and kept his faith even when the factory closed. Miles achieved a sort of fame when the place he worked went on strike and stayed out for a couple of years; after they were sacked he became a postman. Funeral in Berlin, the Manics' biggest rivals, had quite a bit of success in Eastern Europe before the wall came down.

And, of course, the Manics didn't get their record deals in Blackwood or Cardiff. In fact they were the most desperate to get out. No false sentiment, they knew the score. Home advantage is nothing in Wales, that's why you lose your accent until you're rich or make up a strange one like Shirley Bassey.

The Manics were never nationalistic. Our domain was the Valleys, that was our Wales. How could you revere poverty, and sing anthems to squalor? We would scorn the cynical manipulation of national fervour that bled away dole money when Wales played rugby.

And this is something I can't figure now about the Manics. They were passionate, always and ever, about injustice. Petty nationalism was a sideline, a diversion from things that mattered. Iniquities were wrapped in flags. Radicals should burn flags not wave them. So why did the Manics hoist the Welsh dragon? Maybe they wanted to demand recognition of where they were from? (After all, they promote you when you're famous, make you British.) I know the Manics detest jingoism and

In the Beginning

distrust patriotism, so why drape the flag? Maybe as a symbol of the oppressed but undefeated? Sure, stand up and take another kicking, this time from the nationalists because you don't speak Welsh.

Wales is the poor relation in Britain; the Valleys are the paupers of Wales, and the Manics' music is dyed through with the experience of growing up there. But their music resonates with people in very different lands because they articulate universal feelings about despair, need and longing.

In the Beginning

These letters were sent to a good friend of Richey's, Steven Gatehouse, in his pre-Manics days.

3 Mirador Crescent

Uplands

Swansea

Dear Steve,

Hope you had a good time in London. What's the news with the job? Did you find any bargins in Camden? I haven't seen anyone from Blackwood down here this term, which is probably a good thing. After all the whole point of going away is to meet new people. That's also the point of looking for a job outside Wales which I've got to start doing soon.

The careers office are hassling me but I'm not going to rush into anything I'm not sure of. At the moment it feels like I'm at a crossroads 'My life.' I can either do my degree get a job etc or do what I really want to do and that's something to do with music. I know that if I don't do something soon I'll just end up in a job I don't want.

So I've bought myself a guitar and it's not that difficult, I just wish I'd started earlier. I think it, probably too late fo me to start a band now but that's not the point. If I don't even try I probably wouldn't survive in a 9 to 5 job thinking 'What If...'

Nothing totally inspiring has happened this term — just the usual stuff — films, bar, Cinders, parties, etc. Oh me and Dan did have a total punk rock experience at the College Bar on Friday when 2 massive cunts tried to beat us up but Dan talked them out of it. Personally, I think my dm's scared them off.

Jenny Watkins-Isnardi

Have you been to Metro's and are you going to Clare Forward's birthday party at the Top Club in Risca? Also are you coming to see the Pogues? (I'm not going; I don't think they're worth £7). I'm also defiantly going to the Godfathers and maybe to the Wedding Present / Flatmates are supporting them. AAAH.

Also the money situation is dire after buying a guitar.

Anyway, see you soon

Richard

In the Beginning

3 Mirador Crescent

Uplands

Swansea

Dear Steve,

Glad to see everythings groovey (with Rachey especially). I've had some bad hassle with girls as you shall hear later...

I wish I'd come to see the concerts but money + time + energy is tight and well, I dunno. I don't mind missing Darling Buds etc cos Fraser etc keeps giving me earache about how he discovered them, etc. I really regret not seeing the Godfathers tho — LOVE IS DEAD, I WANT EVERYTHING are 2 absolute post punk classics.

I think you might be disappointed with the LPs tho; especially the 2nd one — a bit Hm in parts.

On Thursday everyone down here was estatic that TOTP had Primitives, Mosser, Mish and Sisters. So was I BUT they were calling it a MOVEMENT and in truth they have nothing in common. I don't see how they can deny it. At the best it'll just be another Echo, Simple Minds, Big Country, U2 'movement':- which is very very good but there should be more. As good ol' Dave Rimmer said 'Like Punk Never Happened.' Oh yeah — did you hear the Joy Division thingy on the radio on Saturday — fucking mega. When you think about the classics they were producing when Ian started hanging about his kitchen in Maccelfield you realise his swinging suicide was the greatest loss in music history.

About Port Talbot — the best band they're having this term — SHAMEN — have been and gone and I missed them. We've the likes of JAZZ BUTCHER and MIGHTY MIGHTY etc coming soon but no one's going. I just want to see McCARTHY or WOLFHOUNDS.

Jenny Watkins-Isnardi

A couple of weeks we had ROACHFORD — pile of crap — I've come to the conclusion that MANDELA BAR is a crap place for bands to play. So has everyone else (that counts.) So far they've sold 2 'Men they Couldn't Hang' tickets and it'll probably cancel. Pogues sold out but it's going to be so violent.

Let me explain.

Last Saturday at Cinders (I was there!) there was a riot between our rugby team and townies. It ended up with a towny in intensive care — MEATHEAD AND BOOTHY (in hall with me last year) kicked his nose into his brain. Bastards. So since then they've been some serious repercussions. The next Saturday there was no-one there and so the townies simply started beating students in the street. I don't blame them tho.

It makes a change to report that everyone seems happy down here — Becca, Sally, Ade, Jill + Scott — not that I see them tho — I tend to see Becca for about 5 minutes every week for about 2 minutes and she gives me a running commentary on the state of things. I was having a mega time till last Monday and things have got a bit (only a bit) shit since then. But before we get onto that it's true what you said about Capricorns being late starters in life.

I spend have my day thinking... " why didn't I start playing years ago." But I've already had 3 very serious offers from bands to join but they can fuck off. I've got to be in a band that's going somewhere. On top of that people like Fraiser keep asking me to come up Hendre 'for a jam'. No thank you.

Most of the bands will get nowhere — oh yeah — did you see the Bowlheads from Cardiff in NME — James Brown did a piece on them. Wales is moving at last (but POOH STICKS will, I'm afraid, be destined to become our BABY AMPHETAMINE).

Heavy deep psyche stuff coming up boy.

On Monday 15th I was in the Doctors getting some zit

cream and this mega girl comes. Sounds stupid but it 100% total love. I spent every night that week searching for her — to no avail. I was going out of my mind. Then on Saturday 21st I give it a go by going to the RAG BALL (like a posh version of the Tech Dance) I didn't go to the Rag Ball last year as I hate things that have dress restrictions and are student only affairs. Anyway I compromised all my principles for her; ethics went out of the window. I really would die for this shining beacon in a sea of mediocrity, well she was there (but so was I) and she was with a boy. I was so upset. I drank a bottle of vodka and then humiliated myself all night. At the end of the evening I was on my knees being sick and she walks in front of me.

"DON'T WALK AWAY IN SILENCE" Ian Curtis

But she did and I was left there with puke dribbling down my borrowed jacket, tie, shirt etc. How can reality be so hard. She is totally dominating my life.

On a real downer then till Tuesday when I go to Cinders and she is there. I thought her boyfriend was coming and I got completely pissed again to ease the blackness and just danced all night but then she comes and dances by me for about an hour. On the way home I got to talk to her but vodka has killed my throat and I end up just saying 'sorry...sorry' and she leaves me at 2AM on top of Mumbles pier. FUCKING HELL.

Since then I've spent every day looking for her. When something happens I'll let the whole world know. Not much else to say except go out and get em boy!

Love + Fishes

Richey

Jenny Watkins-Isnardi

3 Mirador Crescent
Uplands
Swansea

YO Stevey Boy!

Ta very much for the letter. It arrived on a very grey, northern day when the sun refused to show itself. Firstly apologies for this paper — it's shit I know but blame the government. After all I didn't vote for her. Well... glad to hear things are cool with Rachey. After all love is the sinews of life, but then again so is hate.

KAPOW. My baby doll has left me but I feel OK.

Never mind, she snivelled too much for my liking anyway. So here I am — loneliness shot straight through — and I feel better than ever. Sorrow the humble oppressed us. It's going to be a long hot summer. Take it to extremes and by September something quite significant just might have happened.

KAPOW. From now on I shall not put girls on pedestals, I shall pore peroxide on their foundations. Turn around to a NEW EUROPEAN WAY of LIFE.

Anyway, glad things are going well but remember some important rules

— EMOTIONS ARE JUST CHEMICAL REACTIONS — (Wolfhounds)

— IS IT AN ADMITTANCE OF FAILURE TO RELY ON ANOTHERS BODY?

(Moi, but you'll have to discover the answer yourself.)

Turn around to EXAM FEVER. I've just realised my exams begin in less than a week and I have an ocean full of notes to revise. But with my memory I know these exams, like them all, are a piece of piece(?) Only one thing to remember about exams — if you know you're intelligent why worry? To consider failure during a 3 hour exam is to admit you are intellectually inadequate. That has been the basis of my academic life (but then it has been helped, especially down here, by being in a classful of zero sidewalk bores, writing intellectual cheques that they're brain cannot cash) If only you knew how privileged we were to go to CROSSKEYS COLLEGE. I know I didn't go anywhere / speak to anyone in college but I knew they were some worthy souls to be found amongst the morons of empty, soulness lives. Down here I just feel DISGUST, HATE, SCORN for my classmates. LISTEN — Swansea University has 4000 students — the University Shop orders 10 copies of NME / Melody Maker / Sounds etc each week cos thats all they can sell. Pathetic isn't it? I might have disliked the vast majority in Crosskeys but at least they knew something...

Turn around to music. Pretty bad year huh. The dreams of C86 smashed incandescently on the brittle edges of Thatchers Britain.

Who succeeded? The Weddoes? Soupies? MLD? etc etc all fucked it up. All my dreams hang around me and they ALL let me down.

Pah! All I had left was McCarthy + Wolfhounds. NOW I HAVE NOTHING — except LES THUGS / G.L.F. (But I love Liverpool F. C. song just as I love Derek B and S EXPRESS and BOMB THE BASS) KAPOW. I am Neil Kinnock — the neutered triumph of Mid 70's morality. Still reading, most people get bored by this point.

AAAARRGHH. Here we come to 'IMPACT'

Now there's been a lot of uninspired, boring, monotonous, foolish, oppressive talk about this magazine and its all true. My letter? What letter? "ACADEMIC INSPIRATION YOU GAVE ME NONE" — Ode to Davnia.

KAPOW — so they didn't like the letter or weren't impressed. WHY ARE THEY SO BLIND — I knew they'd hate it but the purpose was not to impress them. It was a mere letter — why read anything more than that into it? I have many things to do that bore my empty mind but none so nauseatng as the thought of trying to impress some magazine. PAH! PAH! PAH!

Jenny Watkins-Isnardi

But saying that — how do you know they were unimpressed — I think I know who informed you but you shouldn't take things at face value all the time (You were right tho — FIERCE tho he is informs me that they despise me) — Oh and I thought they'd send me flowers. It's a shame tho — Wales' only true Youth Magazine and you give them the biggest story of their fucking lives and they turn it down (or did they?).

Anyway — enough said but do watch out for details in the press soon.

June 2ND — Yeah MSP are playing but why did you take the piss? I thought XMAS was behind me. Since then no one from back home has written to me and I hardly ever see Becca, Sally etc. I wonder why...

I just wish people would realise, they never let me explain. I HAVE ALWAYS, ALWAYS ONLY SANCTIONED MUSIC WITH A MORAL PURPOSE. Ask anyone in school, or anyone in college. At XMAS I got slagged off constantly for everything I said.

EXAMPLES — a symptom of consensus mediocrity I know, but they are necessary.

1. I HATE DOORS / SISTERS / MISSION / etc. YOU KNOW THAT — did you ever hear me say anything different??? So how come Den etc bite my head off for repeating myself.

2. Please someone deny bands like SMITHS / SOUP DRAGONS / WEDDOES have changed. Of course they fucking have. LOOK — if you like a RED WALL and overnight someone paints it BLUE do you still like the wall??

NO — the wall is still there but its different.

I can't be bothered to write this letter to anyone else because I think only YOU of everyone back home may understand. Say PUNK ROCK (a bad example I know).

When the majority think of 'punk' they think of that oaf in Sid 'n' Nancy (brilliant film tho it is) To me Punk is ISAAC NEWTON.

In the Beginning

OK — MANIC STREET PREACHERS — I don't know why everyone HATES me for associating with them. I really don't understand it (or maybe I know only too well)

You know what NIETZCHE (sorry — wrong spelling) said about pathological hatred...

Whatever you think of them its obvious that they got the songs to smash this fucking apathy

Take DEF II — SPINELESS WHITE AVERAGES — Soup Dragons and those other countless bores NO MORE. And then Top of The Pops — Prefab Sprout (Why take the piss out of 'mean arsed rock 'n' roll? — its cos he can't fucking write a decent ORIGINAL song. CRITICISM is the EASY OPTION. And as for Billy Braggs 'amazing' performance... DRAP DEAD..."

Anyway... what to say. I happen to think MSP are a good band (just listen to the last 2 demos — MOTORCYCLE EMPTINESS / SUNGLASS AESTHETIC / ENGLAND IS STILL A BITCH and RUTHLESS / WHISKEY PSYCHOSIS / COLT 45 RUSTY JAMES) and if you ever hear these songs you'll love them as well. I guarantee that 100% Now MSP may HATE ME but that's not the point. That doesn't detract from the point that they are GOOD

Yeah, all this SELF INDUCED INADEQUACY doe's no one any good — they've taken it to extremes which is all well and good — BUT you see THATS THE POINT. No one knows how to say FUCK OFF these days.

Well, this is the end — I'm popping up to see Adrian soon. It's quite strange actually that, just like college, everyone seems to be taking the piss. It's good news. I mean — REALLY — what do people like, I dunno, everyone, know about music... All those 1986 Smiths fans suddenly discovering the Primitives when Mosser wears their T-shirt. It's so fucking sick to even be funny. Anyway, all this abuse I've received is good for the soul — Its gives me conscious + direct unity. I AM TIRED OF IDENTITY THRU BIGOTRY

Deutschland Uber Alles

Jenny Watkins-Isnardi

Love + Fishes
Richey
x

Good Luck with the gigs
SPLISH SPLASH SPLOOSH
DROP YOUR LIFE
AND PICK UP YOUR
SOUL